Captain C. F. Hall.

See page 289

NORTH-POLE VOYAGES:

EMBRACING

SKETCHES OF THE IMPORTANT FACTS AND INCIDENTS

IN THE LATEST

AMERICAN EFFORTS TO REACH THE NORTH POLE

FROM THE SECOND GRINNELL EXPEDITION TO THAT OF THE POLARIS.

BY REV. Z. A. MUDGE,

AUTHOR OF "VIEWS FROM PLYMOUTH ROCK," "WITCH HILL," "ARCTIC HEROES," ETC., ETC.

FIVE ILLUSTRATIONS.

NEW YORK:
NELSON & PHILLIPS.
CINCINNATI: HITCHCOCK & WALDEN.
SUNDAY-SCHOOL DEPARTMENT.

PREFACE.

FOR more than three hundred years an intense desire has been felt by explorers to discover and reveal to the world the secrets of the immediate regions of the North Pole. Nor has this desire been confined to mere adventurers. Learned geographers, skillful navigators, and scientific men of broad and accurate study, have engaged in these enterprises with enthusiastic interest. The great governments of the Christian world have bestowed upon them liberally the resources of their wealth and science, and never to a greater extent than within the last three years. Failure seems but to stimulate exertion. Scarcely have the tears dried on the faces of the friends of those who have perished in the undertaking before we hear of the departure of a fresh expedition. Something like a divine inspiration has attended these explorations from the first, and their moral tone has been excellent.

This volume sketches the latest American efforts, second to no others in heroism and success, and abounding in instructive and intensely interesting adventures both grave and gay.

We have followed in this volume, as in its companion volume, "The Arctic Heroes," the orthography of Professor Dall, of the Smithsonian Institution, in some frequently-occurring Arctic words.

CONTENTS.

Illustrations.

NORTH-POLE VOYAGES.

CHAPTER I.

NORTHWARD.

THE readers who have been with us before into the arctic regions will recollect the good American brig Advance, and her wonderful drift during five months, in 1851, from the upper waters of the Wellington Channel, until she was dropped in the Atlantic Ocean by the ice-field which inclosed her. Dr. Kane, then her surgeon, took command of this same vessel, in 1853, for another search for the lost Franklin. We have seen that the place of Franklin's disasters and death was found while Kane was away on this voyage, so the interest of the present story will not connect with that great commander, except in the noble purposes of its heroes.

The Advance left New York on the thirtieth of May, having on board, all counted, eighteen men. Kind hearts and generous purses had secured for her a fair outfit in provisions for the comfort of the adventurers, in facilities for fighting the ice and cold, and in the means of securing desired scientific results. Of the thousands who waved them a kind adieu from the shore many said sadly, "They will never return."

We shall make the acquaintance of the officers and men as we voyage with them, and a very agreeable acquaintance we are sure it will be. The rules by which all agreed to be governed were these and no others: "Absolute obedience to the officer in command; no profane swearing; no liquor drunk except by special order."

The voyagers touched at St. John's, and among other kindnesses shown them was the gift by the governor of a noble team of nine Newfoundland dogs.

At Fiskernaes, the first Greenland port which they entered, they added to their company Hans Christian, an Esquimo hunter, nineteen years of age. Hans was expert with the Esquimo spear and kayak. He will appear often in our story, and act a conspicuous part; he at once, however, prepossesses us in his favor by stipulating with Dr. Kane to leave two barrels of bread and fifty pounds of pork with his mother in addition to the wages he is to receive. The doctor made his cup of joy overflow by adding to these gifts to his mother the present for himself of a rifle and new kayak.

The expedition next touched at Lichtenfels. Dr. Kane obtained here a valuable addition to his outfit of fur clothing. Stopping at Proven, a supply of Esquimo dogs was completed; lying to briefly at Upernavik, the most northern port of civilization, their equipment in furs, ice-tools, and other necessary articles known to arctic voyagers, was rendered still more complete. At this last port the services of Carl Petersen were engaged for the expedition. We have met this intelligent, heroic Dane among our "Arctic Heroes." He will for a long time appear in the shifting scenes of our story.

On the twenty-seventh of July the "Advance" drew near to Melville Bay. The reader who has accompanied the earlier arctic explorers into this region will remember their terrific experience in this bay. Every arctic enemy of the navigator lurks there. Their attacks are made singly and in solid combinations. At one time they steal upon their victim like a Bengal tiger; at other times they rush upon him with a shout and yell, like a band of our own savages. Giant icebergs; fierce storms; cruel nips; silent, unseen, irresistible currents; with ever-changing, treacherous "packs" and "floes," and the all-pervading, relentless cold, are some of these enemies. A favorite movement of these forces is to so adjust themselves as to promise the advancing explorer or whaler a speedy and complete success; then, suddenly changing front, to crush and sink him at once, or to bind him in icy fetters, a helpless, writhing victim, for days, weeks, or months, and finally, perhaps, to bury both ship and men in the dark, deep waters of the bay.

The "Advance" was at this time treated by these guardians of the approach to the North Pole with exceptional courtesy. We suspect that they secretly purposed to follow them into more northern regions, and there to attack them at even greater advantage. This they certainly did.

But just to show them what it could and was minded to do, the evil spirit of the bay invited them at one time to escape impending danger by fastening to a huge berg. This they did, after eight hours of warping, heaving, and planting ice-anchors, a labor of prostrating exhaustion. Hardly had they begun to enjoy the invited hospitality of the berg, when it began to shower upon them, like big drops from a summer cloud, pieces of ice the size of a walnut, accompanied by a crackling, threatening noise from above. A gale from out of its hiding-place on shore came sweeping upon them at the same time, driving before it its icy supporter. Mischief was evidently intended. The "Advance" retreated from the berg with all possible haste, and had barely gone beyond its reach when it launched after it its whole broadside, which came crashing into the water with a roar like a whole park of artillery. Could any thing be rougher? But then it was true to its icebergy character.

The "Advance" was not injured, but the ice held as a trophy more than two thousand feet of good whale line, which had to be cut in the retreat.

These bergs, though thus harsh and treacherous as a rule, *can* do a generous thing. May be, like some people, they are all the more dangerous on account of exceptional generosity. The loose ice, soon after this incident, was drifting south, and would have borne the navigators with it back from whence they had come, perhaps for hundreds of miles. But a majestic berg came along whose sunken base took hold of the deep water current, and so, impelled by this current, it sailed grandly northward, sweeping a wide path through the rotten floes. It condescendingly offered to do tugboat service for the "Advance," and invited its captain to throw aboard an ice-anchor. We wonder he dared to trust it, but he did, and, grappling its crystal sides, made good headway for awhile until other means of favorable voyaging were presented.

Soon after the explorers parted from this bergy friend the midnight sun came out over its northern crest, kindling on every part of its surface fires of varied colors, and scattering over the ice all around blazing carbuncles, sparkling rubies, and molten gold.

August fifth the "Advance," fairly clearing the hated Melville Bay, sailed along the western coast of the "North Water" of Baffin Bay. At Northumberland Island, at the mouth of Whale Sound, their eyes were again delighted by an exhibition of beautiful colors, delicately tinted, but this time not made by a gorgeous sunrise over a gigantic iceberg. The snow of the island and its vicinity bore, over vast areas, a reddish hue, and great patches of beautiful green mosses broke its monotony, while here and there the protruding sandstone threw in a rich shading of brown. So God paints the dreariest lands in colors of great beauty, and scatters over them profusely at times the richest sunlit gems.

On the sixth of August they passed the frowning headland of Smith's Sound, known as Cape Alexander. It stands like the charred trunk and limbs of some mighty oak, at the entrance of an unexplored, gloomy forest, seen in the murky darkness. Cape Alexander seemed a mighty sentinel of evil purpose, toward all who dared pass to the mysterious regions beyond. It inspired the sailors with superstitious fear, and admonished their officers that eternal vigilance must be the price of safety in the waters beyond.

Arriving at Littlěton Island, our explorers built a monument of stones as a conspicuous object from the sea, surmounted by the stripes and stars, put under it a record of their voyage thus far, and, two miles north and east, upon the mainland, deposited a metallic life-boat, with provisions and various stores. These were for a resort in case of accident in their further progress.

While making this deposit they discovered the remains of Esquimo huts, and graves of some of their former occupants. The dead had been buried in a sitting posture, their knees drawn close to their bodies; the few simple implements belonging to the deceased were buried with them. In one grave was a child's toy spear. So even the rude Esquimo child has its toys, and, no doubt, the mother looks upon its trinkets, as she lays them beside its dead body, with tearful interest.

Soon after making these deposits in the life-boat, the "Advance," while making a vigorous struggle with the broken ice, was borne into a land-locked inlet, which Dr. Kane called Refuge Harbor. It was rather a cosy place for an arctic shore, and in it the explorers waited for the movement of the ice.

While here they were much annoyed by their dogs, fifty in number. Two bears had been shot, which were the only game which had been taken for them. They were now on short allowance, and were as ravenous as wolves. They gulped down almost any thing which could go down their throats, even devouring at one time a part of a feather-bed. Dr. Kane's specimens of natural history fared hard at their jaws. He happened once to set down in their way two nests of large sea-fowl. They were filled with feathers, filth, moss and pebbles—a full peck, but the dogs made a rush for them and gobbled down the whole. There were plenty of wolves not far from the brig, on which they delighted to feed. But the hunters had no luck in trying to take them. Rifle balls glanced from their thick hides as if they had been peas from a toy gun. They needed the Esquimo harpoon and the Esquimo skill. But fortunately a dead narwhal, or sea-unicorn, was found. Under its soothing influence, when fed out to them, the dogs became more quiet.

After remaining a few days at Refuge Harbor, a desperate push was made to get the vessel farther north and east. For twelve days they manfully battled with the ice, and made forty miles. This brought them to the bottom of a broad shallow bay, which they named Force Bay. Here they fastened the brig to a shelving, rocky ledge near the shore.

CHAPTER II.

ANCHORED AT LAST.

ON Wednesday, August seventeenth, the heralds of a storm from the South reached the brig. They made their announcement by hurling against her sides some heavy floe-pieces. Understanding this hint of what was coming, the explorers clung to their rocky breakwater by three heavy hawsers. Louder and louder roared the blast, and more fiercely crashed the ice which it hurled against the ledge. At midnight one of the cables, the smaller of the three, parted, and the storm seemed to shout its triumph at this success as it assailed the writhing vessel more vigorously. But the ledge broke the power in a measure of the wind and ice, and was, indeed, a godsend to the imperiled men, so they put it down on their chart as Godsend Ledge.

The next day the huge, human-faced walrus came quite near the brig in great numbers, shaking their grim, dripping fronts. The dovekies, more cheerful visitors, scud past toward the land. Both walrus and fowls proclaimed in their way the terribleness of the increasing tempest. The place of the broken hawser had been supplied, and the worried craft strained away at three strong lines which held on bravely. Everything on board was stowed away, or lashed securely, which could invite an assault by the wind.

Saturday, late in the afternoon, Dr. Kane, wet, and weary with watching, went below and threw himself for rest and warmth into his berth. Scarcely had he done this before a sharp, loud twang brought him to his feet. One of the six-inch hawsers had parted; its sound had scarcely been lost in the uproar before a sharp and shrill "twang! twang!" announced the snapping of the whale line. The brig now clung to the ledge by a single cable—a new ten-inch manilla line, which held on grandly. The mate came waddling down into the cabin as the doctor was drawing on his last article of clothing to go on deck. "Captain Kane," he exclaimed, "she wont hold much longer; it's blowing the devil himself."

All hands now gathered about the brave manilla line on which their fate seemed to depend. Its deep Eolian chant mingled solemnly with the rattle of the rigging and the moaning of the shrouds, and died away in the tumult of the conflicting wind and sea. The sailors were loud in its praises as they watched it with bated breath. It was singing its death song, for, with the noise of a shotted gun, and a wreath of smoke, it gave way, and out plunged the brig into the rushing current of the tempest-tossed ice.

Two hours of hard and skillful labor were bestowed on the vessel to get her back to the ledge; first by beating, or trying to do so, up into the wind; and then by warping along the edge of the solid floe, but all in vain. A light sail was then set, that they might keep command of the helm, and away they scud through a tortuous lead filled with heavy, broken ice.

At seven o'clock on Sunday morning the vessel was heading, under full way, upon huge masses of ice. The heaviest anchor was thrown out to stay her speed. But the ice-torrent so crowded upon the poor craft that a buoy was hastily fastened to the chain, and it was slipped, and away went "the best bower," the sailor's trusted friend in such dangers.

The vessel now went banging and scraping against the floes, one of which was forty feet thick, and many of which were thirty feet. These collisions smashed in her bulwarks, and covered her deck with icy fragments. Yet the plucky little brig returned to the conflict after every blow with only surface wounds.

These assaults failing to turn back or to destroy the little invading stranger, the arctic warriors now brought into the field their mightiest champions. Not far ahead, and apparently closing the lead, was a whole battalion of icebergs. It was an unequal fight, and down upon them, with unwilling haste, came the "Advance." As it approached it was seen that a narrow line of clear water ran between the bergs and the solid, high wall of the floe. Into this the vessel shot, with the high wind directly after it. The sailors, caps in hand, were almost ready to send to the baffled enemy a shout of triumph, when the wind died away into a lull, which amounted, for a moment, to almost a dead calm. But on that moment the fate of the expedition appeared to hang. The enemy saw his opportunity and began to close up. There seemed no possible escape for the brig. On one side was the steep ice-wall of the floe, on which there could be no warping. On the other were the slowly but steadily advancing bergs in a compact line. Just in time, the anxious, waiting, and almost breathless crew, hailed their deliverer. It was a broad, low, platform-shaped berg, over which the water washed. It came sailing swiftly by, and into it they planted an ice-anchor attached to a tow line. Away galloped their crystal racer, outrunning the "pale horse" which followed them! So narrow became the channel between the bergs and floe e'er they reached the open water beyond, that the yards had to be "squared" to prevent them from being carried away, and the boats suspended over the sides were taken on deck to prevent them from being crushed. They came round under the lee of a great berg, making the enemy of a moment ago their protector now. Dr. Kane says: "Never did heart-tried men acknowledge with greater gratitude their merciful deliverance from a wretched death."

But the fight was not over. A sudden flaw puffed the "Advance" from its hiding-place, and drove it again into the drifting ice along the edge of the solid floe. Once she was lifted high in the air on the crest of a great wave, and, as it slipped from under her, she came down with tremendous force against the floe. The masts quivered like reeds in the wind, and the poor craft groaned like a struck bullock.

At last they reached a little pond of water near the shore. They had drifted since morning across Force Bay, ten miles. A berg, with pretended friendliness, came and anchored between the brig and the storm. The situation seemed to warrant a little rest, and the men went below and threw themselves into their bunks. Dr. Kane was yet on deck, distrusting the treacherous ice. Scarcely had the men begun to sleep before the vessel received a thump and a jerk upward. All hands were instantly on deck. Great ice-tables, twenty feet thick, crowding forward from the shore side with a force as from a sliding mountain, pressed the vessel against the shore front of the berg; had this been a perpendicular wall, no wood and iron wrought into a vessel could have prevented a general crash. But the unseen Hand was apparent again. The berg was sloping, and up its inclined plane the vessel went, in successive jerks. The men leaped upon the ice to await the result. Personal effects, such as could be carried and were deemed indispensable, were in readiness in the cabin for leave-taking. Sledge equipments and camping conveniences were put in order and placed at hand. The explorers had experienced a midnight assault, and were ready for the flight. But Dr. Kane bears warm testimony concerning the coolness and self-possession of every man.

While awaiting the fate of the vessel, on which hung their own fate also, not a sound was heard save the roaring of the wind, the crashing ice, and the groaning of the vessel's timbers, as she received shock after shock, and mounted steadily up the ice-mountain. Having attained a cradle high and dry above the sea, the brig rested there several hours. Finally she quietly settled down into her old position among the ice rubbish of the sea.

When the escape was apparent, there was for a moment a deep-breathing silence among the men, before the rapturous outburst of joyful congratulation.

While this last thrilling incident had been transpiring, four of the men were missing. They had gone upon the ice some hours before to carry out a warp, and had been carried away on an ice-raft. When the morning came, and the vessel grounded in a safe place, a rescue party was sent out, who soon returned with them. A little rest was now obtained by all.

CHAPTER III.

THRILLING INCIDENTS.

AFTER a brief rest our explorers continued their voyage. They warped the vessel round the cape near which they found shelter, into a bay which opened to the north and west. Along the shore of this bay they toiled for several days and reached its head. It seemed impossible to go farther, for the ice was already thick and the winter at hand. A majority of the officers, in view of these facts, advised a return south. But Dr. Kane thought they might winter where they were, or further north if the vessel could be pushed through the ice, and their explorations be made with dog-sledges. To learn more fully the practicability of his view he planned a boat excursion. While this was in contemplation an incident came near ending all further progress of the expedition. The brig grounded in the night, and was left suddenly by the receding tide on her beam ends. The stove in the cabin, which was full of burning coal, upset and put the cabin in a blaze. It was choked by a pilot-cloth overcoat until water could be brought. No other harm was done than the loss of the coat and a big scare.

About the first of September the doctor and seven volunteers started in the boat "Forlorn Hope" to see the more northern shore-line. The boat was abandoned at the end of twenty-four hours, all the water having turned to ice, and the party tramped many a weary mile, carrying their food and a few other necessary things. Dr. Kane attained an elevation of eleven hundred feet, from which, with his telescope, he looked north beyond the eightieth degree of latitude, and through a wide extent of country east and west. From this observation he decided that sledging with dogs into and beyond this region was practicable. This had seemed doubtful before. He therefore returned with the decision to put the "Advance" into winter-quarters immediately.

A few facts interesting to the scientific were learned on this excursion. A skeleton of a musk ox was found, showing they had been, at no distant time, visitors to this coast. Additions were made to their flowering plants, and up to this date twenty-two varieties had been found.

The brig was now drawn in between two islands, and the mooring lines carried out. The explorers were in a sheltered, and, as to the ice, safe winter home. They called it Rensselaer Harbor. Near them an iceburg had anchored as if to watch their movements. A fresh-water pond on the upland promised them its precious treasure if they would *cut* for it. An island a few rods distant they named Butler Island, and on this they built a store-house. A canal was cut from the brig to this island, and kept open by renewed cutting every morning. They then run the boat through this canal, thus transferring the stores from the hold to the store-house.

While one party was thus engaged, others were equally busy in other directions. The scientific corps selected a small island which they called Fern Rock, and put up a rude "observatory," from which not only the stars were to be watched, but the weather, the meteors, and the electrical currents were to be noted.

While this outside work was going on Dr. Kane was taxing his ingenuity to arrange the brig, now made roomy by the removal of the stores, so as to have it combine the greatest convenience, warmth, and healthfulness. A roof was put over the upper deck, which was then made to answer for a promenade deck for pleasure and health.

Even the wolfish Esquimo dogs were remembered in this general planning. A nice dog house, cozy and near, was made for them on Butler Island. But the dogs had notions of their own about their quarters. Though so savage at all times as to be willing to eat their masters if not kept in abject fear, yet they refused to sleep out of the sound of their voices. They would leave their comfortable quarters on the island and huddle together in the snow, exposed to the severest cold, to be within the sound of human voices. So they had to be indulged with kennels on deck.

While these matters were being attended to the hunters scoured the country to learn what the prospect was for game. They extended their excursions ninety miles, and returned with a report not very encouraging. They saw a few reindeer, and numerous hares and rabbits. It was plain that hunting would not make large returns.

The winter came on with its shroud of darkness. On the tenth of September the sun made but a short circuit above the horizon before it disappeared again. In one month it would cease to show its disk above the surrounding hills; then would come a midday twilight for a few days, followed by nearly a hundred days of darkness in which no man could work. Even now, at noon, the stars glowed brightly in the heavens, though but few of them were the familiar stars of the home sky.

While the work of which we have spoken was going on Dr. Kane's thoughts were much upon the necessity of establishing, before the winter nights fully set in, provision depots at given distances northward for at least sixty miles. These would be necessary for a good start in the early spring of a dog-sledge journey North Poleward. For the spring work the Newfoundland dogs, of which he had ten, were in daily training. Harnessed to a small, strong, beautifully made sledge called "Little Willie," the doctor drove his team around the brig in gallant style. These Newfoundlanders were a dependence for heavy draught. The Esquimo dogs were in reserve for the long, perilous raids of the earnest exploration into darkness and over hummocks.

While all this busy preparation was going on the morning and evening prayers were strictly maintained, bringing with them a soothing assurance of the Divine care.

On the twentieth of September the provision deposit party started on an experimental journey. It consisted of seven men in all, M'Gary and Bonsall officers. They carried about fourteen hundred pounds of mixed stores for the "cairns." They took these stores upon the strong, thorough-built sledge "Faith," and drew it themselves, by a harness for each man, consisting of a "rue-raddy," or shoulder-belt, and track-line. The men then generously did a service they would in future have the dogs do.

While this party was gone the home work went on, enlivened by several incidents involving the most appalling dangers, yet not without some comic elements.

The first was occasioned by rats. What right these creatures had in the expedition is not apparent; nor do we see what motive impelled them to come at all. If it was a mere love of adventure, they, as do most adventurers, found that the results hardly paid the cost. They were voted a nuisance, but how to abate it was a difficult question. The first experiment consisted of a removal of the men to a camp on deck for a night, and a fumigation below, where the rats remained, of a vile compound of brimstone, burnt leather, and arsenic. But the rats survived it bravely.

The next experiment was with carbonic acid gas. This proved a weapon dangerous to handle. Dr. Hays burnt a quantity of charcoal, and the hatches were shut down after starting three stoves.

The gas generated below rapidly, and nobody was expected, of course, to go where it was. But the French cook, Pierre Schubert, thinking his soup needed seasoning, stole into the cook room. He was discerned by Morton, staggering in the dark; and, at the risk of his own life, he sprung to his relief, and both reached the deck bewildered, the cook entirely insensible.

Soon after this Dr. Kane thought he smelt a strange odor. The hatches were removed and he went below. After a short tour between decks, he was passing the door which led to the carpenter's room, and he was amazed to see three feet of the deck near it a glowing fire. Beating a hasty retreat, he fell senseless to the floor at the foot of the stairs which led to the upper deck. The situation was critical. A puff of air might envelope the hold in flames, with the doctor an easy victim; but the divine Hand still covered him. Mr. Brooks, reaching down, drew him out. Coming to the air the doctor recovered immediately and communicated his startling discovery quietly to those only near him. Water was passed up from the "fire-hole" along side, kept open for just such emergencies. Dr. Kane and Ohlsen went below, water was dashed on, and they were safe.

The dead bodies of twenty-eight rats were the net result of this onslaught with carbonic acid gas. But they were but few among so many. The rat army was yet in fighting order.

The other incident was less serious, yet quite on the verge of fatal consequences. Several Esquimo dogs became the mothers of nice little families. Now these young folks in the kennels were considered intruders by the master of the vessel—rather hard on them since they were not to blame in the matter. But it happens with dogs as with the human race, that they sometimes suffer without fault of their own. Six puppies were thrown overboard; two died for the good their skins might do as mittens; and, alas! seven died more dreadful deaths—they were eaten by their mammas! Whether these puppy calamities bore heavily upon the brains of the dog mothers or not we cannot tell, but the fact recorded is that one of them went distracted. She walked up and down the deck with a drooping head and staggering gait. Finally she snapped at Petersen, foamed at the mouth, and fell at his feet. "She is mad!" exclaimed Petersen. "Hydrophobia!" was the dreadful cry which passed about the deck. Dr. Kane ran for his gun. He was not a moment too soon in reappearing with it. The dog had recommenced her running and snapping at those near. The Newfoundland dogs were not out of her reach, and the hatches leading below were open. But a well-directed shot ended at once her life and the danger.

It was now the tenth of October. The sun, though just appearing above the horizon to the surrounding country, only sparkled along the edge of the hill-tops to the gazers from the "Advance." The depot party had been gone twenty days, and

Dr. Kane was beginning to feel anxious about them. He harnessed four of his best Newfoundlanders into the "Little Willie," and, accompanied by John Blake, started in search of them.

For a little time the party progressed very well. But after awhile the new ice between the broken floes was found thin. The seams thus frozen had to be leaped. Sometimes they were wide, and the dogs in their attempts to spring across broke in. Three times in less than as many hours one had received an arctic bath. The men trotted along side, leaping, walking, running, and shouting to the dogs. Extended and exhausting diversions were made to avoid impassable chasms or too steep hummocks. Thus four days had passed in a fruitless search for the missing ones.

On the morning of the fifth day, about two hours before the transient sun showed his glowing disk, Dr. Kane climbed an iceberg to get a sight of the road ahead. In the dim distance on the snow a black spot was seen. Is it a bear? No, it now stretches out into a dark line. It is the sledge party! They see their leader's tent by the edge of a thinly-frozen lead; into this they launch their boat and come on, singing as they come. The doctor, in breathless suspense, waits until they draw near, and counts them: one, two, three, four, five, six, seven! They are all safe! Three cheers go up from both parties, followed by hearty handshaking and congratulations. The depot enterprise was a success.

CHAPTER IV.

LOST AND RESCUED.

THE sun had disappeared, but the moon completed her circuit in the heavens with great beauty. Her nearest approach to the horizon was twenty-five degrees. For eight days after the return of the party to the vessel it shone with almost unclouded brightness, as if to give them a joyful welcome.

When November came our explorers were well settled in their winter-quarters. They had made them by judicious ventilation and a careful distribution of heat tolerably comfortable. Below decks they had a uniform temperature of sixty-five degrees above zero, and under the housing of the upper deck it never went below zero, while outside the thermometer averaged twenty-five degrees minus.

While shut up in the darkness, relieved only by the light from the sparkling stars and the glowing moon, the daily routine of the ship's duties were strictly performed. Each had his assigned work. The monotonous meals came at the stated hour, and the bell noted the changing watches. The morning and evening prayers, and the religious observance of the Sabbath, were pleasant and profitable prompters to serious thought. These became more and more needed as the inactive season progressed. The continued darkness without, made dense often by heavy clouds, wore upon the spirits of the men; besides, their light within became less cheerful by the failure of the supply of oil. The lamps refused to burn poor lard, and muddy corks and wads of cotton floating as tapers in saucers filled with it gave but a lurid light and emitted an offensive smoke and odor. It would be strange, indeed, if in this ice-imprisoned company there were no homesick ones, however bravely the feeling might be suppressed. Hans, the Esquimo, at one time packed his clothes and shouldered his rifle to bid the brig's company good-bye. A desperate, lone journey homeward he would have had of it! It was whispered that in addition to his drawings to his mother there was at Fiskernes a lady-love. He, however, was persuaded to stay on shipboard, and Dr. Kane gave him for his sickness a dose of salts and promotion. They worked well, and he seems to have been very contented afterward.

The usual resort was had to dramatic performances, fancy balls, and the publication of a paper called the "Ice-blink." A favorite sport was the "fox-chase," in which each sailor in turn led off as fox in a run round the upper deck, followed by the rest in chase. Dr. Kane offered a Guernsey shirt as a prize to the man who held out the longest in the chase. William Godfrey sustained the chase for fourteen minutes, and *wore* off the shirt.

November twenty-seventh the commander sent

out a volunteer party under Bonsall to see if the Esquimo had returned to the huts which had been seen in the fall. The darkness at noonday was too great for reading, and the cold was terrible. The party returned after one night's encamping, the sledge having broken, and the tent and luggage being left behind. A few days after Morton started alone to recover the lost articles. In two days and a half he returned bringing every thing. He tramped in that time, with the cold forty degrees below zero, sixty-two miles, making only three halts. The darkness during the time was such that a hummock of ice fifty paces ahead could hardly be seen.

The effect of the darkness on the dogs was very marked, but so long as there was any sledging for them to do their spirits kept up. One of the Newfoundlands, named Grim, was a character. He was noted for a profound appreciation of his dinner, of which he never had enough, for a disrelish for work, and a remarkable knowledge of the arts of hypocrisy. His cunning fawning, and the beseeching wink of his eye, procured for him warm quarters in the deck-house, and a bed on the captain's fur coat, while his fellows had to be content with their kennel. Though Grim thus proved his knowledge of the best place at the dog-table, and the best bits it afforded, as well as the best place to sleep, he never could understand a call to the sledge-harness. He always happened at such times to be out of the way. Once, when the dog-team was about to start, he was found hid in a barrel, and was bid join the party. But Grim was equal to the occasion. He went limping across the deck, as much as to say, Would you have a poor lame dog go? The joke was so cute that he was allowed to remain at home, and after that he became suddenly lame as soon as a movement toward the sledges was made. Grim thus attained the usual success of shallow-brained, flattering hypocrisy—many favors and universal contempt. His end, too, was very befitting his life. His master, thinking he was becoming too fat in his lazy dignity, commanded him to join a sledge party. Grown presumptuous by indulgence, he refused, and showed his teeth, besides pleading lameness. But the order was peremptory this time, and a rope was put round his body and attached to the sledge, and he was made to trot after his faithful fellows. At the first halt he contrived to break the rope, and, carrying a few feet of it dragging after him, started in the darkness for the ship. Not having come home when the party returned, search was made for him with lanterns, as it was thought the rope might have caught and detained him in the hummock. His tracks were found not far from the vessel, and then they led away to the shore. Old Grim was never seen again.

Grim could be spared, but the explorers were much alarmed soon after his death by a strange disease among the whole pack. They were at times frenzied, and then became stupid. They were taken below, nursed, tended, and doctored with anxiety and care, for on them much depended. But all died except six. Their death threw a cloud over the prospect of further successful exploration.

But a still darker event threatened the explorers. Every man was more or less touched with the scurvy, except two, and some were prostrate. It was with great joy, therefore, that, on the twenty-first of January, 1854, they saw the orange-colored tints of the sun faintly tracing the top of the distant hills. Daylight and game would be important medicines for the sick. A month later and Dr. Kane made a long walk, and a hard scramble up a projecting crag of a headland of the bay, and bathed in his welcome rays. It was about a week later before he was seen from the deck of the "Advance."

A very busy company now was that on board the brig, making preparations for spring work. The carpenter was making and mending sledges; the tinker making and mending cooking apparatus for the journeys; many busy hands were at work on the furs and blankets for a complete renewed outfit for wearing and sleeping. But though March had come, the average cold was greater than at any time before. Still a sledge party was in readiness to start by the middle of the month, to carry provisions for a new deposit beyond those made in the fall. The party consisted of eight men. A new sledge had been made, smaller than the "Faith," and adapted to the reduced dog-team. To this the load was lashed, a light boat being placed on top. The men harnessed in but could hardly start it. The boat was then removed and two hundred pounds of the load, and thus relieved away they went, cheered by the hearty "God bless you!" of their shipmates. Dr. Kane had added to their provisions by the way, as an expression of good-will, the whole of his brother's "great wedding cake."

But as they started their ever watchful commander thought he saw more good-will than ability to draw the load, and a suspicion, too, impressed him that the new sledge was not all right. So he followed, and found them in camp only five miles away. He said nothing about any new orders for the morning, laughed at the rueful faces of some of them, and heard Petersen's defense of *his* new sledge as the best which could be made. He saw them all tucked away in their buffaloes, and returned to the brig. We have before referred to a sledge called the "Faith." It was built by Dr. Kane's order, after an English pattern, except that the runners were made lower and wider. It had been thought too large for the present party. The doctor now called up all his remaining men. The "Faith" was put on deck, her runners polished, lashings, a canvas covering, and track-lines were adjusted to her. By one o'clock that night the discarded two hundred pounds of provisions and the boat were lashed on, and away the men went for their sleeping comrades. They were still sound asleep when the "Faith" arrived. The load of the new boat was quietly placed upon it, all put in traveling order, and it was started off on an experimental trip with five men. The success was perfect. The sleepers were then awakened, and all were delighted at the easier draught of the heavier load. Dr. Kane and his party returned to the vessel with the discarded sledge.

Ten days slipped away, and no tidings from the depot party. The work of clearing up the ship, and putting the finishing touch to the preparation for the distant northern excursion, which was to crown the efforts of the expedition, and unlock, it was hoped, at last, some of the secrets of the North Pole, progressed daily. At midnight of the eleventh day a sudden tramp was heard on deck, and immediately Sontag, Ohlsen, and Petersen entered the cabin. Their sudden coming was not so startling as their woe-begone, bewildered looks. It was with difficulty that they made their sad tale known. Brooks, Baker, Wilson, and Schubert were all lying on the ice, disabled, with Irish Tom Hickey, who alone was able to minister to their wants. The escaped party had come, at the peril of their own lives, to get aid. They had evidently come a long distance, but how far, and where they had left the suffering ones, they could not tell, nor were they in a condition to be questioned.

While the urgent necessities of the new comers were being attended to, Dr. Kane and others were getting ready the "Little Willie," with a buffalo cover, a small tent, and a package of prepared meat called pemmican. Ohlsen seemed to have his senses more than the others, though he was sinking with exhaustion, having been fifty hours without rest. Dr. Kane feeling that he *must* have a guide or fail to find the lost ones, Ohlsen was put in a fur bag, his legs wrapped up in dog-skins and eider down, and then he was strapped on the sledge.

Off dashed the rescue party, nine men besides their commander, carrying only the clothes on their backs. The cold was seventy-eight degrees below the freezing point.

Guided by icebergs of colossal size, they hurried across the bay, and traveled sixteen hours with some certainty that they were on the right track. They then began to lose their way. Ohlsen, utterly exhausted, had fallen asleep, and when awakened was plainly bewildered. He could tell nothing about the way, nor the position of the lost ones. He had before said that it was drifting heavily round them when they were left. The situation of the rescue party was becoming critical, and the chance of helping the lost seemed small indeed; they might be anywhere within forty miles.

Thus situated Dr. Kane moved on ahead, and clambered up some ice-piles and found himself upon a long, level floe. Thinking the provision party might have been attracted by this as a place to camp, he determined to examine it carefully. He gave orders to liberate Ohlsen, now just able to walk, from his fur bag, and to pitch the tent; then leaving tent, sledge, and every thing behind, except a small allowance of food taken by each man, he commanded the men to proceed across the floe at a good distance from each other. All obeyed cheerfully and promptly, and moved off at a lively step to keep from freezing; yet somehow, either from a sense of loneliness, or involuntarily, there was a constant tendency of the men to huddle together. Exhaustion and cold told fearfully upon them; the stoutest were seized with trembling fits and short breath, and Dr. Kane fell twice fainting on the snow. They had now been eighteen hours out without food or rest, and the darkness of their situation seemed to have no ray of light, when Hans shouted that he thought he saw a sledge track. Hardly daring to believe that their senses did not deceive them, they traced it until footsteps were apparent; following these with religious care they came after awhile in sight of a small American flag fluttering from a hummock. Lower down they espied a little Masonic banner hanging from a tent pole barely above the drift. It was the camp of the lost ones! It was found after an unfaltering march of twenty-one hours. The little tent was nearly covered by the drift.

Dr. Kane was the last to come up, and when he reached the tent his men were standing in solemn silence upon each side of it. With great kindness and delicacy of feeling they intimated their wish that he should be the first to go in.

He lifted the canvas and crawled in, and in the darkness felt for the poor fellows, who were stretched upon their backs. A burst of welcome within was answered by a joyful shout without. "We expected you," said one, embracing the doctor; "we *knew* you would come!" For the moment all perils, hunger, and exhaustion were forgotten amid the congratulations and gratitude.

The company now numbered fifteen, the cold was intense, but one half the number had to keep stirring outside while the rest crowded into the little tent to sleep. Each took a turn of two hours, and then preparations were made to start homeward.

They took the tent, furs for the rescued party, and food for fifty hours, and abandoned every thing else. The tent was folded and laid on the sledge, a bed was then made of eight buffalo skins, the sick, having their limbs carefully sewed up in reindeer skins, were then put in a reclining position on the bed, and other furs and blanket bags thrown around them. The whole was lashed together, allowing only a breathing place opposite the mouth. This *embalming* of the sufferers, and getting them a good meal, cost four hours of exposure in a cold that had become fifty-five degrees minus. Most of the rescuers had their fingers nipped by the frost.

When all was ready the whole company united in a short prayer.

Now commenced the fearful journey. The sledge and its load weighed eleven hundred pounds. The hummocks were many; some of them were high, and long deviations round them must be made; some which they climbed over, lifting the sledge after them, were crossed by narrow chasms filled with light snow—fearful traps into which if one fell his death was almost certain. Across these the sledge was drawn, some of them being too wide for it to bridge them, so it had to be sustained by the rope, and steadily too, for the sick could not bear to be lashed so tight as not to be liable to roll off, and the load was top-heavy.

In spite of these obstacles all went bravely for six hours. The abandoned tent was nine miles ahead, the sledge on which life depended bravely bore every strain, the new floe was gained, and the traveling improved, so that good hope was entertained that the tent, its covert and rest, would be gained. Just then a strange feeling came over nearly the whole party. Some begged the privilege of sleeping. They were not cold, they said; they did not mind the wind now; all they wanted was a little sleep. Others dropped on the snow and refused to get up. One stood bolt upright, and, with closed eyes, could not be made to speak. The commander boxed, jeered, argued, and reprimanded his men to no purpose. A halt was made and the tent pitched. No fire could be obtained, for nobody's fingers were limber enough to strike fire, so no food or water could be had.

Leaving the company in charge of M'Gary, with orders to come on after four hours' rest, Dr. Kane and Godfrey went forward to the tent to get ready a fire and cooked food. They reached the tent in a strange sort of stupor. They remembered nothing only that a bear trotted leisurely ahead of them, stopping once to tear a jumper to pieces which one of the men had dropped the day before, and pausing to toss the tent contemptuously aside. They set it up with difficulty, crept into their fur bags, and slept intensely for three hours. They then arose, succeeded in lighting the cooking lamp, and had a steaming soup ready when the rest arrived.

Refreshed with food and rest, the feeble re-adjusted, they commenced the home stretch. Once the old sleepiness came over them, and they in turn slept three minutes by the watch and were benefited. They all reached the brig at one o'clock P. M. All were more or less delirious when they arrived, and could remember nothing of what had happened on the way, with slight exception. The rescue party had been out seventy-two hours; of this time only eight hours were spent in halting. They had traveled about eighty-five miles, most of the distance dragging their sledge.

Dr. Hayes took the sick in hand. Two lost one or more toes; and two, Jefferson Baker, a boyhood playfellow of Dr. Kane, and Pierre Schubert, the French cook, died.

CHAPTER V.

MORE HEROIC EXCURSIONS.

ON the seventh of April, a week after the return of the party just noted, our explorers were startled by shouts from the shore. Dark figures were seen standing along the edges of the land ice, or running to and fro in wild excitement. It was not difficult to make them out as a company of Esquimo. Dr. Kane, seeing by their wild gesticulations that they were unarmed, walked out and beckoned to a brawny savage, who seemed to be a leader, to approach. He understood the sign, and came forward without fear. He was full a head taller than the doctor, and his limbs seemed to have the strength of those of the bear. He was dressed with a fox skin, hooded jumper, white bear-skin trousers, and bear-skin boots tipped with the claws. Though he had evidently never before seen a white man, he manifested no fear. His followers soon crowded around and began to use great freedom, showing an inclination to rush on board the ship. This they were made to understand they must not do. Petersen came out and acted as interpreter, and matters went on more smoothly. The leader, whose name was Metek, was taken on board, while the rest remained on the ice. They brought up from behind the floes fifty-six dogs and their sledges, and, thrusting a spear into the ice, picketed them about the vessel.

While Dr. Kane and Metek were having their interview in the cabin, word was sent out that others might come on board. Nine or ten mounted the ladder with boisterous shouts, though ignorant of how Metek had fared. They went every-where, handled every thing, talked and laughed incessantly, and stole whatever they could. Finally all hands had to be mustered, and restraint laid upon the Esquimo to keep them within due bounds. This they took good naturedly; ran out and in the vessel, ate, and finally *sat* down like tired children, their heads drooping upon their breasts, and slept, snoring the while most famously.

In the morning, before they departed, the commander assembled them on deck for an official interview. He enlarged upon his wonderful qualities as a chief, and the great benefits to his visitors of his friendship. He then entered into a treaty with them, the terms of which were very few and simple, that it might be understood, and the benefits mutual, that it might be kept. He then showed his beneficence by buying all their spare walrus meat and four dogs, enriching them in compensation with a few needles, beads, and treasures of old cask staves. The Esquimo were jubilant. They voted, in their way, Dr. Kane a great captain, promised vociferously to return in a few days with plenty of walrus meat, and loan their dogs and sledges for the great northern journey, all of which they never remembered to do.

When the visitors had gone, it was ascertained that an ax, a saw, and some knives, had gone with them. Besides, the store-house on Butler Island had been entered, and a careful survey of the vicinity revealed the fact that a train of sledges were slyly waiting behind some distant hummocks for a freight of its treasures.

All this had a hard look for friendly relations with the Esquimo; but our explorers felt that conciliation, with quiet firmness, was their best policy. The savages could do their sledge excursions much harm, and, if they would, could greatly aid them.

The next day there came to the vessel five natives—two old men, a middle aged man, and two awkward boys. They were treated with marked kindness, some presents were given them, but they were told that no Esquimo would in future be admitted to the brig until every stolen article was restored. They were overjoyed at the gifts, and departed, lifting up their hands in holy horror on the mention of theft; yet in passing round Butler Island they bore away a coal barrel. M'Gary was watching them, and he hastened their departure by a charge of fine shot. Notwithstanding all this, one of the old men, known afterward as Shung-hu, made a circuit round the hummocks, and came upon an India-rubber boat which had been left upon the floe, and cut it in pieces and carried off the wood of the frame-work.

Soon after this a sprightly youth, good-looking, with a fine dog team, drove up to the vessel in open day. When asked his name, he replied promptly, "Myouk I am." He spoke freely of his place of residence and people, but when asked about the stolen articles he affected great ignorance. Dr. Kane ordered him to be confined in the hold. He took this very hard, at first refusing food. He soon after began to sing in a dolorous strain, then to talk and cry, and then to sing again. The hearts of his captors were made quite tender toward him, and when in the morning it was found that the prisoner had lifted the hatches and fled, taking his dogs with him, even the commander secretly rejoiced.

April twenty-fifth, M'Gary and five men started with the sledge "Faith," on another exploring excursion. They took a small stock only of provisions, depending on the supply depots which had been made in the fall. The plan this time was, to follow the eastern coast line a while, which run north and west, cross over Smith Sound to the American side, where it was hoped smooth ice would be found; and once on such a highway, they anticipated that the Polar Sea would greet their delighted vision, and may be speak to them of the fate of the lost Franklin.

Two days after M'Gary's party left, Dr. Kane and Godfrey followed with the dog sledge loaded with additional comforts for the journey, the men trotting by its side. Only three dogs remained of the original supplies, which, harnessed with the four purchased of the Esquimo, made a tolerable team.

Ten men, four in health and six invalids, were left to keep the vessel. Orders were left by the commander to treat the Esquimo, should they come again, with fairness and conciliation, but if necessity demanded to use fire arms, but to waste no powder or shot. The credit of the gun must be sustained as the bearer of certain death to the white man's enemies.

Dr. Kane and his companions overtook the advanced party in two days. They pushed forward together with tolerable success for four days more, when they all became involved in deep snow-drifts. The dogs floundered about nearly suffocated, and unable to draw the sledge. The men were compelled to take the load on their backs, and kick a path for the dogs to follow. In the midst of these toils the scurvy appeared among the men, and some of the strongest were ready to yield the conflict altogether. The next day, May fourth, Dr. Kane, while taking an observation for latitude fainted, and was obliged to ride on the sledge. Still the party pushed on; but they soon met with an obstacle no heroism could overcome. They were without food for further journeying! The bears had destroyed their carefully deposited stores. They had removed stones which had required the full strength of three men to lift. They had broken the iron meat casks into small pieces. An alcohol cask, which had cost Dr. Kane a special journey in the late fall to deposit, was so completely crushed that a whole stave could not be found.

On the fifth of May Dr. Kane became delirious,

and was lashed to the sledge, while his brave, though nearly fainting, men took the back track. They arrived at the brig in nine days, and their commander was borne to his berth, where he lay for many days, between life and death, with the scurvy and typhoid fever. Thus closed another effort to unlock the secrets of the extreme polar region.

Hans made himself exceedingly useful at this time. He was promoted to the post of hunter, and excused from all other duties; he was besides promised presents to his lady-love on reaching his home at Fiskernaes. He brought in two deer, the first taken, on the day of this special appointment. The little snow-birds had come, of which he shot many. The seal, too, were abundant, and some of them were added to the fresh provisions. These wonderfully improved those touched by the scurvy.

One day Hans was sent to hunt toward the Esquimo huts, that he might get information concerning the nearness to the brig of clear water. He did not come back that night, and Dr. Hays and Mr. Ohlsen were sent with the dog-sledge to hunt him up. They found him lying on the ice about five miles from the vessel, rolled up in his furs and sound asleep. At his side lay a large seal, shot, as usual, in the head. He had dragged this seal seven hours, and, getting weary, had made his simple camp and was resting sweetly.

May twentieth, Dr. Hays and Godfrey started with the dog team, to make another attempt to cross Smith Strait and reach, along the American side, the unknown north. The doctor was a fresh man, not having been with any previous party. The dogs were rested, well fed, and full of wolfish energy. The second day he fortunately struck into a track free from heavy ice, and made fifty miles! But this success was after the arctic fashion, made to give bitterness to immediate failure. On the third day they encountered hummocks, piled in long ridges across their path; some of them were twenty feet high. Over some of these they climbed, dragging after them both sledge and dogs. Long diversions were made at other times, and their path became in this way so very tortuous that in making ninety miles advance northward they traveled two hundred and seventy miles!

Snow-blindness seized Dr. Hays in the midst of these toils. But, nothing daunted, after short halts, in which his sight improved, he pushed on. But Godfrey soon broke down, though one of the hardiest of explorers. Their dogs, too, began to droop; the provisions were running low, and so the homeward track was taken. Before they reached the vessel they were obliged to lighten their load by throwing away fifty pounds weight of furs, the heaviest of which had been used as sleeping bags.

This excursion resulted in valuable additions to the extreme northern coast-line survey.

On the afternoon of June fourth, M'Gary, with four men, started on a last desperate effort to push the survey, on the Greenland side, a hundred miles farther, by which Dr. Kane thought the limits of the ice in that direction might be reached. Morton, one of the company, was to keep himself as fresh as possible, so that when the rest came to a final halt he might be able to push on farther. Hans was kept at the vessel until the tenth, four days later, when he started light with the dog-sledge to join them. His part was to accompany Morton on the final run.

The hunter of the vessel being gone, Dr. Kane, who was now much better, took his rifle to try his skill at seal hunting. This animal is not easily taken by unpracticed game seekers. He lies near the hole which he keeps open in the ice, and at the slightest noise plunges out of sight. Seeing one lying lazily in the sun, the doctor lay down and drew himself along softly behind the little knobs of ice. It was a cold, tedious process, but finally getting within a long rifle shot, the seal rolled sluggishly to one side, raised his head, and strained his neck, as if seeing something in an opposite direction. Just then the doctor saw with surprise a rival hunter. A large bear lay, like himself, on his belly, creeping stealthily toward the game. Here was a critical position. If he shot the seal, the bear would probably have no scruples about taking it off his hands, and, perhaps, by way of showing that might makes right, take him before his rifle could be reloaded. While the doctor was debating the matter the seal made another movement which stirred his hunter blood, and he pulled the trigger. The cap only exploded. The seal, alarmed, descended into the deep with a floundering splash; and the bear, with a few vigorous leaps, stood, a disappointed hunter, looking after him from the edge of the hole. Bruin and Dr. Kane were now face to face. By all the rules of game-taking the bear should have eaten the man; he was the stronger party, the gun was for the moment useless, he was hungry, and had lost his dinner probably by the intrusive coming of the stranger, and, as to running, there was no danger of his escape in that way. But the bear magnanimously turned and ran away. Not to be outdone in courtesy, Dr. Kane turned and ran with all his might in the opposite direction.

On the twenty-sixth, M'Gary, Bonsall, Hickey, and Riley returned. The snow had almost made them blind; otherwise they were well. They had been gone about three weeks, had made valuable surveys, and fully satisfied the expectations of their commander. Hans caught up with them after two weeks of heroic travel alone with his dogs and sledge. He and Morton had, in accordance with the programme, pressed on farther northward.

The returned party had their adventure with a bear to tell. They had all lain down to sleep in their tent after a wearisome day of travel. The midnight hour had passed when Bonsall felt something scratching at the snow near his head, and, starting up, ascertained that a huge bear was making careful observations around the outside of the tent. He had, in looking round, already observed, no doubt, the important fact that the guns, and every thing like a defensive weapon, were left on the sledge some distance off, though perhaps the importance to him of this fact he did not appreciate. There was consternation, of course, in the camp, and a council of war was called. It had hardly convened before bruin, as a party concerned, thrust his head into the tent door. A volley of lucifer matches was fired at him, and a paper torch was thrust into his face. Without minding these discourteous acts, the bear deliberately sat down and commenced eating a seal which had been shot the day before and happened to be in his way. By the laws of arctic hospitality this should have been considered fair by the tent's company, for strangers are expected to come and go as they please, and eat what they find, not even saying, "By your leave." But the stranger did not conform to the usage of the country. Tom Hickey cut a hole in the back of the tent, seized a boat-hook, which made one of its supporters, and attacked the enemy in the rear. He turned on his assailant and received a well-aimed blow on his nose, by which he was persuaded to retire beyond the sledge and there to pause and consider what to do next. While the bear was thus in council with himself, Hickey sprang forward, seized a rifle from the sledge, almost under the nose of the enemy, and fell back upon his companions. Bonsall took the deadly weapon and sent a ball through and through the bear, and the disturber of the rest of our explorers afforded them many bountiful repasts.

CHAPTER VI.

THE OPEN SEA.

MORTON and Hans returned to the brig on the tenth of July, after having been on their separate exploration three weeks and a half. Their story is full of thrilling incidents and important results.

The first day they made twenty-eight miles, and were greatly encouraged. The next day the arctic enemies of exploration appeared on the field, skirmishing with deep snow through which dogs and men had to wade. Next came a compact host of icebergs. They were not the surface-worn, dingy-looking specimens of Baffin Bay, but fresh productions from the grand glacier near which they lay. Their color was bluish white, and their outlines clearly and beautifully defined. Some were square, often a quarter of a mile each side. Others were not less than a mile long, and narrow. Now and then one of colossal size lifted its head far above its fellows, like a grand observatory. Between these giant bergs were crowded smaller ones of every imaginable size and form.

Through these our explorers had to pick their way. Beginning one night at eight, they dashed along through a narrow lane, turning this way and that, for seven hours. Then they came against the face of a solid ice-cliff, closing the path altogether. Back they urged their weary dogs, and their own weary selves, looking for an opening by which they might turn north, but none appeared until they reached the camp from which they had started. Resting awhile, they commenced anew.

Sometimes they climbed over an ice hillock, making a ladder of their sledge. Morton would climb up first, and then draw up the dogs, around whose bodies Hans tied a rope; then the load was passed up; lastly Hans mounted, and drew up the sledge.

Having broken through the bergy detachment of their arctic foes and reached smoother ice, other opposing columns met them. Dense mists, giving evidence of open water, chilled and bewildered them; but the welcome birds, giving other proof of the nearness of the Polar Sea, cheered them on.

The next attack was in the form of insecure ice. The dogs were dashing on in their wild flight when it began to yield beneath them. The dogs trembled with fear and lay down, as is their habit in such cases. Hans, by a skillful mingling of force and coaxing, succeeding in getting the party out of the danger.

At one time a long, wide channel presented its protest to their farther progress. To this they were obliged so far to yield as to go ten miles out of their way to reach its northern side.

Their right of way was also challenged by seams in the ice often four feet deep, filled with water, and too wide for their best jumping ability. These they filled up by attacking the nearest hummocks with their axes and tumbling the fragments into it until a bridge was made. This work often caused hours of delay.

The signs of open water became more and more apparent. The birds were so plenty that Hans brought down two at one shot. Soon they struck the icy edge of a channel. Along this they coasted on the land side. It brought them to a cape around which the channel run close to a craggy point. Here they deposited a part of their provisions to lighten the sledge. Morton went ahead to learn the condition of the land-ice round the point. He found it narrow and decaying, so that he feared there would be none on their return; yet, forward! was the word. The dogs were unloosed and driven forward alone; then Hans and Morton tilted the sledge edgewise and drew it along, while far below the gurgling waters were rushing southward with a freight of crushed ice.

The cape passed, they opened into a bay of clear water extending far and wide. Along its shore was a wide, smooth ice-belt. Over this the dogs scampered with their sledge and men with wonderful fleetness, making sixty miles the first day! The land grew more and more sloping to the bay as they advanced until it opened from the sea into a plain between two elevated rocky ranges. Into this they entered, steering north, until they struck the entrance of a bay; but the rugged ice across their path forbid farther sledge-travel in that direction. So they picketed, securely, as they thought, the dogs, took each a back load of provisions, and went forward. Their trusty rifles were in hand, and their boat-hook and a few scientific instruments were carefully secured to their persons. Thus equipped, they had tramped about nine miles from the last camp when an exciting scene occurred. It was a bear fight, shaded this time with the tender and tragic. A mother-bear and her child came in sight. They were a loving couple, and had plainly been engaged in a frolic together. Their tracks were scattered profusely about, like those of school children at recess in a recent snow. There were also long furrows down the sloping side of an ice-hill, upon and around which the footprints were seen. Morton declared that they had been coasting down this slope on their haunches, and this opinion was supported by the fact that Dr. Kane did, at another time, see bears thus coasting!

Five of the dogs had broken away from their cords and had overtaken their masters. So they were on hand for the fight.

Mother and child fled with nimble feet, and the dogs followed in hot pursuit. The bear, being overtaken by her enemies, began a most skillful and heroic skirmishing. The cub could not keep up with its mother, so she turned back, put her head under its haunches and threw it some distance ahead, intimating to it to run, while she faced the dogs. But the little simpleton always stopped just where it alighted, and waited for mamma to give it another throw! To vary the mode of operation, she occasionally seized it by the nape of the neck and flung it out of harms way, and then snapped at the dogs with an earnestness that meant business. Sometimes the mother would run a little ahead and then turn, as if to coax the little one to run to her, watching at the same time the enemy.

For a while the bear contrived to make good speed; but the little one became tired and she came to a halt. The men came up with their rifles and the fight became unequal, yet the mother's courage was unabated. She sat upon her haunches and took the cub between her hind legs, and fought the dogs with her paws. "Never," says Morton, "was animal more distressed; her roaring could have been heard a mile! She would stretch her neck and snap at the nearest dog with her shining teeth, whirling her paws like the arms of a windmill." Missing her intended victim, she sent after him a terrific growl of baffled rage.

When the men came up the little one was so far rested as to nimbly turn with its mother and so keep front of her belly. The dogs, in heartless mockery of her situation, continued a lively frisking on every side of her, torturing her at a safe distance for themselves.

Such was the position of the contending parties when Hans threw himself upon the ice, rested upon his elbows, took deliberate aim, and sent a ball through the heroic mother's head. She dropped, rolled over, relieved at once of her agony and her life.

The cub sprung upon the dead body of its mother and for the first time showed fight. The dogs, thinking the conflict ended, rushed upon the prostrate foe, tearing away mouthfuls of hair. But they were glad to retreat with whole skins to their own backs. It growled hoarsely, and fought with genuine fury.

The dogs were called off, and Hans sent a ball through its head; yet it contrived to rise after falling, and climbed again upon its mother's body. It was mercifully dispatched by another ball.

The men took the skin of the mother and the little one for their share of the spoils, and the dogs gorged themselves on the greater carcass.

After this incident the journey of our explorers soon ended. Hans gave out, and was ordered to turn leisurely aside and examine the bend of the bay into which they had entered. Morton continued on toward the termination of a cape which rose abruptly two thousand feet. He tried to get round it, but the ice-foot was gone. He climbed up its sides until he reached a position four hundred and forty feet, commanding a horizon of forty miles. The view was grand. The sea seemed almost boundless, and dashed in noisy surges below, while the birds curveted and screamed above. Making a flag-staff of his walking-stick, he threw to the wind a Grinnell flag. It had made the far southern voyage with Commodore Wilkes, and had come on a second arctic voyage. It now floated over the most northern known land of the globe.

Feasting his eyes with the scenery for an hour and a half, Morton struck his flag and rejoined Hans. The run home had its perils and narrow escapes, but was made without accident, and with some additional surveys.

CHAPTER VII.

AN IMPORTANT MOVEMENT.

IT was now well into July. The last proposed survey was made, and all hands were on shipboard. But the arctic fetters still bound the "Advance," with no signs of loosening. The garb of midwinter was yet covering land and sea, and in every breeze there was a dismal whisper to the explorers of another winter in the ice. The thought was appalling to both officers and men. They had neither health, food, nor fuel for such an experience. To abandon the vessel and try to escape with the boats and sledges was impossible in the prostrate condition of the men.

Having carefully studied the situation Dr. Kane resolved to try to reach Beechy Island, and thus communicate with the British exploring expedition, or by good luck with some whaler, and so secure relief. This island we have often visited in our voyages with the "Arctic Heroes." It is, it will be recollected, at the mouth of Wellington Channel.

When this plan was announced to the officers it was approved cordially. Both officers and men were ready to volunteer to accompany him; he chose five only—M'Gary, Morton, Riley, Hickey, and Hans. Their boat was the old "Forlorn

Hope." The outfit was the best possible, though poor enough. The "Hope" was mounted on the sledge "Faith;" the provisions were put on a "St. John's sledge." The "Faith" started off ahead; the smaller sledge, to which Dr. Kane and two of the men attached themselves, followed.

It took five days of incessant toil, with many head flows, to reach the water and launch the "Hope," though the distance from the brig was only twenty miles.

The boat behaved well, and they reached Littleton Island, where they were rejoiced to see numerous ducks. Watching their course as they flew away, the explorers were led to several islets, whose rocky ledges were covered with their nests, and around which they hovered in clouds. The young birds were taking their first lesson in flying, or were still nestling under their mothers' wings. In a few hours over two hundred birds were taken, the gun bringing down several at one shot, and others were knocked over with stones. But the men were not the only enemies of the ducks. Near by was a settlement of a large, voracious species of gull. They swooped down, seized, gobbled up, and bore away to their nests the young eiders, without seeming to doubt that they were doing a fair and, to themselves, a pleasant business. The gulls would seize the little eiders with their great yellow bills, throw their heads up, and then their victims would disappear down their throats, and in a few moments after they would be ejected into their nests and go down the throats of their young. The ducks fought the gulls bravely in the interests of their brood, but the victory was with the stronger.

Our voyagers pitied, of course, the bereaved eider mothers, despised the cormorant gulls, but gladly increased their stock of needed provisions with both. They filled four large india rubber bags with these sea-fowl after cleaning and rudely boning them.

Leaving this profitable camping place, the boat was soon in the open sea-way. One day's pleasant sailing was quite as much in that way as experience taught them to expect. A violent storm arose, the waves ran high, and their clumsy boat, trembling under the strain, was in danger of sinking at any moment. The safety of the whole company depended entirely upon the skill and nerve of M'Gary. For twenty-two successive hours he held in his strong grasp the steering oar and kept the head of the boat to the sea. A break of the oar or a slip from his hand and all was lost! They finally grappled an old floe in a slightly sheltered place, and rode out the storm.

For twelve days heroic exertions were made to get the boat through the pack which now beset them, with the view of working south and west. Little progress was made and the men, wet, weary, and worn, began to fail. In view of this state of things the commander directed his course to Northumberland Island, near which they were coasting. Here they found three recently occupied, but now forsaken, Esquimo huts. The foxes were abundant, and their young ones greeted the strangers with vociferous barking. They found here, too, what was more valuable—the scurvy grass. Rest, fresh fowl, and cochlearia greatly refreshed the whole party. Seeing the utter impossibility of going south, they made the best of their way back to the brig. It was a sad and joyful meeting with their old comrades. Their return safely was joyful, but the return spoke of another winter.

By great exertions the brig was loosened from her icy cradle and warped to a position more favorable for an escape should the open water reach the vicinity. On the seventeenth of August, instead of a glad breaking up of the old ice, came the formation of new ice, thick enough to bear a man. The question of an escape of the brig seemed settled. The allowance of wood was fixed to six pounds a meal; this gave them coffee twice a day and soup, once. Darkness was ahead, and if the fuel utterly failed it would be doubly cheerless. The Sabbath rest and devotions became more solemn. The prayer, "Lord, accept our gratitude and bless our undertakings," was changed to, "Lord, accept our gratitude and restore us to our homes."

Affairs looked so dark that Dr. Kane deemed it wise to leave a record of the expedition on some conspicuous spot. A position was selected on a high cliff which commanded an extensive view over the icy waste. On its broad, rocky face the words, "'Advance,' A. D. 1853–54," were painted in large letters which could be read afar off. A pyramid of heavy stones was built above it and marked with a cross. Beneath it they reverently buried the bodies of their deceased companions. Near this a hole was worked into the rock, and a paper, inclosed in a glass vessel sealed with lead, was deposited. On this paper was written the names of the officers and crew, the results in general thus far of the expedition, and their present condition. They proposed to add to the deposit a paper containing the date of their departure, should they ever get away, and showing their plans of escape.

Now, more earnestly than ever, the winter and what to do was looked in the face. Some thought that an escape to South Greenland was still possible, and even the best thing to do. The question of detaching a part of the company to make the experiment was debated, but the commander arrived at a settled conviction that such an enterprise was impracticable.

In the mean time the ice and tides were closely examined for a considerable distance, for the slightest evidence of a coming liberation of the poor ice-bound craft.

As early as August twenty-fourth all hopes of such a liberation seemed to have faded from every mind. The whole company, officers and crew, were assembled in council. The commander gave the members his reasons in full for deeming it wise to stand by the vessel. He then gave his permission for any part of the company who chose to do so to depart on their own responsibility. He required of such to renounce in writing all claims upon the captain and those who remained. The roll was then called, and nine out of the seventeen decided to make the hazardous experiment. At the head of this party was Dr. Hayes and Petersen. Besides the hope of a successful escape, they were influenced in the course they were taking by the thought that the quarters in the brig were so straitened that the health and comfort of those remaining would be increased, and the causes of disease and death diminished by their departure; and still further, if the withdrawing party perished, an equal number was likely to die if all remained.

The decision having been made, Dr. Kane gave them a liberal portion of the resources of the brig, a good-bye blessing, with written assurances of a brother's welcome should they return. They left August twenty-eight.

Those who remained with Dr. Kane were Brooks, M'Gary, Wilson, Goodfellow, Morton, Ohlsen, Hickey, and Hans. The situation of these was increasedly dreary on the departure of half of their companions. They felt the necessity of immediate systematic action to drive away desponding thoughts, as well as to make the best possible preparation for the coming struggle with darkness, cold, poverty, and disease. The discipline of the vessel, with all its formality of duties, was strictly maintained. The ceremonies of the table, the religious services, the regular watching, in which every man took his turn unless prevented by sickness, the scientific observations of the sky, the weather and the tides, the detailed care of the fire and the lights, all went on as if there was no burdens of mind to embarrass them.

In view of the small stock of fuel, they commenced turning the brig into something like an Esquimo igloë or hut. A space in the cabin measuring twenty feet by eighteen was set off as a room for all hands. Every one then went to work, and, according to his measure of strength, gathered moss. With this an inner wall was made for the cabin, reaching from the floor to the ceiling. The floor itself was calked with plaster of Paris and common paste, then two inches of Manilla oakum was thrown over it, and upon this a canvas carpet was spread. From this room an avenue three feet high, and two and a half feet wide, was made. It was twelve feet long, and descended four feet, opening into the hold. It was moss-lined, and closed with a door at each end. It answered to the *tossut* of the Esquimo hut, or the sort of tunnel through which they creep into their one room. All ingress and egress of our explorers were through this avenue on their hands and knees. From the dark hold they groped their way to the main hatchway, up which, by a stairway of boxes, they ascended into the open air.

The quarter-deck also was well padded with turf and moss. When this was done, no frost king but the one presiding over the polar regions could have entered. Even he had to drop his crown of icicles at the outer door of the avenue.

The next step was to secure, so far as possible, a supply of fuel for the coming darkness. A small quantity of coal yet remained for an emergency. They began now, September tenth, to strip off some of the extra planking outside of the deck, and to pile it up for stove use.

Having thus put the brig itself into winter trim, they went diligently to work to arrange its immediate vicinity on the floe. Their beef-house came first, which was simply a carefully stowed pile of barrels containing their water-soaked beef and pork. Next was a kind of block-house, made of the barrels of flour, beans, and dried apples. From a flag-staff on one corner of this fluttered a red and white ensign, which gave way on Sundays to a Grinnell flag. From the block-house opened a traveled way, which they called New London Avenue. On this were the boats. Around all this was a rope barrier, which said to the outside world, Thus far only shalt thou come! Outside of this was a magnificent hut made of barrel frames and snow, for the special use of Esquimo visitors. It was in great danger of a tearing down for its coveted wood.

CHAPTER VIII.

TREATY MAKING.

THE stock of fresh provisions was now alarmingly low. To secure a fresh supply, Dr. Kane and Hans started with the dog team on a seal hunt. The doctor was armed with his Kentucky rifle, and Hans with a harpoon and attached line. They carried a light Esquimo boat to secure the prey if shot. They expected to find seal after a ten miles' run, but the ice was solid until they had traveled another hour. Now they entered upon an icy plain smooth as a house floor. On the dogs galloped, in fine spirits, seeming to anticipate the shout which soon came from Hans—"Pusey, puseymut!"—seal, seal! Just ahead were crowds of seals playing in the water. But the joy of the hunters was instantly turned into a chill of horror. The ice was bending under the weight of the sledge, and rolling in wavy swells before it, as if made of leather. To pause was certain death to dogs and men. The solid floe was a mile ahead. Hans shouted fiercely to his dogs, and added the merciless crack of his whip to give speed to his team; but the poor creatures were already terror-stricken, and rushed forward like a steam-car. A profound silence followed, as painful as the hush of the wind before the destructive tornado. Nothing more could be done; the faithful dogs were doing their utmost to save themselves and their masters. They passed through a scattered group of seals, which, breast-high out of water, mocked them with their curious, complacent gaze. The rolling, crackling ice increased its din, and, when within fifty paces of the solid floe the frightened dogs became dismayed, and they paused! In went the left runner and the leading dog, then followed the entire left-hand runner. In the next instant Dr. Kane, the sledge and dogs, were mixed up in the snow and water. Hans had stepped off upon ice which had not yet given way, and was uttering in his broken English, piteous moans, while he in vain reached forward to help his master. He was ordered to lay down, spread out his hands and feet, and draw himself to the floe by striking his knife into the ice. The doctor cut the leader's harness and let him scramble out, for he was crying touchingly, and drowning his master by his caresses. Relieved of the dog he tried the sledge, but it sunk under him; he then paddled round the hole endeavoring to mount the ice, but it gave way at every effort, thus enlarging the sphere of operation most uncomfortably, and exhausting his strength. Hans in the mean time had reached solid footing, and was on his knees praying incoherently in English and Esquimo, and at every crushing-in of the ice which plunged his master afresh into the sea exclaimed, "God!" When the fatal crisis was just at hand, deliverance came by a *seeming* accident.

How often does God deliver by such seeming accidents! One of the dogs still remained attached to the sledge, and in struggling to clear himself drew one of the runners broadside against the edge of the circle. It was the drowning man's last chance. He threw himself on his back so as to lessen his weight, and placed the nape of his neck on the rim of the ice opposite to but not far from the sledge. He then drew his legs up slowly and placed the ball of his moccasin foot against the runner, pressing cautiously and steadily, listening the while to the sound of the half-yielding ice against which the other runner rested, as to a note which proclaimed his sentence of life or death. The ice, holding the sledge, only faintly yielded, while he felt his wet fur jumper sliding up the surface; now his shoulders are on; now his whole body steadily ascends; he is safe.

Hans rubbed his master with frantic earnestness until the flesh glowed again. The dogs were all saved, but the sledge, Esquimo boat, tent, guns, and snow-shoes were all left frozen in to await a return trip. A run of twelve miles brought them, worn and weary, but full of gratitude, to the brig. The fire was kindled, one of the few remaining birds cooked, a warm welcome given, so that the peril was forgotten except in the occasion it gave for increased love to the *Deliverer*.

We have had no occasion to notice the Esquimo since the escape from prison of young Myouk. Soon after Dr. Hayes's party left, three natives came. They had evidently noted the departure of half of the number of the strangers, and came to learn the condition of those left behind. It was Dr. Kane's policy to conciliate them, while carrying toward them a steady, and when needed, as it was often, a restraining hand.

These visitors were quartered in a tent in the hold. A copper lamp, a cooking-basin, and a full supply of fat for fuel, was given them. They ate, slept, awoke, ate and slept again. Dr. Kane left them eating at two o'clock in the morning when he retired to the cabin to sleep. They seemed soon after to be sleeping so soundly that the watch set over them also slept. In the morning there were no Esquimo on board. They had stolen the lamp, boiler, and cooking-pot used at their feast; to these they added the best dog—the only one not too weary from the late excursion to travel. Besides, finding some buffalo robes and an india-rubber cloth accidentally left on the floe, they took them along also.

This would not do. The savages must be taught to fear as well as to respect and love the white men. Morton and Riley, two of the best walkers, were sent in hot pursuit. Reaching the hut at Anoatok, they found young Myouk with the wives of two absent occupants, the latter making themselves delightfully comfortable, having tailored already the stolen robes into garments worn on their backs. By searching, the cooking utensils, and other articles stolen from the brig but not missed, were found.

The white officers of the law acted promptly,

as became their dignity. They stripped the women of these stolen goods and tied them. They were then loaded with all the articles stolen, to which was added as much walrus meat of their own as would pay their jail fees. The three were then marched peremptorily back to the brig; though it was thirty miles they did not complain, neither did their police guardians in walking the twice thirty. It was scarcely twenty-four hours after these thieves had left the brig with their booty before they were prisoners in the hold. "A dreadful white man" was placed over them as keeper, who never spoke to them except in words of terrifying reproof, and whose scowl exhibited a studied variety of threatening and satanic expressions. The women were deprived of the comfort of even Myouk's company. He was dispatched to Metek, "head-man of Etah and others," "with the message of a melo-dramatic tyrant," to negotiate for their ransom. For five long days the women sighed and cried, and sung in solitary confinement, though their appetites continued excellent. At last the great Metek and another Esquimo notable arrived, drawing quite a sledge load of returned stolen goods. Now commenced the treaty making. There were "big talks," and a display on the part of Dr. Kane of the splendors and resources of his capital, its arts and sciences, not forgetting the "fire-death," whose terrific power so amazed the Etah dignitaries. On the part of the Esquimo there were many adjournments of the diplomatic conferences to eat and sleep. This was well for the explorers no doubt, as plenty of sleep and a good dinner are very pacific, it is well known, in their influence even on savages. In the final result the Esquimo agreed: Not to steal, to bring fresh meat, to sell or lend dogs, to attend the white men when desired, and to show them where to find the game. On the part of *Kablunah* (the white men) Dr. Kane promised: Not to visit the *Inuit* (Esquimo) with death or sorcery; to shoot for them on the hunt; to welcome them on board the ship; to give them presents of needles, pins, two kinds of knives, a hoop, three bits of hard wood, some kinds of fat, an awl, and some sewing-thread; to trade with them of these, and all other things they might want, for walrus and seal meat of the first quality.

Dr. Kane sent Hans and Morton to Etah, on the return of Metek, as his representatives, and this treaty was there ratified in a full assembly of its people.

This treaty was really of much importance to the famishing, ice-bound, scurvy-smitten strangers. It was faithfully kept on the part of the natives, but it was believed that the example of the white man's prodigious power given by Morton and Riley, in the tramp of sixty miles in twenty-four hours, had quite as much to do with its faithful observance as any regard to their promise. They might not understand the binding nature of promises however solemnly made, but they could comprehend the meaning of strong arms and swift feet.

Having made peace with the Etahites, Dr. Kane

sent M'Gary and Morton to the hut at Anoatok on a like errand. They found there of men, Myouk, Ootuniah, and Awatok—Seal Bladder—who were at first shy. The rogue, Myouk, suspected their visit might mean to him another arrest. Seeing it did not, all went merry as a marriage-bell. The treaty was ratified by acclamation.

CHAPTER IX.

ARCTIC HUNTING.

EARLY in October the Esquimo disappeared from the range of travel from the brig. Hans and Hickey were sent to the hunting grounds, and they returned with the unwelcome news, no walrus, no Esquimo. Where could they have gone? Were they hovering on the track of the escaping party under Dr. Hayes? and where were these? Would the natives return from a trip south, and bring any news of the battle they were fighting with the ice and cold?

While such queries may have been indulged by the brig party, they had serious thoughts concerning their own condition. Their fresh provisions were nearly exhausted. Without walrus or bear meat, their old enemy, scurvy, would come down upon them like an armed man. There was now plainly another occasion for one of those accidental occurrences, through which the eye of a devout Christian sees God's kind hand. In the midst of these painful thoughts the shout by Hans was heard ringing through the brig: "Nannook! nannook!"

"A bear! a bear!" chimed in Morton.

The men seized their guns and ran on deck. The dogs were already in battle array with the bear, which was attended by a five-months-old cub. Not a gun was in readiness on the instant, and while they were being loaded the canines were having rough sport with bruin. Tudla, a champion fighter, had been seized twice by the nape of his neck, and made to travel several yards without touching the ground. Jenny, a favorite in the sledge, had made a grand somerset by a slight jerk of the head of the bear, and had alighted senseless. Old Whitey, brave but not bear-wise, had rushed headlong into the combat, and was yelping his utter dissatisfaction with the result while stretched helpless upon the snow. Nannook considered the field of battle already won, and proceeded, as victors have always done, to a very cool investigation of the spoils. She first turned over a beef barrel, and began to nose out the choice bits for herself and child. But there was a party interested in this operation whom she had not consulted. Their first protest was in the form of a pistol ball in the side of her cub. This, to say the least, was rather a harsh beginning. The next hint was a rifle ball in the side of the mother, which she resented by taking her child between her hind legs and retreating behind the beef-house. Here, with her strong forearms, she pulled down three solid rows of beef barrels which made one wall of the house. She then mounted the rubbish, seized a half barrel of herring with her teeth, and with it beat a retreat. Turning her back on the enemy was not safe, for she immediately received, at half pistol range, six buck shots

She fell, but was instantly on her feet again, trotting off with her cub under her nose. She would have escaped after all but for two of the dogs. These belonged to the immediate region, and had been trained for the bear hunt. They embarrassed her speed but did not attack her. One would run along ahead of her, so near as to provoke the bear to attempt to catch him, and then he would give her a useless chase to the right or left, the other one, at the right moment, making a diversion by a nip in her rear. So coolly and systematically was this done that poor Nannook was hindered and exhausted without being able to hurt her tormentors in the least.

This game of the dogs brought again Dr. Kane and Hans on the field of conflict. They found the bear still holding out in the running fight, and making good speed away from the brig. Two rifle balls brought her to a stand-still. She faced about, took her little one between her fore legs, and growled defiance. It took six more balls to lay her lifeless on the blood-stained snow!

This method of conquering the foe was no doubt, from the bear point of view, mean and cowardly; instead of the hand-to-paw fight, recognized as the Arctic lawful way of fighting, it was sending fire-death at a safe distance for the attacking party. With her own chosen weapons—two powerful arms, and a set of almost resistless teeth—the bear was the stronger party. But then it was the old game of brains against brute force, with the almost sure result. As to the cruelty, the bear had no reason to complain. She came to the brig seeking, if haply she might find, a man, or men, to appease her craving hunger and feed her child. The men sought and obtained her life that they might stay the progress of their bitter enemy, the scurvy, and save their own lives!

When the mother fell, her child sprung upon her body and made a fierce defense. After much trouble, and, we should think, some danger from her paws and teeth, both of which she used as if trained for the fight, she was caught with a line looped into a running knot between her jaws and the back of her head, somewhat as farmers catch hogs for the slaughter. She was marched off to the brig and chained outside, causing a great uproar among the dogs.

The mother-bear's carcass weighed when cleaned three hundred pounds; before dressing, the body weighed six hundred and fifty. The *little* one weighed on her feet one hundred and fourteen pounds. They both proved most savory meat, and were eaten with gratitude, as the special gifts of the great Giver.

This bear capture was soon followed by one no less exciting and truly Arctic in its character. It was the hunt and capture of a walrus, the lion of the sea, as the bear is the tiger of the ice. The story is as follows:—

About the middle of October Morton and Hans were sent again to try to find the Esquimo. They reached on the fourth day a little village beyond Anoatok, seventy miles from the brig. Here they found four huts, two occupied and two forsaken. In one was Myouk, his parents and his brother and sister; in the other was Awahtok, Ootuniah, their wives, and three young children. The strangers were made to feel at home. Their moccasins were dried, their feet rubbed, two lamps set ablaze to cook them a supper, and a walrus skin spread on the raised floor for them to stretch and rest their weary limbs. The lamps and the addition to the huts' company sent the thermometer up to ninety degrees above zero, while outside it was thirty below. The natives endured this degree of heat finely, as the men and children wore only the apparel nature gave them, and the women made only a slight, but becoming, addition to it. The strangers after devouring six small sea-birds a piece enjoyed a night of profuse perspiration and sound sleep.

In the morning Morton perceived that Myouk and his father were preparing for a walrus hunt, and he cordially invited himself and Hans to go with them. The two strangers accepted the invitation thus given, and the party of four were soon off.

A large size walrus is eighteen feet long, with a tusk thirty inches. His whole development is elephantine, and his look grim and ferocious.

The Esquimo of this party carried three sledges; one they hid under the snow and ice on the way, and the other two were carried to the hunting ground at the open water, about ten miles from the huts. They had nine dogs to these two sledges, and by turns one man rode while the other walked.

As they neared the new ice, and saw by the murky fog that the open water was near, the Esquimo removed their hoods and listened. After a while Myouk's countenance showed that the wished-for sound had entered his ear, though Morton, as attentively listening, could hear nothing. Soon they were startled by the bellowing of a walrus bull; the noise, round and full, was something between the mooing of a cow and the deep baying of a mastiff, varied by an oft-repeated quick bark. The performer was evidently pleased with his own music, for it continued without cessation while our hunters crept forward stealthily in single file. When within half a mile of some discolored spots showing very thin ice surrounded by that which was thicker, they scattered, and each man crawled toward a separate pool, Morton on his hands and knees following Myouk. Soon the walruses were in sight. They were five in number, at times rising altogether out of the deep, breaking the ice and giving an explosive puff which might have been heard, through the thin, clear atmosphere, a mile away. Two grim-looking males were noticeable as the leaders of the group.

Now came the fight between Myouk, the crafty, expert hunter, and a strong, maddened, persistent walrus. Morton was the interested looker-on, following the hunter like a shadow, ready, if it had been wanted, to put in his contribution to the fight in the form of a rifle-ball. When the

Walruses—A Family Party.

walrus's head is above water, and peering curiously around, the hunter is flat and still. As the head begins to disappear in the deep he is up and stirring, and ready to dart toward the game. From his hiding-place behind a projecting ice knoll the hunter seems not only to know when his victim will return, but where he will rise. In this way, hiding and darting forward, Myouk, with Morton at his heels, approaches the pool near the edge of which the walruses are at play. Now the stolid face of Myouk glows with animation; he lies still, biding his time, a coil of walrus hide many yards in length lying at his side. He quickly slips one end of the line into an iron barb, holding the other, the looped end, in his hand, and fixes the barb to a locket on the end of a shaft made of a unicorn's horn. Now the water is in motion, and only twelve feet from him the walrus rises, puffing with pent up respiration, and looks grimly and complacently around. What need *he* fear, the mighty monarch of the Arctic sea! Myouk coolly, slowly rises, throws back his right arm, while his left arm lies close to his side. The walrus looks round again and shakes his dripping head. Up goes the hunter's left arm. His victim rises breast-high to give one curious look before he plunges, and the swift, barbed shaft is buried in his vitals! In an instant the walrus is down, down in the deep, while Myouk is making his best speed from the battle-field, holding firmly the looped end of his harpoon-line, at the same time paying out the coil as he runs. He has snatched up and carries in one hand a small stick of bone rudely pointed with iron; he stops, drives it into the ice and fastens his line to it, pressing it to the ice with his foot.

Now commence the frantic struggles of the wounded walrus. Myouk keeps his station, now letting out his line, and then drawing it in. His victim, rising out of the water, endeavors to throw himself upon the ice, as if to rush at his tormenter. The ice breaks under his great weight, and he roars fearfully with rage. For a moment all is quiet. The hunter knows what it means, and he is on the alert. Crash goes the ice, and up come two walrusses only a few yards from where he stands; they aimed at the very spot but will do better next time. But when the game comes up where he last saw the hunter he has pulled up his stake and run off, line in hand, and fixed it as before, but in a new direction. This play goes on until the wounded beast becomes exhausted, and is approached and pierced with the lance by Myouk.

Four hours this fight went on, the walrus receiving seventy lance thrusts, dangling all the while at the end of the line with the cruel harpoon fixed in his body. When dying at last, hooked by his tusk to the margin of the ice, his female, which had faithfully followed all his bloody fortune, still swam at his side; she retired only when her spouse was dead, and she herself was pricked by the lance.

Morton says the last three hours wore the

aspect of a doubtful battle. He witnessed it with breathless interest.

The game was, by a sort of "double purchase," a clever contrivance of the Esquimo, drawn upon the ice and cut up at leisure. Its weight was estimated at seven hundred pounds.

The intestines and the larger part of the carcass, were buried in the crevices of an iceberg—a splendid ice-house! Two sledges were loaded with the remainder, and the hunters started toward home. As they came near the village the women came out to meet them; the shout of welcome brought all hands with their knives. Each one having his portion assigned, according to a well understood Esquimo rule, the evening was given up to eating. In groups of two or three around a forty pound joint, squatting crook-legged, knife in hand, they cut, ate, and slept, and cut and ate again. Hans, in his description of the feast to Dr. Kane, says: "Why, Cappen Ken, sir, even the children ate all night. You know the little two-year-old that Aroin carried in her hood—the one that bit you when you tickled it?"

"Yes."

"Well, Cappen Ken, sir, that baby cut for herself, sir, with a knife made out of an iron hoop, and so heavy it could hardly lift it, cut and ate, sir, and ate and cut, as long as I looked at it."

Morton and Hans returned to the brig with two hundred pounds of walrus meat and two foxes, to make glad the hearts of their comrades.

Besides these Arctic monsters of the sea, and

shaggy prowlers of the land and ice, there was another sort of game, requiring a different kind of hunting, found nearer home.

We have related the experiment, a year before this, of the explorers with the rats. They had failed to smoke them out by a villainous compound, and, as the experience came near burning up the vessel, it was not repeated. They bred like locusts in spite of the darkness, cold, and short rations, and went every-where—under the stove, into the steward's drawers, into the cushions, about the beds, among the furs, woolens, and specimens of natural history. They took up their abode among the bedding of the men in the forecastle, and in such other places as seemed to them cosy and comfortable. When their rights as tenants were disputed they fought for them with boldness and skill.

At one time a mother rat had chosen a bear-skin mitten as a homestead for herself and family of little ones. Dr. Kane thrust his hand into it not knowing that it was occupied, and received a sharp bite. Of course his hand left the premises in rather quick time, and before he could suck the blood from his finger the family had disappeared, taking their home with them.

Rhina, a brave bear-dog, which had come out of encounters with his shaggy majesty with special honors, was sent down into the citadel of the rats. She lay down with composure and slept for a while. But the vermin gnawed the horny skin of her paws, nipped her on this side, and bit her on that, and dodged into their hiding-places. They were so many, and so nimble, that poor Rhina yelled in vexation and pain. She was taken on deck to her kennel, a cowed and vanquished dog.

Hans, true to his hunter's propensity, amused himself during the dreary hours of his turn on the night watch, by shooting them with his bow and arrow. Dr. Kane had these carefully dressed and made into a soup, of which he educated himself to eat, to the advantage of his health. No other one of the vessel's company cared to share his pottage.

Hans had one competitor in this "small deer" hunting, as the sailors called it. Dr. Kane had caught a young fox alive, and domesticated it in the cabin. These "deer" were not quick enough to escape his nimble feet and sharp teeth. But unfortunately he would kill only when and what he wanted to eat.

December came in gloomily. Nearly every man was down with the scurvy. The necessary work to be done dragged heavily. The courage of the little company was severely taxed but not broken. But where were the escaping party under Dr. Hayes? Were they yet dragging painfully over their perilous way? were they safe at Upernavik? or had they perished?

While such queries might have occupied the thoughts of the dwellers in the "Advance," on the seventh of the month Petersen and Bonsall of that party returned; five days later Dr. Hayes arrived, with the remainder of his company. Their adventures had been marvelous, and their escape wonderful. It will be a pleasant fancy for us to consider ourselves as sitting down in the cabin of the "Advance," and listening to their story from the lips of one of their party.

CHAPTER X.

THE ESCAPING PARTY.

HAVING, as has been seen, provided for all the contingencies of our journey as well as circumstances permitted, we moved slowly down the ice-foot away from the brig. The companions we were leaving waved us a silent adieu. A strong resolution gave firmness to our step, but our way was too dark and perilous for lightness of heart. At ten miles distance we should reach a cape near which we expected to find open water, where we could exchange the heavy work of dragging the sledges for the pleasanter sailing in the boat. This we reached early the second day. But here we experienced our first keen disappointment. As far as the eye could reach was only ice. Before us, a thousand miles away, was Upernavik, at which we aimed, the first refuge of a civilized character in that direction. As we gazed at this intervening frozen wilderness it did indeed seem afar off. Yet every man stood firm through fourteen hours of toil before we encamped, facing a strong wind and occasional gusts of snow. After this the shelter of our tent, and a supper of cold pork and bread with hot coffee, made us almost forget the wind, which began to roar like a tempest.

We looked out in the morning, after a good night's

rest, hoping to see the broken floe fleeing before the gale, giving us our coveted open sea. But no change had taken place. We had no resort but to weary sledging. We carried forward our freight in small parcels, a mile on our journey, finally bringing up the boat.

We took from under a cliff of the cape the boat "Forlorn Hope," which Dr. Kane had deposited there. It was damaged by the falling of a stone upon it from a considerable height. Petersen's skillful mending made it only a tolerable affair. Thus wearied and baffled in our efforts at progress, we returned early to our tent, and slept soundly until three o'clock in the morning, when we were aroused by shouting without. It came from three Esquimo, a boy eighteen years old, and two women. The boy we had before seen, but the women were strangers. They were filthy and ragged—in fact scarcely clothed at all. The matted hair of the women was tied with a piece of leather on the top of the head; the boy's hair was cut square across his eyebrows. One of the women carried a baby about six months old. It was thrust naked, feet foremost, into the hood of her jumper, and hung from the back of her neck. It peered innocently out of its hiding-place, like a little chicken from the brooding wing of its mother.

They shivered with cold, and asked for fire and food, which we readily gave them, and they were soon off down the coast in good spirits.

These visitors were only well started when Hans rushed into our camp, excited and panting for breath. He was too full of wrath to command his poor English, and he rattled away to Petersen in his own language. When he had recovered somewhat his breath, we caught snatches of his exclamations as he turned to us with, "Smit Soun Esquimo no koot! no koot! all same dog! Steal me bag! steal Nalegak buffalo."

The fact finally came out that our visitors had been to the brig and stolen, among other things, a wolf-skin bag and a small buffalo skin belonging to Hans, presents from Dr. Kane. Hans took a lunch, a cup of coffee, and continued his run after the thieves.

The ice had now given way a little, and small leads opened near us. Loading the boat, we tried what could be done at navigation. But the water in the lead soon froze over and became too thick for boating, while yet it was too thin for sledging; so after trying various expedients we again unloaded the boats and took to the land-ice. But this was too sloping for the sledges, so we took our cargo in small parcels on our backs, carrying them forward a mile and a half, and finally bringing the sledges and boat. Bonsall had, on one of these trips, taken a keg of molasses on the back of his neck, grasping the two ends with his hands. This was an awkward position in which to command his footing along a sideling, icy path. His foot slipped, the keg shot over his head, and glided down into the sea. Coffee without molasses was not pleasant to think of, and then it was two hours after our day's work was done before we could find even water. Our supper was not eaten and we ready to go to bed until ten. We slept the better, however, from hearing, just as we were retiring, that Bonsall and Godfrey had recovered the keg of molasses from four feet of water.

The next morning we resolved to try the floe again. It was plain we could make no satisfactory progress on the land-ice, so we loaded first the small sledge and run it safely down the slippery slope. Then the large sledge, "Faith," was packed with our more valuable articles. Cautiously it was started, men in the rear holding it back by ropes. But the foothold of the men being insecure, they slipped, lost their control both of themselves and the sledge, and away it dashed. The ice as it reached the floe was thin; first one runner broke through, now both have gone down; over goes the freight, and the whole is plunged into the water! Fortunately every thing floated. A part of our clothes were in rubber bags and was kept dry; all else was thoroughly wet. No great damage was done except in one case. Petersen had a bed of eider-down, in which he was wont snugly to stow himself at night. When moving it was compressed into a ball no larger than his head. It was a nice thing, costing forty Danish dollars. It was, of course, spoiled. So rueful was his face that, though we really pitied him, we could not repress a little merriment as he held up his dripping treasure. Seeing a smile on Dr. Hayes's face, he hastily rolled it up into a wad, and, in the bitterness of his vexation, hurled it among the rocks, muttering something in Danish, of which we could detect only the words "doctor" and "Satan."

Our situation seemed gloomy enough. The men's courage was giving way, and one took a final leave and returned to the "Advance." Yet we pressed forward; we were not long in readjusting the load of the "Faith," and met with no further accident during the day; but our fourteen hours toil left us six more hours of ice-travel before we could reach what seemed to be a long stretch of clear sea.

Hans returned from his pursuit, having overtaken the thieves, but did not find about them the stolen goods. He proposed to remain and help us, but we could go no farther that night. We encamped, and obtained much needed rest and sleep.

We were awakened at midnight to a new and unexpected discouragement. M'Gary and Goodfellow arrived from the "Advance" bringing a peremptory order from Dr. Kane to bring back the "Faith." We could not understand this. We had been promised its use until we reached the open sea. We had only one other, which was very poor and utterly insufficient for our purpose. We were sure it was not needed at the brig; what could the order mean? But there it was in black and white, so we delivered it up, and the messengers returned with it on the instant.

This journey of Goodfellow and M'Gary was a wonderful exhibition of endurance. They had worked hard all day; having eaten supper, they were dispatched with the message. They were back to the brig to breakfast, having traveled in all to and fro thirty miles without food or rest.

Our sledging, almost insufferable before, was more difficult now. Petersen exhausted his skill in improving our poor sledge with little success. We made about six miles during the day, gained the land at the head of Force Bay, and pitched our tent. We had shipped and unshipped our cargo, and had experienced the usual variety of boating and sledging. Several of us had broken through the ice and been thoroughly wet. Old rheumatic and scurvy complaints renewed their attacks upon the men.

While the supper was cooking, three of the officers climbed a bluff and looked out upon the icy sea. To our joy they reported the open water only six miles away. With a good sledge we could reach it in one day's pull. With our shaky affair it would take three. Indeed, it seemed a hopeless task to make at all six miles with it. Such was the situation when our supper was eaten and we had lain down to sleep. Its solace had scarcely come to our relief when Morton's welcome voice startled us. He had come to bring back the "Faith." How timely! And then he brought also a satisfactory explanation of its being taken away. Dr. Kane had been informed that a dissension existed among us, and that the sledge was not in the hands of the officers. The next morning the good sledge "Faith" was loaded, and the men, now in good spirits, made fine speed toward the open sea. Morton pushed on after the thieves. Late in the afternoon he returned with them. He had overtaken them where they had halted to turn their goods into clothing. They had thrown aside their rags, and were strutting proudly in the new garments they had made of the stolen skins. Morton soon left, with his prisoners, to return to the "Advance."

We did not reach the open water until midnight. Every thing was now put on board the boat, and we sailed about two miles and drew up against Esquimo Point, pitched our tent on a grounded ice-raft, and obtained brief rest.

In the morning, Riley, who had been sent to us for that purpose, returned to the "Advance" with the "Faith." We packed away eight men and their baggage in the "Forlorn Hope." It was an ordinary New London whale-boat rigged with a mainsail, foresail, and a jib. Her cargo and passengers on this occasion brought her gunwale within four inches of the water. But for five miles we made fine progress. Then suddenly the ice closed in upon us, compelling us to draw the "Hope" up upon a solid ice-raft, where we encamped for the night. Near was a stranded berg from which we obtained a good supply of birds, of which we ate eight for supper.

In the morning, while our breakfast was cooking, the ice scattered and a path for us through the sea was again opened, and we bore away joyously for the capes of "Refuge Harbor." With varying fortune, we passed under the walls of

Cape Heatherton, and sighted the low lands of Life-boat Bay. There, as has been stated, in August, 1853, Dr. Kane left a Francis metallic life-boat. Could we reach this bay and possess ourselves of this life-boat, a great step would have been taken, we thought, toward success. For awhile all went well; then came the shout from the officer on the lookout, "Ice ahead!" We run down upon it before a spanking breeze, and got into the bend of a great horseshoe, while seeking an open way through the floe. We could turn neither to the right nor left, and we were too deep in the water to attempt to lay-to. The waves rolled higher and higher, and the breeze was increasing to a tempest. Our cargo, piled above the sides of the boat, left no room to handle the oars, if they had been of any use. There was no resort but to let her drive against the floe. John sat in the stern, steering-oar in hand; Petersen stood on the lookout to give him steering orders; Bonsall and Stephenson stood by the sails; the rest of us, with boat-hooks and poles, stood ready to "fend off." The sails were so drawn up as to take the wind out of them. Petersen directed the boat's head toward that part of the ice which seemed weakest, and on we bounded. "'See any opening, Petersen!' 'No sir.' An anxious five minutes followed. 'I see what looks like a lead. We must try for it.' 'Give the word, Petersen.' On flew the boat. 'Let her fall off a little—off! Ease off the sheet—so—steady! A little more off—so! Steady there—steady as she goes.'"

Petersen, cool and skillful, was running us through a narrow lead which brought us into a small opening of clear water. We were beginning to think that we should get through the pack when he shouted, "I see no opening! Tight every-where! Let go the sheet! Fend off."

Thump went the boat against the floe! But the poles and boat-hooks, in strong, steady hands, broke the force of the collision. Out sprang every man upon the ice.

No serious damage was done to our craft. Our first thought was that we were in a safe, ice-bound harbor. But no! See, the floe is on the move! We unshipped the cargo in haste, and drew up the "Hope" out of the way of the nips. The stores were next removed farther from the water's edge, the spray beginning to sprinkle them. The whole pack was instantly in wild confusion, ice smiting ice, filling the air with dismal sounds. But it was a moment for *action*, not of moping fear. Our ice-raft suddenly separated, the crack running between the cargo and the "Hope!" This would not do! A boat without a cargo, or a cargo without a boat, were neither the condition of things we desired; but as the ice bearing the boat shot into the surging water, it was evident no *human* power could hinder it. Yet *divine* power could and did prevent it—just that Hand always so ready to help us in our time of need, and seeming now almost visible. The boat's raft, after whirling in the eddying waters, swung round, and struck one corner of ours. In a minute of time the "Hope" was run off, and boat, cargo, and men were once more together.

Soon the commotion brought down a heavy floe against that on which we had taken refuge, and no open water was within a hundred yards of us

CHAPTER XI.

A GREEN SPOT.

WE seemed now to be in a safe resting-place. Dr. Hayes and Mr. Bonsall, accompanied by John and Godfrey, took the advantage of this security to go in search of the life-boat, which they judged was not more than two miles away.

After a walk over the floe of one hour they found it. It had not been disturbed, and the articles deposited under it were in good order. There were, besides the oars and sails, two barrels of bread, a barrel of pork, and one of beef; thirty pounds of rice, thirty pounds of sugar, a saucepan, an empty keg, a gallon can of alcohol, a bale of blankets, an ice anchor, an ice chisel, a gun, a hatchet, a few small poles, and some pieces of wood. They took of these a barrel of bread, the saucepan filled with sugar, a small quantity of rice, the gun, the hatchet, and the boat's equipments. They were to carry this cargo, and drag the life-boat, back to the camp, unless a fortunate lead should enable them to take to the boat.

They ascended a hill, before starting, to get a view of the present state of the fickle ice. All was fast in the direct line through which they came. But, a mile away, washing a piece of the shore of Littleton Island, was open water. They concluded to push forward in that direction, and wait the coming of their companions in the "Hope."

They reached this open water in six hours—a slow march of one mile—but it must be remembered that they had to carry their cargo, piece by piece, then go back and draw along the boat, thus going over the distance many times. Besides, they had to climb the hummocks with their load, and lower it down the other side and tumble about generally over the rough way.

The island thus reached was three fourths of a mile in diameter. They landed in a tumultuous sea, which only a life-boat could survive. There was no good hiding-place from the storm, which was increasing. They were completely wet by the spray, and ready to faint with cold and hunger. In a crevice of the rock a fire was kindled, the saucepan half filled with sea water, and an eider duck John had knocked over with his oar was put into it to stew. To this was added four biscuit from the bread barrel. The hot meal thus cooked refreshed them, but it was their only refreshment. Bonsall and Godfrey crept under the sail taken from the boat, and, from sheer exhaustion, fell asleep. John and Dr. Hayes sought warmth in a run about the island. Dr. Hayes wandered to a rocky point, which commanded a view of the channel between the island and the "Hope." He watched every object, expecting to see her and her crew adrift. He had not watched long before a dark object was seen upon a whirling ice-raft. After a close and careful second look, he saw that it was John. He called but received no answer. John's raft now touched the floe and away he went, jumping the fearful cracks, and disappearing in the darkness. What could inspire so reckless an adventure? Had he seen the "Hope" in peril, and was this a manly effort to save her and his comrades? He was going in the direction in which he had left them.

Bonsall and Godfrey were soon frozen out of their comfortless tent, and joined Dr. Hayes on the rocky point. They took places of observation a short distance apart, and watched with intense anxiety both for the "Hope" and John. The morning came, the sea grew less wild, and the wind subsided, but nothing was seen of the boat.

Leaving Dr. Hayes and his party thus watching on the island, we will glance at the experience of those of us who were left in the camp.

Soon after they left, the wind and the waves played free and wild. The spray wet our clothes, buffaloes, and blankets, as it flew past us in dense clouds. Our bread-bag, wrapped in an india rubber cloth, was kept dry. We pitched our tent in the safest place possible, but were driven out by the increasing deluge of spray. We tried to cook our supper, but the water put out the lamp. So we obtained for thirty hours neither rest nor a warm meal. Dry, hard bread without water, was our only food. Finally the floe broke up, and, hastily packing, ourselves and stores into the "Hope," we went scudding through the leads, earnestly desiring but scarcely daring to hope that we should fall in with Dr. Hayes and his party. As we approached Littleton Island the lead closed, and the pack for a moment shut us in. As we waited and watched, we saw a dark object moving over the floe in the misty distance. Had we been on the lookout for a bear, we might have sent a bullet after it at a venture. But a moment only intervened before John, nimbly jumping the drifting ice-cakes, sprung into the boat! He brought the welcome news of the whereabouts of our companions with the life-boat, and his needed help in our peril. Soon a change of tide brought open water, through which, with all sails set, we bore down on the island. About eight o'clock we saw Dr. Hayes watching for our coming from his bleak, rocky lookout.

So rough was the sea that we could not land, but rowed round Cape Ohlsen, the nearest main-land, where we found a snug harbor with a low beach. The life-boat and her crew followed. The cargoes were taken from the boats, and they were hauled up. From a little stream of melted snow which trickled down the hill-side our kettles were filled. The camp was set ablaze, some young eiders and a burgomaster, shot just before we landed, were soon cooked, a steaming pot of coffee served up, and we talked over our adventures as we satisfied our craving hunger. John was questioned concerning his wild adventure. He had not seen the "Hope," nor did he know where she was. But he was concerned about her, and "wanted to hunt her up."

After dinner we set ourselves at work, preparing the boats for a renewed voyage, which we had some reason to hope would be one of fewer interruptions. The "Hope" was repatched and calked by Petersen. A mast and sail was put into the life-boat, which we named the "Ironsides." The heavier part of the freight was put on board the "Hope," of which Petersen took command, with Sontag, George Stephenson, and George Whipple as companions and helpers. Dr. Hayes commanded in the "Ironsides," with whom was Bonsall, John, Blake, and William Godfrey.

Having spread our sails to a favoring breeze, we gave three cheers and bore away for Cape Alexander, about fourteen miles distant. As we sped onward the scene was delightful. On our left was Hartstene Bay, with its dark, precipitous shore-line, and white glacier fields in the background. The outlines of Cape Alexander grew clearer over our bows, and cheered us onward. But a dark, threatening cloud crept up the northern sky, sending after us an increasing breeze, and tipping the waves with caps of snowy whiteness. The storm-king came on in frequent squalls, giving earnest of his wrath. We could not turn back, nor did such a course at all accord with our wishes; nor could we run toward the shore on the left, where only frowning rocks awaited us. We could only scud before the tempest toward Cape Alexander, come what would. The wind roared louder and the waves rolled higher, yet on we flew. We came within half a mile of the cape unharmed. Now the current, as it swept swiftly round the cape, produced a "chopping sea." The "Hope," being made for a heavy sea, rounded the point in good style. The "Ironsides" was shorter, stood more out of the water, and was, therefore, less manageable. John, who was intrusted with the steering-oar, in minding the business of Bonsall and Godfrey instead of his own, let it fly out of the water, and so permitted the boat to come round broadside to the current. Of course the sea broke over us at its pleasure, filling every part which could be filled and sinking us deep in the water. But for its metallic structure and air-tight apartment we should have sunk; as it was we held fast to the sides and mast to prevent being washed overboard, and thus we drifted ingloriously round the cape.

Here we found our consort, ready to come to our assistance; but as the water was smooth under sheltering land, we bailed out our boat, took in our sails, unshipped the mast, and rowed for a small rock called Sutherland's Island, hoping to find a harbor. But we found none, nor was it safe to land anywhere upon the island. There was nothing to do but to pull back again in the face of the wind. The men were weary and disheartened; the sun had set and it was growing dark; our clothes were frozen and unyielding as a coat of mail; cutting sleet pelted our faces, and we were often compelled to lose for a moment part of what we had with such toil gained. But the sheltering main-land of the cape was at last gained, and we coasted slowly along for some distance looking for a haven. We finally came to a low rocky point, behind which lay a snug little harbor. "A harbor! here we are boys; a harbor!" shouted the lookout. The men responded with a faint cheer—they were too much exhausted for "a rouser."

The boats were unladen and drawn upon the land. Every thing in the "Ironsides" was wet, but the stores of the "Hope" were in perfect order. We pitched our tent, cooked our supper, and lay down to sleep. The sea roared angrily as its waves broke upon the rocky coast, and the wind howled as it came rushing down the hill-side; but they did but lull us to rest as we slept away our weariness and disappointment.

Two days we were detained in this place. Once a little fox peered at us from the edge of the cliff, which set our men upon a fruitless hunt for either his curious little self or some of his kindred. We greatly desired a fox stew, but fox cunning was too much for us.

We started for Northumberland Island on the eighth of September. To reach it we must pass through a wide expanse of sea which was now clear; not a berg greeted our vision, no fragments of drifting ice-packs met our sight. The wind was nearly "after us," and the boats glided through the waves as gloriously as if carrying a picnic party in our own home waters. The spirits of the men run over with glee. "Isn't this glorious?"

cried Whipple as the boats came near enough together to exchange salutations; "we have it watch and watch about."

"And so have we," replied Godfrey.

"We're shipping a galley and mean to have some supper," shouted Stephenson.

"And we have got ours already!" exclaimed John. "Look at this!" he added, flourishing in the air a pot of steaming coffee.

But these joys were emphatically of the *arctic* kind, which are in themselves prophecies of ill. Bergs were soon seen lifting their unwelcome heads in the distance, and sending through the intervening waters their tidings of evil. Next came long, narrow lines of ice; then these were united together by a thin, recent formation. We were now compelled to dodge about to find open lanes. Coming to a full stop, the officers climbed an iceberg to get a view of the situation. The pack was every-where, though in no direction was it without narrow runs of open water. Then and there they were compelled, after careful consultation, to decide a question deeply concerning our enterprise. It was this: Should we take the outer passage, or the one lying along shore. The first would afford a better chance of open water, but if this failed us, as it was even likely to do at this late season, we must certainly perish. The second gave us a smaller chance of boating, but some chance to live if it failed. But we were on a desperate enterprise, and were inclined to desperate measures. But Petersen, who had twenty years' experience in these waters, counseled the inner route, and by his counsel the officers felt bound to abide.

While this consultation was going on the sea became calm, and the boats could be urged only by the oars. It was night before we found a sheltered, sloping land behind a projecting rock. The boats were anchored in the usual way— by taking out their loads and lifting them upon the land.

The tents were pitched upon a terrace a few yards above the boats. This terrace, we were surprised to find, was covered with a green sod, full of thrifty vegetation. The sloping hill-side above had the same greenness. A little seeking brought to our wondering sight an abundant supply of sorrel and "*cochlearia*," anti-scurvy plants which our men much needed. Some of the men soon filled their caps with them. A fox had been shot and was already in the cook's steaming pot, to which a good supply of the green plants was added. Such a supper as we had! Nothing like it had been tasted since we left home! Our scurvy plague spots disappeared before its wonderful healing power. The men became as hilarious as boys when school is out. They reveled and rolled upon the green arctic carpet like young calves in a newly found clover field. They smoked their pipes, "spun yarns," and laughed cheerily, as if their lives had not just now been in peril, and as if no imminent dangers lay at their door. Our camp had indeed been pitched by the all-guiding Hand in a goodly place. The men declared on retiring that they felt the healing *cochlearia* in their very bones, and it is certain that we all felt the glow of our changed condition throughout our whole being.

The next day two of us climbed the highest land of the island for a glance at our situation. We found it as depressing as our paradise of greenness had been encouraging. We could see southward the closed ice-pack for twenty miles, and faint indications of the same condition of the sea could be discerned for twenty more miles.

We returned, and a council was called in which all, men and officers, were called upon freely to discuss, and finally to decide by vote, the question, Shall we go forward or attempt to return to the "Advance." All the facts so far as known were fairly brought out. Upernavik was six hundred miles in a straight line; the brig was four hundred. Dangers, if not death, were everywhere, yet none desponded. Whipple, or "Long George," as his messmates called him, made a heroic speech which expressed the feelings of all. He exclaimed: "The ice can't remain long; I'll bet it will open to-morrow. The winter is a long way off yet. If we have such luck as we have had since leaving Cape Alexander, we shall be in Upernavik in two weeks. You say it is not more than six hundred miles there in a straight line. We have food for that time and fuel for a week. Before that's gone we'll shoot a seal."

We voted with one voice—"Upernavik or nothing." The decision was made.

CHAPTER XII.

NETLIK.

WE were unwillingly detained on the island several days more. During the detention we were visited by an Esquimo, who came most unexpectedly upon us. His name was Amalatok. He had been at the ship last winter, and had seen Dr. Kane in his August trip. His dress was strikingly arctic—a bird-skin coat, feathers turned in; bear-skin pants, hair outward; seal-skin boots; and dog-skin stockings. He carried in his hand two sea birds, a bladder filled with oil, some half-putrid walrus flesh, and a seal thong. He sat down on a rock and talked with animation. While thus engaged he twisted the neck from one of the birds, inserted the fore-finger of his right hand under the skin of its neck, drew it down its back, and thus instantly skinned it. Then running his long thumb nail along the breastbone, he produced two fine fat lumps of flesh, which he offered in turn to each of our company. These were politely declined, to his great disgust, and he bolted them down himself, sending after them a hearty draught of oil from the bladder. The other bird, the remaining oil, and the coil of seal-hide we purchased of him for three needles.

Soon after Amalatok's wife came up with a boy

—her nephew. The woman was old, and exceedingly ugly looking; the boy was fine looking, wide-awake, and thievish—we watched him narrowly. In the evening the Esquimo left for their home on the easternly side of the island.

In the afternoon of the fourteenth of September we left the island, and set our course toward Cape Parry. The sky had been clear, the air soft and balmy, and the open sea invited us onward. But a cold mist soon settled down upon us, succeeded by a curtain of snow, shutting out all landmarks, and leaving us in great doubt as to our course. The compass refused to do its office, the needle remaining where it was placed. We struck into an ice-field and became perfectly bewildered. As we groped about we struck an old floating ice-island, about twelve feet square. On this we crawled and pitched our tent. The cook contrived, with much perseverance and delay, to light the lamp, melt some snow, and make a pot of coffee. This warmed and encouraged us. But as the snow fell faster and faster, we could not unwrap our bedding without getting it wet; so we huddled together under the tent to keep each other warm. None slept, and the night wore slowly away as our ice-island floated we knew not whither. There was great occasion for despondency, but the men were wonderfully cheerful. Godfrey sung negro melodies with a gusto; Petersen told the stories of his boyhood life in Copenhagen and Iceland; John gave items of a "runner's" life in San Francisco; Whipple related the horrors of the forecastle of a Liverpool packet; and Bonsall "brought down the house" by striking up,

"Who wouldn't sell his farm and go to sea?"

During this merriment a piece of our raft broke off, and came near plunging two of the men into the sea.

The morning dawned and showed the dim outlines of some large object near us, whether iceberg or land we could not tell. Before we could well make it out we were near a sandy beach covered with bowlders. We tumbled into the boats and were soon ashore. As we landed, Petersen's gun brought down two large sea-fowl. We were in a little time high on the land, our tent pitched, and all but John, the cook, lay down in the dry, warm buffalo-skins and slept away our weariness. John in the meantime contended through six long hours with the wind, which put out his lamp, the snow, which wet his tinder when he attempted to relight it, and the cold, which froze the water in the kettle during the delay, as well as chilled his fingers and face, and cooked us at last a supper of sea-fowl and fox. As we ate with appetites sharpened by a fast of twenty-four hours, we heard the storm, which raged fearfully, with thankfulness for our timely covert. God, and not our wisdom, had brought us hither.

When the morning broke we learned that we had drifted far up Whale Sound, and were camped on Herbert Island. After a little delay we entered our boats, rowed for several hours through "the slush" the snow had created near the shore, and then spreading our canvas, we sailed for the mainland. We struck the coast twenty miles above Cape Parry.

We had scarcely time to glance at our situation before we heard the "Huk! Huk! Huk!" of Esquimo voices. It was the hailing cry of a man and a boy who came running to the shore. While Petersen talked with the man, the boy scampered off.

The man was Kalutunah, "the Angekok" or priest of his tribe. He had been, as will be recollected, at the ship in the winter. He said the village was only a short distance up the bay, where was plenty of blubber and meat, which we might have if we would allow him to enter our "oomiak" and pilot us there!

While we were talking with Kalutunah, the boy had spread the news of our visit through the village. On came a troop of men, women, and children, rushing along the shore, and throwing their arms about, and shouting merrily, with howling dogs at their heels. The "Kablunah" and "Oomiak"—white men and ship—had come and they were happy.

We took on board Kalutunah from a rocky point, before the crowd could reach it, and pushed off and rowed up the bay. Our passenger was delighted, having never before voyaged in this wise. He stood up in the boat and called to his envious countrymen who ran abreast of us along the shore, exclaiming, "See me! See me!"

We landed in a little cove, at the head of which

we pitched our tent. The sailors drew up the boat over the gentle slope, shouting, "Heave-oh!" At this the natives broke out into uproarious laughter. Nothing of all the strange shouts and sights brought to their notice so pleased them. They took hold of the ropes and sides of the boats, and tugged away shouting, "I-e-u! I-e-u! I-e-u!" the nearest approach they could make to the strange sound of the white faces.

A short distance from the beach, on the slope, stood the *settlement*—two stone huts twenty yards apart. They were surrounded by rocks and bowlders, looking more like the lurking places of wild beasts than the abodes of men.

The entertainment given us by our new friends was most cordial. A young woman ran off to the valley with a troop of boys and girls at her heels, and filled our kettles with water. Kalutunah's wife brought us a steak of seal and a goodly piece of liver. The lookers-on laughed at our canvas-wick lamp, as it sputtered and slowly burned, and the chief's daughter ran off and brought their lamp of dried moss and seal fat.

We gave them some of our supper, as they expected of course that we would. They made wry faces at the coffee, and only sipped a little; but Kalutunah with more dignity persevered and drank freely of it. We passed round some hard biscuit, which they did not regard as food until they saw us eat them. They then nibbled away, laughing and nibbling awhile until their teeth seemed to be sore. They then thrust them into their boots, the general receptacles of curious things.

After supper the white men lighted their pipes. This to the natives was the crowning wonder. They stared at the strangers, and then looked knowingly at each other. The solemn faces of the smokers, the devout look which they gave at the ascending smoke from their mouths as it curled upward, impressed the Esquimo that this was a religious ceremony. They, too, preserved a becoming gravity. But the ludicrous scene was too much for our men, and their faces relaxed into smiles. This was a signal for a general explosion. The Esquimo burst into loud laughter, springing to their feet and clapping their hands. The religious meeting was over.

The "Angekok," who seemed desirous to show his people that he could do any thing which the strangers could, desired to be allowed to smoke. We gave him a pipe, and directed him to draw in his breath with all his might. He did so, and was fully satisfied to lay the pipe down. His awful grimaces brought down upon him shouts and laughter from his people.

The mimic puffs, and the poorly executed echoes of the sailors' "Heave-oh," went merrily round the village.

Having established good feeling between ourselves and the Esquimo, we entered upon negotiations for such articles of food as they could spare. But they in fact had only a small supply. They wanted, of course, our needles, knives, wood, and iron, and were profuse in their promises of what they would do, but their game was in the sea.

It was midnight before the Esquimo retired and we lay down to sleep. Dr. Hayes and Stephenson remained on guard, for our very plausible friends were not to be trusted where any thing could be stolen. The stars twinkled in the clear atmosphere while yet the twilight hung upon the mountain, and all nature was hushed to an oppressive silence, save when it was broken by the sudden outburst of laughter from the Esquimo, or the cawing of a solitary raven.

Leaving Stephenson on guard, Dr. Hayes walked toward the huts. Kalutunah hearing his footsteps came out to meet him, expressing his welcome by grinning in his face and patting his back. The huts were square in front and sloped back into the hill. They were entered by a long passage-way—tossut—of twelve feet, at the end of which was an ascent into the hut through an opening in the floor near the front. Into this the chief led the way, creeping on all fours, with a lighted torch of moss saturated with fat. Snarling dogs and half-grown puppies were sleeping in this narrow way, who naturally resented in their own amiable way this midnight disturbance. Arriving at the upright shaft, the chief crowded himself aside to let his visitor pass in. A glare of light, suffocating odors, and a motley sight, greeted the doctor. Crowded into the den, on a raised stone bench around three sides, were human beings of both sexes, and of all ages. They huddled together still closer to make room for the stranger, whom they greeted with an uproarious laugh. In one of the front corners, on a raised stone bench, was a mother-dog with a family of puppies. In the other corner was a joint of meat. The whole interior was about ten feet in diameter, and five and a half high. The walls were made of stone and the bones of animals, and chinked with moss. They were not arched, but drawn in from the foundation, and capped above with slabs of slate-stone.

The doctor's visit was one of curiosity, but the curiosity of the Esquimo in reference to him was more intense and must first be gratified. They hung upon his arms and legs and shoulders; they patted him on the back, and stroked his long beard, which to these beardless people was a wonder. The woolen clothes puzzled them, and their profoundest thought was at fault in deciding the question of the kind of animal from whose body the material was taken. They had no conception of clothing not made of skins.

The boys' hands soon found their way into the doctor's pockets, and they drew out a pipe, which passed with much merriment from hand to hand, and mouth to mouth.

Kalutunah drew the doctor's knife from its sheath, pressed it fondly to his heart, and then with a mischievous side glance stuck it into his own boot. The doctor shook his head, and it was returned with a laugh to its place. A dozen times he took it out, hugged it, and returned it to its place, saying beseechingly, "Me! me! give me!" He did want it *so much!* The visitor's pistol was handled with great caution and seriousness. They had been given a hint of its power at the sea-shore, where Bonsall had brought a large sea-fowl down into their midst by a shot from his gun.

While this examination of the doctor was going on he examined more closely the objects about him. There was a window, or opening, above the entrance, over which dried intestines, sewed together, were stretched to let in light. The wall was covered with seal and fox skins stretched to dry.

There were in the hut three families and one or two visitors, in all eighteen or twenty persons. The female head of each family was attending in different parts of the hut, to her family cooking. They had each a stone, scooped out like a clam shell, in which was put a piece of moss soaked in blubber. This was both lamp and stove, and was kept burning by feeding with fat. Over this a stone pot was hung from the ceiling, in which the food was kept simmering. These, and the animal heat of the inmates, made the hut intensely warm. Seeing the white man panting for breath, some boys and girls laid hold of his clothes to strip him, after their own fashion. This act of Esquimo courtesy he declined. They then urged him to eat, and he answered, "Koyenuck"—I thank you—at which they all laughed. Though he had dreaded this invitation, he did not think it good policy to declare it. A young girl brought him the contents of one of the stone pots in a skin dish, first tasting it herself to see if it was too hot.

All eyes were upon the visitor. Not to take their proffered pottage would be a great affront. To him the dose seemed insufferable, though of necessity to be taken. Shutting his eyes, and holding his nose, he bolted it down. He was afterward informed that it was one of the delicacies of their table, made by boiling together blood, oil, and seal intestines!

After thus partaking of their hospitality, the doctor left the Esquimo quarters, escorted by "the Angekok" and his daughter.

We were astir at dawn, preparing to leave this little village known as Netlik. We had obtained a valuable addition to our slender store of blubber, and a few pairs of fur boots and mittens, for which we amply paid them.

Knowing that the Esquimo had never heard of the commandment, "Thou shalt not covet," and that they did not understand well the law of "mine" and "thine," we watched them closely as our stores were being passed into the boat. When we were ready to push off it was ascertained that the hatchet was missing. Petersen openly charged them, as they stood upon the shore, with the theft. They all threw up their hands with expressions of injured innocence. "My people *never* steal!" exclaimed the affronted chief.

One fellow was so loud in his protestations of innocence that Petersen suspected him. The Dane approached him with a flash of anger in his eye, which told its own story. The Esquimo stepped back, stooped, picked up the hatchet, on which he had been standing, and gave it to Petersen with one hand, and with the other presented him a pair of mittens as a peace-offering.

We pushed off, and they stood shouting upon the beach until their voices died away in the distance as we pulled across the bay.

CHAPTER XIII.

THE HUT.

WE now made for Cape Parry with all speed, though this was slow speed. The young ice which covered the bay was too old for us, or, at any rate, it was too strong for easy progress. It was sunset when we reached the cape. Beyond this there had been open water seen by us for many days past, from the elevated points of observation which we had sought. From this point, therefore, we expected free sailing southward, and rapid progress toward safety and our homes. But here we were at last at Cape Parry against a pack which extended far southward. In our desperation we tried to force the boats through. The "Ironsides" was badly battered, and the "Hope" made sadly leaky by the operation, and no progress was made. We then pushed slowly down the shore through a lead, and having gone about seven miles, darkness and the ice brought us to a stand, and we drew up for the night.

In the morning we observed a lead going south from the shore at a point twelve miles distant. For six days, bringing us to the twenty-seventh of September, we fought hard to reach the lead, but failed. We could now neither retreat nor go forward. Ice and snow were every-where. The sun was running low in the heavens, seeming to rise only to set; and soon the night, which was to have no sunrise morning until February, would be upon us. Our food was sufficient for not more than two weeks, and our fuel of blubber for the lamp only was but enough for eight or ten days. Our condition seemed almost without hope, but it had entered into our calculations as a possible contingency, and we girded ourselves for the struggle for life, trusting in the Great Deliverer.

We were about sixteen miles below Cape Parry, and about midway between Whale Sound and Wolstenholme Sound. We pitched our tent thirty yards from the sea on a rocky upland. After securing in a safe place the boats and equipments, we began to look about us for a place to build a hut. It was, indeed, a dreary, death-threatening region. Time was too pressing for us to think of building an Esquimo hut, if, indeed, our strength and skill was sufficient.

While we were looking round and debating what to build and where, one of our party found a crevice in a rock. This crevice ran parallel with the coast, and was opposite to, and near, the landing. It was eight feet in width, and level on the bottom. The rock on the east side was six feet high, its face smooth and perpendicular, except breaks in two places, making at each a shelf. On the other—the ocean side—the wall was scarcely four feet high, round and sloping; but a cleft through it made an opening to the crevice from the west.

We at once determined to make our hut here,

as the natural walls would save much work in its construction. The only material to be thought of was rocks. These we had to find beneath the snow, and then loosen them from the grasp of the frost. For this we fortunately had an ice-chisel —a bar of iron an inch in diameter and four feet long, bent at one end for a handle, and tempered and sharpened at the other. With this Bonsall loosened the rocks, and others bore them on their shoulders to the crevice. When a goodly pile was made we began to construct the walls. Instead of mortar we had sand to fill in between the stones. This was as hard to obtain as the stones themselves, as it had to be first picked to pieces with the ice-chisel, then scooped up with our tin dinner plates into cast-off bread-bags, and thus borne to the builders.

This work was done by four of us only, the other four being engaged in hunting, to keep away threatened starvation. In two days our walls were up. They run across the crevice, that is, east and west, were fourteen feet apart, four feet high, and three thick. The natural walls being eight feet apart, our hut was thus in measurement fourteen feet by eight. The entrance was through the cleft, from the ocean side. We laid across the top of this door-way the rudder of the "Hope," and erected on it the "gable." One of the boat's masts was used for a ridgepole, and the oars for rafters. Over these we laid the boats' sails, drew them tightly, and secured them with heavy stones. Being sadly deficient in lumber, Petersen constructed a door of light frame-work and covered it with canvas; he hung it on an angle, so that when opened it shut of its own weight. A place was left for a window over the door-way, across which we drew a piece of old muslin well greased with blubber, and through which the somber light streamed when there was any outside.

We then endeavored to thatch the roof and "batten" the cracks every-where with moss. But to obtain this article we had to scour the country far and near, dig through the deep snow, having tin dinner plates for shovels, wrench it from the grip of the frost with our ice-chisel, put it in our bread-bags and "back it" home.

In four days, in spite of all obstacles, our hut assumed a homelike appearance—at least homelike compared with our present quarters. We said: "To-morrow we shall move into it and be comparatively comfortable. "But that day brought the advance force of a terrific storm of wind and snow. It caught some of us three miles from the tent. We huddled together in our thin hemp canvas tent and slept as best we could. Two of our company crawled out in the morning to prepare our scanty meal. They found the hut half full of snow, which had sifted through the crevices. But they brought to the tent's company a hot breakfast after some hours' toil; we ate and our spirits revived.

We tried all possible expedients to pass away the time, but the hours moved slowly. The storm continued to howl and roar about us with unceasing fury for four days. Our little stock of food was diminishing, our hut was unfinished, and winter was upon us in earnest. Our situation was one of almost unmitigated misery.

On Friday, October sixth, the storm subsided, and nature put on a smiling face. We renewed our work on the hut, clearing it of snow with our dinner-plate shovels, and then, under greater difficulties than ever, because the snow was deeper and our strength less, we finished it. The internal arrangements were as follows: an aisle or floor, three feet wide, extended from the door across the hut. On the right, as one entered, was a raised platform of stone and sand about eighteen inches high. On this we spread our skins and blankets. Here five of us were to sleep. On the back corner of the other side was a similar platform, or "breck" as the Esquimo would call it; here three men were to sleep. In the left-hand corner, near the door, Petersen had extemporized a stove out of some tin sheathing torn from the "Hope," with a funnel of the same material running out of the roof. This sort of fire-place stove held two lamps, a saucepan, and kettle. On a post which supported the roof hung a small lamp.

Into this hut we moved October ninth. Compared with the tent it was comfortable. It was evening when we were settled. At sundown Petersen came in with eight sea-fowl, so we celebrated the occasion with a stew of fresh game, cooked in our stove with the staves of our blubber kegs, and we added to our meal a pot of hot coffee.

The supper done, we talked by the dim light of our moss taper. A storm, which was heralded during the day, was raging without in full force, burying us in a huge snow-bank. We discussed calmly our duties and trials, and we all lay down prayerfully to sleep.

What shall we do now? was the question of the morning. Indeed, it was the continual question. John reported our stores thus: "There's three quarters of a small barrel of bread, a capful of meat biscuit, half as much rice and flour, a double handful of lard—and that's all." Our vigilant hunting thus far had resulted in seventeen small birds; that was all. Some of us had tried to eat the "stone moss," a miserable lichen which clung tenaciously to the stones beneath the snow. But it did little more than stop for awhile the gnawings of hunger, often inducing serious illness; yet this seemed our only resort.

The storm still raged. We were all reclining upon the brecks except John, who was trying to cook by a fire which filled our hut with smoke, when we were startled by a strange sound. "What is it?" we asked. We could not get out, so we listened at the window. "It was the wind," we said, for we could hear nothing more. In a half hour it was repeated clearer and louder. We opened the door by drawing the snow into the house, and made a little opening through the drift so we could see daylight. "It was the barking of a fox," says one. "No," said another, "it was the growling of a bear." Whipple, who was half asleep, muttered, "It was just nothing at all."

While these remarks were being made the Esquimo shout was clearly recognized. Petersen put his mouth to the aperture in the snow and shouted, "Huk! huk! huk!" After much shouting, two bewildered Esquimo entered our hut. They were from Netlik, the village we had last left, and one was Kalutunah. Their fur dress had a thick covering of snow, and, hardy though they were, they looked weary almost to faintness. They each held in one hand a dog-whip, and in the other a piece of meat and blubber. They threw down the food, thrust their whip-stocks under the rafters, hung their wet outer furs upon them, and at once made themselves at home. The chief hung around Dr. Hayes, saying fondly, "Doctee! doctee!"

John put out his smoking fire, at the Angekok's request, and used his blubber in cooking a good joint of the bear meat. We all had a good meal at our guests' expense. Necessity was more than courtesy with hungry men.

While the cooking and eating were going on, we listened to the marvelous story of the Esquimo. They left Netlik, forty miles north, the morning of the previous day on a hunting excursion with two dog-sledges. The storm overtook them far out upon the ice in search of bear, and they sheltered themselves in a snow hut for the night. Fearing the ice might break up they turned to the land, which they happened to strike near our boats and tent. Knowing we must be near, they picketed their dogs under a sheltering rock and commenced tramping and shouting.

The supper eaten, the story told, and the curiosity of our visitors satisfied in closely observing every thing, we made for them the best bed possible, tucked them in, and they were soon snoring lustily.

In the morning we tunneled a hole from our door through the snow. Kalutunah and Dr. Hayes went to the sea-shore. The dogs were howling piteously, having been exposed to all the fury of the storm during the night without the liberty of stirring beyond their tethers. Besides, they had been forty-eight hours without food, having come from home in that time through a widely deviating track. Every thing about them was carefully secured which could be eaten, and they were loosened.

Dr. Hayes turned toward the hut, and having reached the snow-tunnel he was about to stoop down to crawl through it, when he observed the whole pack of thirteen snapping, savage brutes at his heels. Had he been on his knees they would have made at once a meal of him. They stood at bay for a moment, but seeing he had no means of attack, one of them commenced the assault by springing upon him. Dr. Hayes caught him on his arm, and kicked him down the hill. This caused a momentary pause. No help was near, and to run was sure death. It was a fearful moment, and his blood chilled at the prospect of dying by the jaws of wolfish dogs, whose fierce and flashing eyes assured him that hunger had given them a terrible earnestness. His eye improved the moment's respite in sweeping the circle of the enemy for the means of escape, and he caught a glimpse of a dog-whip about ten feet off. Instantly he sprang as only a man thus situated could spring, and clearing the back of the largest of the dogs, seized the whip. He was now master of the situation. Never amiable, and terribly savage when prompted by hunger, yet the Esquimo dog is always a coward. Dr. Hayes's vigorous blows, laid on at right and left with much effect and more sound and fury, sent the pack yelping away.

In our discussions of the question of subsistence, we had about decided that we must draw our supplies from the Esquimo or perish. Our hunting was a failure, and our supply of food was about exhausted. So when Kalutunah came back we proposed to him through Petersen to purchase blubber and bear meat with our treasures of needles, knives, etc., so valuable in the eyes of the natives. He looked at our sunken cheeks and desolate home with a knowing twinkle of his eye, and a crafty expression on his besotted face. This was followed by the questions, "How much shoot with mighty guns? how much food you bring from ship?" These questions, and the speaking eye and tell-tale face, were windows through which we saw into the workings of his dark heathen mind. They meant, as we understood them, "If you are going to starve we had better let you. We shall then get your nice things without paying for them."

But Petersen understood and outmanaged the crafty chief.

"How we going to live?" he boldly exclaimed, facing the questioner. "Live! Shoot bear when we get hungry, sleep when we get tired; Esquimo will bring us bear, we shall give them presents, and sleep all the time. White man easily get plenty to eat. Always plenty to eat, plenty sleep."

The glory of life from the Esquimo point of view is plenty to eat and nothing to do. They held those who had attained to this high estate in profound respect. The starving could scarcely be brought within the range of their consideration. Hence the policy adopted by Petersen, and it had its desired effect. Kalutunah and his companion tarried another night, and departed promising to return with such food as the hunt afforded, and exchange it for our valuables.

Two weeks—days of misery—passed before their return. We set fox-traps, constructed much after the style of the rabbit-traps of the boys at home, tramping for this purpose over the coast-line for ten miles. One little prisoner only rewarded our pains, while the saucy villains showed themselves boldly by day, barking at us from the top of a rock, dodging across our path at the right and left, and even following us within sight of the hut. But all this was done at a safe distance from our guns.

Petersen went far out to sea on the ice, but neither bear nor seal rewarded his toil. We had burned up our lard keg for our semi-daily fire to cook our scanty meals, and now, with a sorrow that went to our hearts, began to break up the "Hope." We knew this step argued badly for the future, but what could we do? Besides, it was poor, water-soaked fuel, and would last but a little while. We saved the straightest and best pieces for trade with the Esquimo.

Our scanty meals, badly helped by the stone moss, told upon our health. Stephenson gasped for breath with a heart trouble; Godfrey fainted, and was happily saved a serious fall by being caught in John's arms.

CHAPTER XIV.

QUIMO TREACHERY.

THE kind Providence which had interfered for us in so many cases came with timely help. October twenty-sixth, Kalutunah and his companion returned. They had been south to Cape York, nearly a hundred miles, calling on their way at the village called Akbat, thirty miles off. They had killed three bears, the most of which they had upon their sledges. They sold us, reluctantly, enough for a few days. We ate of the refreshing meat like starving men, as we really were. Our sunken eyes and hollow cheeks *seemed* to leave us at a single meal. The faint revived, and our despondency departed. Our past sufferings were for the moment at least forgotten, and we looked hopefully upon the future.

The next day the Esquimo called and left a little more meat and blubber. We caught two small foxes, one of them in a trap, and the other was arrested by a shot from Dr. Hayes's gun. The audacious little fellow run over the roof of our hut and awoke the doctor, who, without dressing, seized his double-barreled gun, and bolted into the cold without. It was dark, and he fired at random. The first shot missed, but the second wounded him, and he went limping down the hill.

The doctor gave chase and returned with the game, but came near paying dear for his prize, barely escaping without frozen feet.

On Sunday, the twenty-ninth, in the midst of pensive allusions, and more pensive thoughts, concerning home, in which even Petersen's weather-beaten face betrayed a tear, an Esquimo boy came in from Akbat. His bearing was manly, his countenance fresh and agreeable, if not handsome, and his dress, of the usual material, was new. He drove a fine team with decided spirit. He was evidently somebody's pet, and we thought we saw a mother's partial stamp upon him. He was on his way to Netlik, and our curious inquiries brought from him the blushing acknowledgment that he was going "a courting!" He was nothing loath to talk of his sweetheart, and he bore her a bundle of bird-skins to make her an under garment as love-token. We gave him a pocket-knife and a piece of wood, to which we added two needles for his lady-love. He was full of joy at this good fortune, but when Sontag added a string of beads for her his cup run over. He had on his sledge two small pieces of blubber, a pound of bear's meat, a bit of bear's skin. These he laid at our feet, and dashed off toward Netlik in fine spirits.

When he was gone we renewed our ever-returning, perplexing, never-settled question, What shall we do? We could agree on no plans of escape, for all seemed impossible of execution. Yet we did agree in the expediency of opening a communication with the brig. But how to do it was the question.

Our dependence upon the Esquimo growing more humiliatingly absolute every day, pained us. We feared their treachery, of which we already saw some signs. "What *shall we do?*" was ever repeated.

While thus perplexed, Kalutunah made his appearance. With him were a young hunter, and a woman with a six months' old baby. The little one was wrapped in fox-skin, and thrust into its mother's hood, which hung on her neck behind. It peered out of its hiding-place with a contented and curious expression of face. Its mother had come forty miles, sometimes walking over the hummocky way, with the thermometer thirty-eight degrees below zero, with a liability of encountering terrific storms, and all to see the white men and their *igloë*. Mother and child arrived in good condition.

We conversed with the chief about our plan of going to Upernavik on sledges, and proposed to buy teams of his people, or hire them to drive us there. He received the proposal with a decided dissent, amounting almost to resentment. His people, he said, would not sell dogs at any price; they had only enough to preserve their own lives.

This we knew to be false. We offered a great price, but he scorned the bribe, and talked with an expression of horror about our plan of passing with sledges over the Frozen Sea, as he called Melville Bay.

While we were urging the sale by him of dogs and sledges he looked quizzically at our emaciated forms and sunken cheeks, and turning to the woman with a significant twinkle in his eye, he sucked in his cheeks. She returned the knowing glance, and sucked in her cheeks. This meant: We shall get all the white men's coveted things without paying when we find them starved and dead. This was a comforting view of the case—for them.

We dropped the plan of going south, and proposed to the chief to carry some of our party to the ship. This he readily assented to, and said at least four sledges should go with Petersen, if to each driver should be given a knife and piece of wood. We closed the bargain gladly, and Petersen was to start in the morning.

Guests and entertainers now sought rest. We gave the mother and child our bed in the corner. This was to us a self-denying act of courtesy, compelled by policy. We had usually given a good distance between us and such lodgers on account of certain specimens of natural history which swarmed upon their bodies, which, though starving, we did not desire. But to put her in a meaner place would be a serious affront, for which we might be obliged to pay dearly.

About midnight voices were heard outside, and soon our young lover, the boy-hunter, entered, accompanied by a widow who was neither young nor beautiful. The hut was in instant confusion. There was but little more sleep for the night, which was peculiarly hard on Petersen, who was to start in the morning on his long journey.

We had no food with which to treat our guests, which they saw, and so supped upon the provisions which they brought. The widow ate raw young birds, of which she brought a supply saved over from the summer. The Angekok had decided that her husband's spirit had taken temporary residence in a walrus, so she was forbidden that animal. She chewed choice bits of her bird and offered them to us. We tried *politely* to decline the kindness, but our refusal plainly offended her.

The widow's husband had been carried out to sea on an ice-raft on the sudden breaking up of the floe, and had never been heard from. Whenever his name was mentioned she burst into tears. Petersen told us that, according to Esquimo custom in such cases, we were expected to join in the weeping.

At the first attempt our success was very indifferent. On the next occasion we equaled in sincerity and naturalness the expressed sorrow of the heirs of a rich miser over his mortal remains. Even the tears we managed so well that the widow, charitably forgetting our former affront, offered us more chewed meat.

In the morning Petersen was off, Godfrey accompanying him at his own option.

The same evening John and Sontag went south with the widow and young hunter. Thus four of us only were left in the hut, and of these, one,

Stephenson, was seriously sick. His death at any time would not have been a surprise to us. The hut was colder than ever, and our food nearly gone. A few books, among which was a little Bible, the gift of a friend, were a great source of comfort.

In a few days John and Sontag returned. They had fared well during their absence. They were accompanied by two Esquimo, who brought us food for a few days, for which they demanded an exorbitant price. They, like people claiming a higher civilization, took advantage of our necessity. When they were about to depart on a bear hunt, Dr. Hayes proposed that two of us accompany them with our guns, but they declined. We went with them to the beach, saw them start, watched them as they swiftly glided over the ice, and, dodging skillfully around the hummocks, faded into a black speck in the distance.

The day was spent as one of rest by four of our number, while two of us visited the traps, returning as usual with nothing. The evening came. A cup of good coffee revived us. The temperature of our den *came up* to the freezing point. We were in the midst of this feast of hot coffee and increased warmth, when we heard a footfall. We hailed in Esquimo, but no answer. Soon the outer door of our passage way opened, a man entered and fell prostrate with a deep moan. It was Petersen. He crept slowly in as we opened the door, staggered across the hut, and fell exhausted on the breck.

Godfrey soon followed, even more exhausted. They both called piteously for "water! water!"

They were in no condition to explain what had happened. We stripped them of their frozen garments, rubbed their stiffened limbs, and rolled them in warm blankets. We gave them of our hot coffee, and the warmth of the hut and dry clothes revived them, but the sudden and great change was followed by a brief cloud over their minds. They fell into a disturbed sleep, and their sudden starts, groans, and mutterings, told of some terrible distress.

Petersen, while sipping his coffee, had told us that the Esquimo had thrown off their disguise and had attempted to murder them; that he and Godfrey had walked all the way from Netlik with the Esquimo in hot pursuit. We must watch, he said, for if off our guard they might overwhelm us with numbers.

This much it was necessary for us to know; the details of their terrible experience he was in no mood to give.

We immediately set a watch outside, who was relieved every hour; he was armed with Bonsall's rifle. Our other guns we fired off and carefully reloaded, hanging them upon their pegs for instant use.

Petersen and Godfrey awoke once, ate, and lay down to their agitated sleep. No others slept, or even made the attempt. The creak of the boots of the sentinel as he tramped his beat near the hut, on a little plain cleared of snow by the wind, was the only sound which broke the solemn silence. The enemy would not dare attack us except unawares, knowing, as they did, that there were eight of us, armed with guns. At midnight noises were heard about the rocks of the coast. They were watching, but seeing the sentinel, and finding it a chilling business to wait for our cessation of vigilance, they sneaked away. In the morning one of our men visited the rocky coverts and found their fresh tracks.

We received at the earliest opportunity the details of Petersen's story. They left us on the third of November, and were gone four days. They arrived in Netlik in nine hours, and were lodged one in each of the two *igloës*. Their welcome had a seeming heartiness. They had a full supply set before them of tender young bear-steak and choice puppy stew. Many strangers were present, and they continued to come until the huts were crowded.

The next day the hunters all started early on the chase, to get, as Kalutunah said, a good supply for their excursion to the ship, as well as a store for their families. This looked reasonable, but when night came the chief and a majority of the men returned not, nor did they appear the next day. The moon had just passed its full, no time could be spared for trifling, and Petersen grew uneasy. This feeling was increased by the strangers which continued to come, the running to and fro of the women, the side glances, and the covert laugh among the crowd.

Kalutunah returned on the evening of the third day of our men at the hut. Several sledges accompanied him, and one of them was driven by a brawny savage by the name of Sipsu. He had shown his ugly face once at our hut. He was above the usual height, broad-chested and strong limbed. He had a few bristly hairs upon his chin and upper lip, and dark, heavy eyebrows overshadowed his well set, evil-looking eyes. He was every inch a savage. While the crowd laughed, joked, and fluttered curiously about the strangers, Sipsu was dignified, sullen, or full of dismal stories. He had, he said, killed two men of his tribe. They were poor hunters, so he stole upon them from behind a hummock, and harpooned them in the back.

Whatever shrewdness Sipsu possessed, he did not have wit enough to hide his true character from his intended victims.

About twelve sledges were now collected, and Petersen supposed they would start early in the morning for the "Advance," so he ventured to try to hurry them a few hours by suggesting midnight for the departure. To this suggestion they replied that they would not go at all, and that they never intended to go. The crowd in the hut greeted this announcement with uproarious laughter.

Petersen maintained a bold bearing. He rose and went to the other hut and put Godfrey upon the watch, telling him what had happened. He then returned and demanded good faith from the chiefs. They only muttered that they could not go north; they could not pass that "blowing place"—Cape Alexander. He then asked them to sell him a dog-team; he would pay them well. They evaded this question, and Sipsu said to Kalutunah, in a side whisper, "We can get his things in a cheaper way."

Now commenced the game of wait and watch between the two parties; the chiefs waited and watched to kill Petersen, and he waited and watched not to be killed. He had his gun outside, because the moisture of the hut condensing on the lock might prevent it from going off. He had told the crowd that if they touched it it might kill them, and this fear was its safety. Those inside thought he had a pistol concealed under his garments. They had seen such articles, and witnessed their deadly power. Their purpose now was to get possession of this weapon, and Sipsu was the man to do it.

Petersen, cool as he was prompt and skillful, had not betrayed his suspicions of them; so he threw himself upon the breck and feigned himself asleep, to draw out their plans.

The strategy worked well. The gossiping tongues of men, women, and children loosened when they thought him asleep, and they revealed all their secrets. Petersen and Godfrey were to be killed on the spot, and our hut was to be surprised before Sontag and John returned from the south. Sipsu the while moved softly toward Petersen to search for the pistol. Just at this moment Godfrey came to the window and hallooed to learn if his chief was alive. Petersen rose from his sham sleep and went out. A crowd were at the door and about the gun, but they dared not touch it. The intended victims kept a bold front, and coolly proposed a hunt. This the natives declined, and they declared they would go alone.

It was late in the night when our beset and worried men started. They were watched sullenly until they were two miles away, and then the sledges were harnessed for the pursuit. Fifty yelping dogs mingled their cries with those of the men, and made a fiendish din in the ears of the flying fugitives. What could they do if the dogs were let loose upon them, having only a single rifle! One thing they intended should be sure; Sipsu or Kalutunah should die in the attack.

When the pursuers seemed at the very heels of our men, *that one gun* made cowards of the Esquimo chiefs. They seemed to understand *their* danger. The whole pack of dogs and men turned seaward, and disappeared among the hummocks. They meant a covert attack.

Keeping the shore and avoiding the hiding-places, Petersen and Godfrey pressed on. The night was calm and clear, but the cold was over fifty degrees below zero. When half way, at Cape Parry, they well-nigh fainted and fell. But encouraging each other, they still hurried onward, and made the fifty miles (it was forty in a straight line) in twenty-four hours. The reader understands why they arrived in such distress and exhaustion.

CHAPTER XV.

LIGHTS AND SHADOWS.

DURING the two days following the return of Petersen and Godfrey we spent our working hours in building a wall about our hut. It was made of frozen snow, sawed in blocks by our small saw. This wall served a double purpose, that of breaking the wind from our hut, and as a defense against the Esquimo. It gave our abode the appearance of a fort, and we called it Fort Desolation. John muttered: Better call it Fort Starvation! This was in fact no unfitting designation. Our food was nearly gone. Those who alone could keep us from starving were seeking our lives. A feeble, flickering light made the darkness of our hut visible. Darkness, and dampness, and destitution were within, and without were fears. We could not be blamed, perhaps, if the death which threatened us seemed more desirable than life. Yet we could not forget Him who had so often snatched us from the jaws of our enemies — cold, hunger, and savages — and we trusted him to again deliver us. And this he did, for the next day Kalutunah and another hunter appeared. They did not come as enemies, but as angel messengers of mercy from the All-Merciful!

The chief was at first shy, nor could he so far lay aside the cowardice of conscious guilt as to lay down for a moment his harpoon, at other times left at the hut door. He brought, to conciliate us, a goodly piece of walrus meat. After spending an hour with us he dashed out upon the ice on a moonlight hunt for bears.

Petersen spent the day in making knives for the Esquimo, in anticipation of restored friendship. With an old file he filed down some pieces of an iron hoop, punching rivet holes with the file, and whittling a handle from a fragment of the "Hope." Though the knife, when done, was not like one of "Rogers's best," it was no mean article for an Esquimo blubber and bear meat knife.

The next day four sledges and six Esquimo made us a call. One of them was our old friend the widow, with her bundle of birds under her arm.

They were all shy at first, showing a knowledge at least of the wrong intended us, but we soon made them feel at home. It was indeed for our interest to do so. They bartered gladly walrus, seal, bear, and bird meat, a hundred pounds in all. It made a goodly pile, enough for four days, but, alas! the duty of hospitality, which we could not wisely decline, compelled us to treat our guests with it, and they ate one third! In three hours they were off toward Netlik.

The next day an Esquimo man came from Northumberland Island; we had not seen him before, and he did not appear to have been in the council of the plotters against us. He sold us walrus meat, blubber, and fifty little sea fowl.

Our health absolutely demanding a more generous diet, we ate three full meals, such as we had not had since leaving the ship. Our new friend's name was Kingiktok—which is, by interpretation, a rock. Mr. Rock was a man of few words, and of very civil behavior. We fancied him, and courted his favor by a few presents for himself and wife. They were gifts well bestowed, for he at once opened his mouth in valuable and startling communications. He said that he and his brother Amalatok were the only two men in the tribe who were friendly to us. Amalatok was the man we met on Northumberland Island, who will be remembered as skinning a bird so adroitly, and offering us lumps of fat scraped from its breast-bone with his thumb nail.

Mr. Rock's talk run thus: He and this brother were in deadly hostility to Sipsu. The reason of this hostility was very curious. The brother's wife, whom we thought decidedly hag-like in her looks, was accounted a witch. *Why* she was so regarded was not stated. Now the law of custom with this people is that witches may be put to death by any one who will do it by stealth. She may be pounced upon from behind a hummock and a harpoon or any deadly weapon may deal the fatal blow in the back, but a face to face execution was not allowed. It was understood that Sipsu assumed the office of executioner, and was watching the favoring circumstances. On the other hand the husband, and his brother, Mr. Rock, watched with courage and vigilance in behalf of the accused, while she lacked neither in her own watching. Thus the family had no fraternal relations with the villagers, though visits were exchanged between them.

Concerning the conspiracy, Mr. Rock thus testified: Sipsu had for a long time counseled the tribe not to visit nor sell food to the white men, holding that they could not kill the bear, walrus, and seal, and would soon starve, and so all the coveted things would fall into Esquimo hands. Kalutunah, on the other hand, held that their "booms"—guns—could secure them any game, and that our poverty of food was owing to a dislike of work.

There had arisen, too, a jealousy about the presents we gave. Sipsu's let-alone policy caused his wife to complain that she only of the women was without even a needle. This drove him to a reluctant visit to us in which he got but little, so the matter was not bettered.

Besides this, the condition of apparent starvation, in which the visitors found us from time to time, finally gave popularity to Sipsu's position, and Kalutunah yielded to the older and stronger chief.

When Petersen and Godfrey arrived at Netlik, Kalutunah went fifty miles to inform Sipsu at his home of the good occasion offered to kill them. Sipsu was to lead the attack, and Kalutunah follow. The arrangement was as we have stated, but failed on account of Sipsu's fear of the "au-leit"—pistol. Having failed, his chagrin and anger led to the hot pursuit, in which he intended to set the dogs upon our men. But this failed when he saw how near he must himself venture to the "*boom*."

This story agreed so well with what Petersen and Godfrey saw and suspected that we fully believed it.

Mr. Rock left us in the morning, and that evening eleven natives, one of whom was Kalutunah, called upon us on their way from Akbat to Netlik. The Angekok was full of talk and smiles. He gave us a quarter of a young bear, for which we gave him one of Petersen's hoop-iron knives. He was not pleased with it, for he had learned before the difference between iron and steel. He attempted to cut a piece of frozen liver with it and it bent. He then bent it in the form of a U, and threw it spitefully away, grunting, "No good." We satisfied him with a piece of wood to patch his sledge.

Among our guests were two widows having each a child. One of the little ones was stripped to the skin, and turned loose to root at liberty. It was three years old, and plainly the dirt upon its greasy skin had been accumulating just that length of time.

One of the hunters was attended by his wife and two children—a girl four, and boy seven years old.

The fat fires of the several families were soon

in full blaze, which, added to the heat of nineteen persons, warmed our hut as it was never warmed before. The heat set the ceiling and walls dripping with the melted frost-work, and every thing was wet or made damp. Besides, the air became insufferable with bad odors. It was now Fort Misery.

But the frozen meat at which we had been nibbling was soon thrown aside for hot coffee, steaming stew, and thawed blubber. Strips of blubber varying from three inches to a foot in length and an inch thick circulate about the hut. Strips of bear and walrus also go round. These strips are seized with the fingers, the head is thrown back, and the mouth is opened, one end is thrust in a convenient distance, the teeth are closed, it is cut off at the lips, and the piece is swallowed quickly, with the least possible chewing, that dispatch may be made, and the process repeated. The seven-year-old boy stood against a post, astride a big chunk of walrus, naked to the waste, as all the guests were. He was sucking down in good style a strip of blubber, his face and hands besmeared with blood and fat, which ran in a purple stream off his chin, and from thence streamed over the shining skin below. Our disconsolate widow supped apart, as usual, on her supply of sea-fowls. Four, each about the size of a half-grown domestic hen, was all she appeared to be able to eat!

We all ate, and had enough. Then followed freedom of talk such as is wont to follow satisfied appetites, and jokes and songs went round. Godfrey amused the women and children with negro melodies, accompanied by a fancied banjo. Dr. Hayes and Kalutunah try to teach each other their languages. Bonsall looks on and helps. The chief is given "yes" and "no," and taught what Esquimo word they stand for. He tries to pronounce them, says "ee's" and "noe," and inquiringly says, "*tyma?*" (right?) Dr. Hayes nods, "tyma" with an encouraging smile, at which the chief laughs at the "*doctee's*" badly pronounced Esquimo.

They try to count, and the Angekok says "*une*" for one, strains hard at "too" for two, and fails utterly at the "th" in three.

The "doctee" tries the Esquimo one, gets patted on the back with "tyma! tyma!" accompanied with merry laughs. The chief tries again, gets prompted by punches in the ribs, and significant commendation in twitches of his left ear.

Having reached ten, the Esquimo numerals are exhausted. Sontag, with the help of Petersen, questions one of the hunters about his people's astronomy. The result in part is as follows, and is very curious.

The heavenly bodies are the spirits of deceased Esquimo, or of some of the lower animals. The sun and moon are brother and sister. The stars we call "the dipper" are reindeer. The stars of "Orion's belt" are hunters who have lost their way. The "Pleiades" are a pack of dogs in pursuit of a bear. The *aurora borealis* is caused by the spirits at play with one another.

It has other teachings on the science of the heavens equally wise. But they are close observers of the movements of the stars. We went out at midnight to look after the dogs, and Petersen asked Kalutunah when they intended to go. He pointed to a star standing over Saunders Island, in the south. Passing his finger slowly around to the west he pointed at another star, saying, "When that star gets where the other is we will start."

Our guests at last lay down to sleep, but we could not lie down near them nor allow them our blankets; so we watched out the night.

CHAPTER XVI.

DRUGGED ESQUIMO.

THE visitors left in the morning. We were now all well except Stephenson. Though we had just eaten and were refreshed, in a few days we might be starving, so we renewed our planning. To open a communication with the "Advance" seemed a necessity. Petersen volunteered to make another effort if he could have one companion. Bonsall promptly answered, "I will be that companion," at which we all rejoiced, as he was the fittest man for the journey next to the Dane.

A dog-team and a sledge were an acquisition now most needed for the proposed enterprise. In a few days an old man came in whom we had never seen, belonging far up Whale Sound; then came a hunter from Akbat with his family. Of these men after much bartering we purchased four dogs. Petersen commenced at once the manufacture of a sledge out of the wood left of the "Hope." All of his excellent skill was needed to make a serviceable article with his poor tools and materials.

On the twentieth of November the sledge was nearly finished, and a breakfast on our last piece of meat assured us that what was done for our rescue must be done soon. But God's hand was, as usual, opened to supply us; in the evening a fox was found in our trap. Stephenson, who had been cheered by our tea, received the last cup.

We were reduced to stone-moss, boiled in blubber, and coffee, and a short allowance of these, when two hunters left us three birds, on which we supped.

We were now out of food. The Esquimo had, most of them, gone north, owing to the failure of game at the south; soon all would be gone. Further discussion led us to the conclusion that we must all return to the "Advance," and start soon unless we chose to die where we were. So we commenced preparations for the desperate enterprise.

To carry out this plan it was absolutely necessary to have two more dogs, for which we must trust to our Esquimo visitors. A sledge drawn by six dogs could convey our small outfit and poor invalid Stephenson. We purposed to direct our course straight for Northumberland Island, which we hoped to reach by lodging one night in a snow-hut. For each person there must be a pair of blankets. Our clothing was wholly insufficient for such a journey, so we set at work to improve it the best we could. Our buffalo robes had been spread upon the stone breck for beds. They were of course frozen down; in some places solid ice of several inches' thickness had accumulated, into which they were imbedded. When disengaged, as they had to be with much care and great labor, the under side was covered with closely adhering pebble-stones. The robes were hung up to dry before we could work upon them. We now slept on a double blanket spread on the stones and pebbles—a sleeping which refreshed us as little as our moss food.

We now, under the instructions of Petersen, cut up the buffalo robes and sewed them into garments to wear on our journey. We refreshed ourselves with frequent sips of coffee, of which, fortunately, we had a plenty, and made out one meal at night on walrus hide boiled or fried in oil, as we fancied. It was very tough eating.

At the close of the second day's tailoring four hunters came in from Akbat, with five women and seven children. We stowed them all away for the night, and gladly did so for the opportunity of purchasing forty-eight small birds, a small quantity of dried seal meat, and some dried seal intestines imperfectly cleansed; but better, if possible, was the purchase of two dogs. Our team of six was complete. The hand of the great Provider was plainly manifested.

The visitors were soon gone, but the four hunters came back the next day. They were bent on mischief. They stole, or tried to steal, whatever they saw, and seemed glad to annoy us. Unfortunately for us, close upon their heels came another party, from the south also, and equally bent on mischief. Among them was an old evil-eyed woman. Whatever she saw she coveted, and all that she could she stole. Going to her sledge as the party was about to start, we found a mixed collection of our articles, some of which could have been of no use to her. But we had missed two drinking cups which we could not find. We charged her with the theft, but she protested innocence. We threatened to search her sledge, and she straightway produced them, and, to conciliate us, threw down three sea-fowl. We were gladly thus conciliated.

The whole party became so troublesome that we were compelled to drive them away. The hunters lingered about, intending, we feared, to steal our dogs, two of which were purchased of them. We set a watch until they seemed to have left the vicinity, but no sooner was the sentinel's back turned than one of them and one of the dogs were seen scampering off together. Bonsall seized his rifle, and a sudden turn round a rock by the thief saved him from the salutation of an ounce of lead.

On the twenty-ninth of November we were ready for a start. Our outfit was meager enough. It consisted of eight blankets, a field lamp and kettle, two tin drinking cups, coffee for ten days, eight pounds of blubber, and two days' meat. This last consisted of sea-fowls boiled, boned, and cut into small pieces. They were frozen into a solid lump. We hoped to be at Northumberland Island in two days, and get fresh supplies.

The sled was taken out through the roof of the hut, loaded, and the load well secured, and poor Stephenson carried out and placed on top of it,

The dogs were then harnessed, and we moved away.

The thermometer was forty-four degrees below zero when we left the hut, but it was calm, and the moon shone with a splendid light. We were weary and ready to faint at the end of one hour, how then could we endure days of travel! The sledge was a poor one, the runners, the best our material afforded, were rough, and the dogs could not drag the sledge without two of us pushed, which we did in turn. We had thus gone about eight miles when Stephenson said he would walk. This we refused to let him do, knowing his extreme weakness. But soon after he slid off the sledge. Dr. Hayes assisted him to rise, and supported his attempt to walk. He had thus gone about a mile when he fell and fainted.

Near us was an iceberg in whose side was a recess something like a grotto. Into this we bore our companion, and added to the shelter by piling up blocks of snow. The lamp was lighted to prepare him hot coffee. For some time he remained insensible, and when he came to himself he begged us to leave him and save ourselves. He could never, he said, reach the "Advance," and he might as well die then as at a later hour.

Go without Stephenson we would not. Go with him seemed impossible. In fact we were all too weary to take another step, so we concluded to camp. But this, after unloading our sledge and making some effort, we could not do. We had no strength to make a hut, and we were already bitten by the frost; so we resolved to repack the sledge and return to the hut.

All arrived at the hut that day, but how and exactly at what time we did not know, only that some were an hour behind others, and that several finished the journey by creeping on their hands and knees. We had just enough consciousness left to bring in our blankets and spread them on those we left on the breck, and to close up the hole in the roof. We then lay down and slept through uncounted hours.

When we awoke it was nearly noon. Though hungry, cold, and weak, we were not badly frost-bitten. The first desirable thing was a fire. The tinder-box with its fixings could not be found. The one having it in charge remembered it was used at the berg, and this we all knew, and that was all any one knew about it. Without this we could have no fire. Never before in all our exigencies was such a feeling of despair expressed on our countenances. In this plight one in attempting to walk across the tent struck something with his foot. We all knew the tinder-box by its rattle. Our lamp was soon lighted, coffee was made, and half of our meat warmed. The other half was given to Petersen and Bonsall, who started immediately to go, as we had once before planned, to the brig, while the rest remained in the hut.

Dr. Hayes and Sontag accompanied them to the shore. The last words of the noble Petersen were: "If we ever reach the ship we will come back to you, or perish in the attempt, so sure as there is a God in heaven."

Four days passed, after our companions left us, of accumulating misery. The hut was colder than ever, and we were in utter darkness the most of the time Our food was now scraps of old hide, so hard that the dogs had refused it.

In this our condition of absolute starvation, three hunters, with each a dog-team, came to us from Netlik, one of whom was Kalutunah. They entered our hut with only two small pieces of meat in their hands, enough for a scanty meal for themselves. We appropriated one piece to ourselves without ceremony. The visitors frowned and protested, but this was not a moment with us for words. We soon satisfied, or seemed to satisfy, them by presents, and both pieces were soon steaming.

Dr. Hayes renewed his proposal for the Netlik people to carry us to the "Advance." Kalutunah refused curtly. Would they *let* teams to us for that purpose? No! The spirit of the refusal was, We wont help you. We know you must starve, and we desire you to do so that we may possess your goods. It was evident they understood our desperate condition perfectly.

These convictions of their purposes and feelings were confirmed when one of our number found buried in the snow, near their sledges, several large pieces of bear and walrus meat. This they were evidently determined we should not taste.

Kalutunah did not pretend that destitution or short supplies at Netlik made a journey to the brig inconvenient, but, as if to taunt us, said that a bear, a walrus, and three seals had been taken the day before.

The case then, as we saw it, stood thus: Six civilized men must die because three savages, who had plenty, choose to let them, that they might be benefited by their death. We at once and unanimously decided that it should not be so, and that the Esquimo should not thus leave us.

Not willing to do them unnecessary harm, Dr. Hayes proposed to give them a dose of opium; then to take the dogs and sledge and push forward to Northumberland Island, leaving them to come along at their leisure when they awoke. We could, we thought, push forward fast enough to be out of the reach of any alarm that might reach Netlik.

To this proposal all agreed. To carry it into execution we became specially sociable, and free with our presents. To crown the freeness of our hospitality we set before them the stew just prepared, into which Dr. Hayes had turned slyly when it was over the fire a small vial of laudanum. To prevent any one getting an over dose it had been turned out into three vessels, an equal portion for each. It was, of course, very bitter.

They at first swallowed it very greedily, but tasting the bitter ingredient only ate half of it.

The next few moments were those of intense anxiety. Would it stupefy them? Soon, however, their eyes looked heavy, and their heads drooped. They begged to lie down, and we tucked them up this time in our blankets.

We were in our traveling suits ready for a start, dog-whips at hand. As a last act Godfrey reached up to a shelf for a cup, and down came its entire contents with a startling noise. Dr. Hayes put out the light with his mitten, and cuddled down instantly by the side of Kalutunah. The chief awoke, as was feared, grunted, and asked what was the matter. The "doctee" patted him and whispered, "Singikok," (sleep.) He laughed, muttered something, and was soon snoring.

Fearing from this incident that we could not trust the soundness nor length of time of their sleep, we carried off their boots, coats, and mittens, that they might be detained in the tent until relief came. Stephenson was, most fortunately, better than he had been for some time, being able to carry a gun and walk. All the firearms being secured, Dr. Hayes stood at one side of the door outside with a double-barrelled shot-gun, and Stephenson on the other with a rifle. The purpose was if they awoke to compel them, at the mouth of the guns, to drive us north.

Sontag and the others brought up the most of the meat which was buried in the snow, and put it in the passage way. This would last five or six days, and keep the prisoners from starving until help came. The dogs being harnessed, we mounted the sledges and once more turned our backs on Fort Desolation.

The dogs objected decidedly to this whole proceeding; they especially disliked their new masters, and were determined on mischief. John and Godfrey were given by their team a ride a mile straight off the coast instead of along-side of it, as they desired to go. Dr. Hayes was worse used by his. They drew in different directions, went pell-mell, first this way, then that, at one time carrying him back nearly to the hut. Finally they became subdued apparently, and sped swiftly in the way they were guided. The other sledges had in the mean time dropped into the desired course. All seemed to be going well, when, just as the doctor's dogs had shot by the other teams, they suddenly turned round, some to the right and others to the left, turning the sledge over backward, and rolling the men into a snow-drift. The doctor grasped firmly the "up-stander" of the sledge, and was dragged several yards before he recovered his feet. As the dogs at this moment were plunging through a ridge of hummocks, the point of the runner caught a block of ice. The traces of all the dogs excepting two snapped, and away went the freed dogs to their imprisoned masters. They yelped a taunting defiance as they disappeared in the distance.

The doctor and Mr. Stephenson, taking each a dog, went to the other teams, and we were again on the fly, leaving the third sledge jammed in the hummock. We reached in safety the southern point of Cape Parry, found a sheltering cave, and camped.

CHAPTER XVII.

BACK AGAIN.

WE tarried in our camp full two hours. We obtained a pot of hot coffee and rest. The whips had been used so freely that they required repairing, for without their efficient help there could be no progress.

All being in readiness, we were about starting when three Esquimo came in sight. They were those we had left asleep in our hut! Dr. Hayes and Mr. Sontag seized their guns, and rushed down the ice-foot to meet them. They stood firm until our men, coming within a few yards, leveled their guns at them. They instantly turned round and threw their arms wildly about, exclaiming in a frantic voice, "Na-mik! na-mik! na-mik!" —don't shoot! don't shoot! don't shoot!

Dr. Hayes lowered his rifle and beckoned them to come on. This they did cautiously, and with loud protestations of friendship. By this time Whipple had come up. Each of our men seized a prisoner, and marched him into the camp. Reaching the mouth of the cave, the doctor turned Kalutunah round toward his sledge, pointed to it with his gun, and then turning north, gave him to understand, mostly by signs, that if he took the whip which lay at his feet, and drove us to the

"Oomeaksoak" (ship) he should have his dogs, sledge, coat, boots, and mittens; but if they did not do so that he and his companions would be shot then and there; and to give emphasis to his words, he pushed him away and leveled his gun.

The chief went sideling off, crying, "Na-mik, na-mik!" at the same time imitated the motion of a dog—driving with his right hand, and pointed north with the other. His declaration was, "Don't shoot! I'll drive you to the ship!"

Dr. Hayes seeing he was understood, told Kalutunah that the dogs and sledges were the white men's until the promise was fulfilled, to which he answered, "tyma"—all right, approaching with smiles and the old familiarity, as though some great favor had been done him. He could respect pluck and strength if nothing else.

The prisoners had been awakened by our escaped dogs, which, on arriving at the hut, run over the roof and howled a startling alarm. Their masters starting up, found means of lighting a lamp, and being refreshed by sleep and the food we left, entered at once on the pursuit. Coming to the abandoned sledge, they harnessed the dogs and made good time on our trail, bringing away with them as many of our treasures as they could well carry.

They were rare looking Esquimo just at this moment. They had cut holes in the middle of our blankets and thrust their heads through. One had found a pair of cast-off boots and put them on; the others had bundled their feet up in pieces of blanket. Neither of them had suffered much from cold.

We expressed our confidence in their promises by restoring their clothes. They jumped into them, happy as Yankee children on the Fourth of July. They were as obedient, too, as recently whipped spaniels. They touched neither dogs, sledge, nor whip until they were bidden. "Onward to Netlik!" we shouted as we mounted our sledges and dashed away. Our distant approach was greeted by the howling of a pack of dogs, which snuffed our coming in the breeze. As we drew nearer, men, women, and children ran out to meet us. As soon as we halted fifty curious and wondering savages crowded around us, pressing the questions why we were brought by their friends, and why we came at all. But our bearing was that of those who came because they pleased to come without condescending to give reasons why. We told Kalutunah that three of us would go to each of the two huts, and stop long enough to eat and sleep, and then we would continue our journey. A renewed leveling at him of our guns, and pointing northward, brought out the prompt "tyma," giving the gaping bystanders a hint of the nature of our arguments for the services of their friends.

When we had entered the huts, the crowd rushed in too, making quite too many for comfort or safety. We told our hosts to order out all but the regular occupants of the huts, as many strangers had come in who were lodging in the adjoining snow-huts.

They did not understand our right to give such a command until a hint about our "booms" convinced them. Ours was the right of self-preservation by superior strength.

We had traveled fifteen successive hours, making in the time fifty miles. So weary were we that even these Esquimo dens, affording as they did refreshment and rest without danger of freezing, were delightful places of entertainment. The women kindly removed our mittens, boots, and stockings, and hung them up to dry. They then brought us frozen meat, which intense hunger compelled us to try to eat, but the air of the hut was one hundred and twenty degrees warmer than that without, and we fell asleep with the food between our teeth. Having taken a short nap we were aroused by the mistress of the house, who had prepared a plentiful meal of steaming bear-steak. We ate and slept alternately until the stars informed us that we had rested twenty-seven hours. We intimated to Kalutunah that we would be going, and in a few moments he had every thing in readiness.

Our next halting place was Northumberland Island, a distance, as we traveled, of thirty miles, which we made in six hours. Here we found two huts belonging to our old friends, Amalatok and his brother, "Mr. Rock." We divided ourselves into companies of threes as before, and made ourselves at home in the two households. Mr. Rock, aided by his wife, and the witch-wife of his brother, was kindly attentive. Our fare was varied by abundant supplies of sea-birds, which in their season swarm here. We tarried until our physical strength was sensibly increased. We learned that Petersen and Bonsall had been at this hospitable halting-place, eaten and rested, and pushed northward under the guidance of Amalatok.

Our next run was to Herbert Island, and, passing round its northwestern coast, we struck across to the mainland, and halted near Cape Robertson, at the village of Karsooit. We were on the northern shore of the mouth of Whale Sound. We had made a run of fifty miles, halting to eat our frozen food only once. We had walked much of the way to prevent being frozen, and to lighten the load of the dogs over a rough way.

The village consisted of two huts half a mile apart. One of them belonged to Sipsu, our old enemy. He received us gruffly, and because he felt that he must. His only kindness was a fear of our *booms*. The huts were crowded, there being here, as at Netlik, many stranger visitors from the south. We were almost suffocated on entering, passing as we did from a temperature of fifty degrees below zero to one seventy-five above. Our entertainers immediately laid hold of our clothes and began to strip us. They were much surprised at our persistence in retaining a certain part of them. We feasted on seal flesh, slept, were refreshed and encouraged.

Our stay was short, and our next run was to a double hut, a distance of thirty miles, which we made in five hours. We had been joined at Karsooit by an old hunter named Ootinah. We were on four sledges, the dogs were in good condition, the ice smooth, the drivers full of merriment and shouts of "Ka! ka!" by which their teams were stimulated onward.

Our next run was to be one of sixty miles, including the rounding of Cape Alexander, and ending at Etah. It was to be a terrific adventure we well knew. At the mention of it our drivers shrugged their shoulders. The natives dread the storms of this cape, with their blinding snows, as the wandering Arabs of the desert do a tempest-cloud of sand.

The first twenty miles was made comfortably. But we were yet many miles from the rocky fortress guarding the Arctic Sea, when we were saluted with a stunning squall. It cut us terribly, though it was but an eddy, for the wind was at our backs; it was only a rough hint of what we might expect when the giant of the cape sent his blast squarely in our faces. The night came on, lighted only by the twinkling stars. The ice was smooth, and the wind at our backs drove our sledges upon the heels of the dogs, who ran howling at the top of their speed to keep out of their way. The cliffs, a thousand feet above us, threw their frowning shadows across our path, pouring upon the plain clouds of snow sand, and shouting in the roaring wind their defiance at our approach. Yet we sped swiftly on, until a dark line was seen ahead with wreaths of "frost-smoke" curling over it. "Emerk! emerk!" shouted the Esquimo. "Water! water!"

echoed our men. Our teams "reined up" within a few yards of a recently opened crack, now twenty feet across and rapidly widening. We were quite near Cape Alexander, but between it and us was ice, across which numerous cracks had opened. Against the cape was open water, whose sullen surges fell dismally upon our ears. It was plain that we could not go forward upon the floe; to mount the almost perpendicular wall to the land above was impossible; to turn back and thus face the storm would be certain death. Our case seemed desperate. Even the hardy Esquimo shrunk at the situation and proposed the return trail, against which to us, at least, ruinous course they could not be persuaded until the pistol argument was used.

In our peering through the darkness for some way of escape we caught a glimpse of the narrow ice-foot, hanging over the water at the bottom of the cliff. Along this we determined to attempt a passage.

We ascended this ice-foot by a ladder made of the sledges. Then we ran along the smooth surface and soon passed the open water below; but we had advanced a short distance only before a glacier barred our progress and turned us to the floe again. A short run on this brought us to another yawning crack with its impassable water. We ran along its margin with torturing anxiety, looking for an ice bridge. Finding a place where a point of ice spanned the chasm, within about four feet, Dr. Hayes made a desperate leap to gain the other side. Lighting upon this point, it proved to be merely a loose, small ice-raft which settled beneath his feet. Endeavoring to balance himself upon it to gain the solid floe beyond he fell backward, and would have gone completely under the water; but Stephenson, standing on the spot from which the doctor jumped, caught him under the arms and drew him out. As it was he had sunk deep into the cold stream, filling his boots and wetting his pants.

In the mean time a better crossing was found, and Dr. Hayes followed the last of the party to the other side.

We returned to the ice-foot and found a level and sufficiently wide drive-way, and made good progress, soon reaching and running along that part of the icy road which overlooked the open water below. We met with no interruption until we came to the extreme rocky projection of the cape. Here the ice-foot was sloping, and for several feet was only fifteen inches wide! Twenty feet directly below was the icy cold, dark water, sending up its dismal roar as it waited to receive any whose foot might slip in attempting the perilous passage. The wind howled fearfully as it swept over the cliff and along the ice-foot in our rear, pelting us incessantly with its snow sand.

"Halt!" was passed along the line, and the whole party, men and dogs, crouched under the overhanging rocks, seeming for the moment like beings doomed to die a miserable death in a horrid place.

There was no time for indecision, and the pause was but for a moment. Dr. Hayes, taking off his mittens, and clinging with his bare hands to the crevices of the rock, was the first to make the desperate experiment. His shout announcing his safe landing on the broad belt beyond the dangerous place, welling up as it did from a heart overflowing with emotions of joy and gratitude, sent a thrill of gladness along the shivering and shrinking line, of which even our poor dogs seemed to partake.

The teams, each driven by its master, were next brought up, as near as safety permitted, to the narrow, slippery pathway. The dogs were then seized by their collars, and one by one dragged across safely. Next the sledges were brought forward. Turning them upon one runner, they were pushed along until the dogs could make them feel the traces; then a fierce shout from their drivers caused a sudden and vigorous spring of the animals, which whirled the sledges beyond the danger of sliding off the precipice. Cautiously, one by one, then came the remaining members of the party, all holding their breath in painful suspense, and each, we trust, in silent prayer, until all were safe over. The Divine arm and eye had been with us! We could not have gone back, nor have turned to the right or left. A few inches less of width in the ice-foot, or slightly more slope, and we had all perished!

Except some frost bites on our fingers, every man was all right. We had traveled five miles on the ice shelf above the foaming sea. We now had a smooth, safe ice-foot, which conducted us soon to the solid ice-field of Etah Bay. Across this, fifteen miles, we scampered with joyous speed, and arrived at the village of our old Esquimo friends, a worn and weary, but thankful party.

Good news met us at the hut. Petersen and Bonsall had, we were told, preceded us, and arrived safely at the ship.

But our trials were not ended. There was a sledge journey of ninety-one miles yet awaiting us. Dr. Hayes's frosted feet gave him intense pain and he could not sleep. There was danger, if the heat of the hut thawed them, that he would lose them altogether. So, after only four hours' rest, he whispered his intention of a speedy departure toward the "Advance," to Sontag, who was to take charge of the party; he then crept stealthily out of the hut, accompanied by Ootinah, the faithful Esquimo from Karsooit. Sontag was not to mention his departure to his comrades until they were rested and refreshed.

He had hardly started before the rest of our company were at his heels. They did not wish their leader to endure the perils of the journey without them; besides, they too had reason for a desire to be speedily at the brig.

The wind was high, the floe full of hummocks, the cold intense, and altogether the journey was not unlike in its dangers that already endured. Whipple, ere they had reached the end, began to whisper that he was not cold, and finally fell from the rear sledge, benumbed and senseless, and was not missed until he was a hundred yards behind. He was lifted again to the sledge, but others gave signs of the approach of the same insensibility.

But the track becoming smoother, the drivers cracked their whips and shouted fiercely, goading onward their teams to their utmost speed in the fearful race for life. Now old familiar landmarks are passed; the hull of the dismantled ship opens in the distance, and its outlines grow clearer until we shout with feeble voices, but in gladness of heart, "*Back again!*" During the last forty hours we had been in almost continual exposure, with the thermometer eighty degrees below zero, in which time we had traveled a hundred and fifty miles. During the run of ninety-one miles from Etah to the "Advance" we encamped once only, but failing to light our lamp, or to secure any protection from the cold, we immediately decamped and finished our run of forty-one miles.

CHAPTER XVIII.

SCARES.

WHEN the Esquimo arrived with Bonsall and Petersen, Dr. Kane resolved at once to send them back with supplies for the remaining portion of Dr. Hayes's company, supposed to be, if living, at the miserable old hut. Petersen and Bonsall were utterly unable to accompany them. Of the scanty ship's store he caused to be cleaned and boiled a hundred pounds of pork; small packages of meat-biscuit, bread-dust, and tea were carefully sewed up, all weighing three hundred and fifty pounds; and the whole was intrusted to the returning convoy, who gave emphatic assurances that these treasures, more precious than gold to those for whom they were intended, should be promptly and honestly delivered. But this promise, we have seen, they did not keep, and, probably, did not intend to keep; they ate or wasted the whole. This untrustworthy trait of the Esquimo character goes far to show that nothing but Dr. Hayes's "boom" could have assured their help in his desperate necessities.

When Dr. Hayes arrived it was midnight. Dr. Kane met him at the gangway and gave him a brother's welcome. All were taken at once into the cabin. Ohlsen was the first to recognize

Hayes as he entered, and, kissing him, he threw his arms around him and tossed him into the warm bed he had just left. The fire was set ablaze, coffee and meat-biscuit soup were prepared, and, with wheat bread and molasses, were set before them. In the mean time their Esquimo apparel was removed and hung up to dry. They ate and slept; but many weary days passed, under skillful treatment by Dr. Kane, and kind care by all, before they fully recovered from the strain of their terrible exposures and fearful journey.

When the returned comrades were duly cared for, Dr. Kane turned his attention to the conciliation of the Esquimo who had accompanied them back. They, of course, had their complaints to make, and, may be, meditated revenge, though they were, as usual, full of smiles. It was the white chief's policy to impress them with his great power and stern justice. He assembled both parties, the Hayes men and their Esquimo, in conference on deck. Both were questioned as if it were a doubt who had been the offenders. This done, he graciously declared to the savage members of the council his approval of their conduct, which he made emphatic, in the Esquimo way, by pulling their hair all around.

The great Nalekok having thus expressed his good will, showed it still further by introducing his guests, now to be considered friends, into the mysterious *igloë* below where they had not before been permitted to enter. Their joy was that of indulged children during a holiday. They were seated in state on a red blanket. Four pork-fat lamps burned brilliantly; ostentatiously paraded were old worsted damask curtains, hunting knives, rifles, chronometers, and beer-barrels, which, as they glowed in the light, astonished the natives. With a princely air, which, no doubt, seemed to the recipients almost divine, he dealt out to each five needles, a file, and a stick of wood. To the two head men, Kalutunah and Shunghu, knives and other extras were given. A roaring fire was then made and a feast cooked. This eaten, buffaloes were spread about the stove, and the guests slept. They awoke to eat, and ate to sleep again. When they were ready to go, the white chief explained that the sledges, dogs, and some furs, which his men had taken, had been taken to save life, and were not to be considered as stolen goods, and he then and there restored them. They laughed, voted him in their way a good fellow, and, in fine spirits, dashed away, shouting to their wolfish dogs. They had taken special care, however, to add to the treasures so generously given, a few stolen knives and forks.

As the whole company are now crowded into the little cabin, and the darkness is without, so that the days pass without much incident, except that all are crowded with heavy burdens upon mind and body, we will listen to a few of the yet untold stories of the earlier winter.

At one time Dr. Kane attempted a walrus hunt. Morton, Hans, Ootuniah, Myouk, and "a dark stranger," Awahtok, accompanied him. He took a light sledge drawn by seven dogs, intending to reach the farthest point of Force Bay by daylight. But as the persistency of the Esquimo had overladen the sledge, they moved slowly, and were overtaken by the night on the floe in the midst of the bay. The snow began to drift before an increasing storm. While driving rapidly, they lost the track they had been following; they could see no landmarks, and in their confusion, turned their faces to the floating ice of the sound.

The Esquimo, usually at home on the floe, whether by night or by day, were quite bewildered. The dogs became alarmed, and spread their panic to the whole party. They could not camp, the wind blew so fiercely, so they were compelled to push rapidly forward, they knew not whither. Checking, after a while, their speed, Dr. Kane gave each a tent-pole to feel their way more cautiously, for a murmur had reached his ear more alarming than the roar of the wind. Suddenly the noise of waves startled him. "Turn the dogs!" he shouted, while at the same moment a wreath of frost smoke, cold and wet, swept over the whole party, and the sea opened to them with its white line of foam, about one fourth of a mile ahead. The floe was breaking up by the force of the storm. The broken ice might be in any direction. They could now guess where they were, and they turned their faces toward an island up the bay. But the line of the sea, with its foaming waves, followed them so rapidly that they began to feel the ice bending under their feet as they ran at the sides of the sledge. The hummocks before them began to close up, and they run by them at a fearful risk as they hurried cautiously forward, stumbling over the crushed fragments between them and the shore. It was too dark to see the island for which they were steering, but the black outline of a lofty cape was dimly seen along the horizon, and served as a landmark. As they approached the shore edge of the floe they found it broken up, and its fragments surging against the base of the ice-foot to which they desired to climb. Being now under the shadow of the land, it was densely dark. Dr. Kane went ahead, groping for a bridge of ice, having a rope tied round his waist, the other end of which was held by Ootuniah, who followed, at whose heels came the rest of the party. The doctor finally succeeded in clambering upon the ice-foot, and the rest one after another followed with the dogs.

The joy of their escape broke out into exultation when they ascertained that the land was Anoatok, only a short distance from the familiar Esquimo huts. God had guided them with his all-seeing eye to where they would find needed refreshment! In less than an hour they were feasting on a smoking stew of walrus meat.

Having eaten their stew and drank their coffee they slept—slept eleven hours! Well they might "after an unbroken ice-walk of forty-eight miles, and twenty haltless hours!" The Esquimo sung themselves to sleep with a monotonous song, in compliment to the white chief, the refrain of which was, "Nalegak! nalegak! nalegak! soak!"—Captain! captain! great captain!"

Without further special incident the party returned to the brig.

At one time an alarm was brought to Dr. Kane that a wolf was prowling among the meat barrels on the floe. Believing that a wolf would be more profitably added to their store of meat than to have him take any thing from it, he seized a rifle and ran out. Yes, there he is, a wolf from the tip of his nose to the end of his tail! Bang goes the rifle, whiz goes the ball, making the hair fly from the back of—one of the sledge-dogs! He was not hurt much, but he came near paying with his life for the crime of running away from Morton's sledge.

The fox-traps made occasion for many long walks, great expectations of game, and grievous disappointment. Dr. Kane and Hans were at one time examining them about two miles from the brig. They were, unfortunately, unarmed. The doctor thought he heard the bellow of a walrus. They listened. No, not a walrus, but a bear! Hark, hear him roar! They sprung to the ice-foot, about ten feet above the floe. Another roar, round and full! He is drawing nearer! He has a fine voice, and, no doubt, is large, and fat, and savory! But then a bear must be killed before he is eaten, and that is just where the difficulty lies. It don't do for two men to run, for that is an invited pursuit, and bears are good runners. "Hans!" exclaimed Dr. Kane, "run for the brig, and I will play decoy!" Hans is a good runner, and this time he did "his level best."

Dr. Kane remains on the ice-foot alone. It is too dark to see many yards off, and the silence is oppressive, for the bear says nothing, and so Kane makes no reply. He queries whether, after all, there is any bear. How easy it is for the imagination to be excited amid these shadowy hummocks, and this dreary waste through which the wind roars so dismally! He gets down from his comparatively safe elevation upon the floe, puts his hand over his eyes, and peers into the darkness. No bear after all! But what's that rounded, shadowy thing? Stained ice? Yes, stained ice! But the stained ice speaks with a voice which wakes the Arctic echoes, and charges on our explorer. It is a hungry bear! Dr. Kane's legs are scurvy-smitten affairs, but this time they credit the fleetness of those of the deer. He drops a mitten, and his pursuer stops to smell of it, to examine it carefully, and to show his disgust at such game, by tearing it to pieces. These bears are famous for losing the bird by stopping to pick up his feathers. The man stops not, but drops another mitten as he flies. Before these articles are duly examined he has reached the brig. Dr. Kane has escaped, and the bear has lost his supper.

It is now bruin's turn to run, for fresh hunters and loaded rifles are after him. He does run, and escapes!

But if there were fears without the brig, there were fightings with a fearful enemy within. The crowded condition of the cabin, after the Hayes party returned, made it necessary for the pork-fat lamps to be set up outside the avenue, in a room parted off in the hold for their use. A watch was set over them, but he deserted his post, the fat flamed over and set the room ablaze. Eight of the men lay in their berths at the time helplessly disabled. The fire was only a few feet from the tinder-like moss which communicated with the cabin. The men able to work seized buckets, and formed a line to the well in the ice always kept open. In the mean time Dr. Kane rushed into the flames with some fur robes which lay at hand, and checked it for the moment. The water then came, and the first bucket full thrown caused a smoke and steam which prostrated him. Fortunately, in falling he struck the feet of the foremost bucket-man. He was taken to the deck, his beard, forelock, and eyebrows singed away, and sad burns upon his forehead and palms. Nearly all received burns and frost-bites, but in a half hour the fire was extinguished. The danger was horrid, and the escape wonderful! Neither wild beasts nor the flames hurt whom God protects!

CHAPTER XIX.

SEEKING THE ESQUIMO.

DECEMBER twenty-fifth came, and our ice-bound, darkness-enshrouded, sick, or, in a measure, health-broken explorers tried to make it a merry Christmas. They all sat down to dinner together. "There was more love than with the stalled ox of former times, but of herbs none." They tried, at least, to forget their discomforts in the blessings they still retained, and to look hopefully on the long distance, and the many conflicts between them and their home and friends.

Immediately after Christmas a series of attempts were commenced to open a communication with the Esquimo at Etah, ninety-one miles away. The supply of fresh meat was exhausted. The traps yielded nothing, and Hans's hunting could not go on successfully in the dark. The scurvy-smitten men were failing for the want of it, and so every thing must be periled to make the journey. The first thing to be done was to put the dogs, if possible, into traveling order. They were now few in number, for fifty had died, and the survivors had been kept on short rations. Their dead companions, which had been preserved in a frozen state, were boiled and fed to them for fresh food.

Dog *did* eat dog, and relished and grew stronger on the diet.

Dr. Kane and Petersen made the first attempt, starting on the twenty-ninth of December. They had scarcely reached the forsaken huts of Anoatok, "the wind loved-spot," so often used as a resting place, when the dogs failed. A storm, with a bitter, pelting snow-drift, confined them awhile. An incident occurred here—one of the many which happened to the explorers—which shows plainly the unseen, but ever present, eye and hand which attended them.

They were just losing themselves in sleep when Petersen shouted: "Captain Kane, the lamp's out!" His commander heard him with a thrill of horror! The storm was increasing, the cold piercing, and the darkness intense. The tinder had become moist and was frozen solid. The guns were outside, to keep them from the moisture of the hut. The only hope of heat was in relighting the lamp. A lighted lamp and heat they *must* have. Petersen tried to obtain fire from a pocket-pistol, but his only tinder was moss, and after repeated attempts he gave it up. Dr. Kane then tried. He says:—

"By good luck I found a bit of tolerably dry paper in my jumper; and, becoming apprehensive that Petersen would waste our few percussion caps with his ineffectual snappings, I took the pistol myself. It was so intensely dark that I had to grope for it, and in doing so touched his hand. At that instant the pistol became distinctly visible.

A pale, bluish light, slightly tremulous but not broken, covered the metallic parts of it, the barrel, lock, and trigger. The stock too was clearly discernible, as if by the reflected light, and, to the amazement of both of us, the thumb and two fingers with which Petersen was holding it, the creases, wrinkles, and circuit of the nails, clearly defined upon the skin. The phosphorescence was not unlike the ineffectual fire of the glowworm. As I took the pistol my hand became illuminated also, and so did the powder-rubbed paper when I raised it against the muzzle.

"The paper did not ignite at the first trial, but the light from it continuing, I was able to charge the pistol without difficulty, rolled up my paper into a cone, filled it with moss sprinkled over with powder, and held it in my hand while I fired. This time I succeeded in producing flame, and we saw no more of the phosphorescence."

When the storm subsided they made further experiment to reach Etah. But dogs and men found the wading impossible, and they returned to the brig, the dogs going ahead and the men walking after them. They made the forty-four miles of their circuitous route in sixteen hours!

Thus closed the year 1854.

The three following weeks were mainly occupied by Dr. Kane in a careful preparation for another attempt to reach Etah, this time with Hans. Old Yellow, one of the five dogs on which success in a measure depended, stalked about the deck with "his back up," as much as to say, "I must have more to eat if I am going." Jenny, a mother dog, had quite a family of little ones. Yellow being very hungry, and not seeing the use of such young folks, gobbled one of them down before his master could say, "Don't you." Dr. Kane taking the hint, and thinking that the puppies would not be dogs soon enough for his use, shared with Yellow the rest of the litter. So both grew stronger for the journey.

The new year, 1855, came in with a vail of darkness over the prospects of our explorers. The sick list was large, and threatened to include the whole party. A fox was caught occasionally, and beyond this stinted supply there was no fresh meat. On Tuesday, January twenty-third, the commander and Hans, with the dog-team, turned their faces toward the Esquimo. All went well for a while, until hope rose of accomplishing the journey, getting savory walrus, and cheering their sinking comrades. Suddenly, Big Yellow, in spite of nice puppy soup, gave out, and went into convulsions. Toodla, the next best animal, failed soon after. The moon went down, and the dark night was upon the beset but not confounded heroes. Groping for the ice-foot, they trudged fourteen wretched hours, and reached the old *igloë* at Anoatok. The inevitable storm arose, with its burden of snow driven by a strange, moistening southeast wind, burying the hut deep and warm. The temperature rose seventy degrees! An oppressive sensation attacked Dr. Kane and Hans, and alarming symptoms were developed. Water ran down from the roof, the doctor's sleeping bag of furs was saturated, and his luxurious eider down, God's wonderful cold defier, was "a wet swab."

After two days in this comfortless hut, the storm having subsided, they once again pushed toward Etah! Their sick, failing comrades were the spur to this desperate effort. But it was in vain, for the deep, moist snow, the hummocks and the wind, defied even desperate courage. They returned to the hut and spent another wretched night.

In the morning, in spite of short provisions, exhaustion, continued snowing, they climbed the ice-foot, and for four haltless hours faced toward the Esquimo! But in vain. Dr. Kane says: "My poor Esquimo, Hans, adventurous and buoyant as he was, began to cry like a child. Sick, worn out, strength gone, dogs fast and floundering, I am not ashamed to admit that, as I thought of the sick men on board, my own equanimity was at fault."

Dr. Kane scrambled up a familiar hill that was near and reconnoitered. He was delighted to see, winding among the hummocks, a level way! He called Hans to see it. With fresh dogs and fresh supplies, they could certainly reach Etah. So, after another night at the hut, they returned to the brig, comforting the sick with the assurance that success would come on the next trial.

The month closed with only five effective men, including the commander, and of these some were about as much sick as well. Dr. Kane could not be spared from his patients, so, February third, Petersen and Hans tried another Etah adventure. In three days they returned, with a sorrowful tale from poor Petersen of heroic efforts ending in exhaustion and defeat.

But God always sent many rays of light through the densest darkness besetting our explorers to cheer them and inspire hope. The yellow tints of coming sunlight were at noonday faintly painted on the horizon. The rabbits prophesied the spring by appearing abroad, and two were shot. They yielded a pint of raw blood, which the sickest drank as a grateful cordial. Their flesh was also eaten raw, and with great thankfulness.

Following these moments of comfort came a dismal and anxious night. Thick clouds overspread the sky, a heavy mist rendered the darkness appalling, followed by a drifting snow and a fearful storm. The wind howled and shrieked through the rigging of the helpless, battered brig, as if in mockery of her condition and the sufferings of her inmates. Goodfellow had gone inland with his gun during the brief day, and had not returned. Roman candles and bluelights were burned to guide him homeward. Altogether it was a night to excite the superstitious fears of the sailors, and they proved to be not beyond the reach of such fears. Tom Hickey, the cook, having been on deck while the gale was in its full strength, to peer into the darkness for him, ran below declaring that he had seen Goodfellow moving cautiously along the land-ice and jump down on the floe. He hurried up his supper to give the tired messmate a warm welcome, but no one came. Dr. Kane went out with a lantern, looked carefully around for some hundreds of yards, but found no fresh footsteps. Tom seriously insisted that he had seen Goodfellow's apparition!

Such was the state of things when one of the sailors went on deck. There was hanging in the rigging an old seal-skin bag containing the remnant of the ship's furs. Its ghostly appearance in ordinary darkness had been the occasion of much jesting. Now, to the excited imagination of the sailor, it pounded the mast like the gloved fist of a giant boxer, glowed with a ghastly light, and muttered to him an unearthly story. He did not stop to converse with it, but hastened below with the expression of his fears. His messmates laughed and jeered at his tale, but their merriment was but the whistling to inspire their own courage.

The morning came and so did Goodfellow, none the worse for his night's experience. The storm subsided, Hans killed three rabbits, they all tasted a little and felt better, and the seal-skin bag was never known from that time to utter a word. *Fears* may endure for a night but joy cometh in the morning! Dr. Kane devoutly remarks: "See how often relief has come at the moment of extremity; see, still more, how the back has been strengthened to its increasing burden, and the heart cheered by some unconscious influence of an unseen POWER."

CHAPTER XX.

DESERTERS.

HANS had been for some time promising the hungry company a deer. He had seen their tracks, and he was watching for them with a good rifle, a keen eye, and a steady hand. He came in on the evening of February twenty-second with the good news that he had lodged a ball in one at a long range, and that he went hobbling away. He was sure he should find him dead in the morning. The morning came and the game was found, having staggered, bleeding, only two miles. He was a noble fellow, measuring in length six feet and two inches, and five feet in girth. He weighed about one hundred and eighty pounds when dressed. The enfeebled men with difficulty drew him on board. His presence caused a thrill of joy, and his luscious flesh sent its invigoration through their emaciated frames.

The following Sunday, as Dr. Kane was standing on deck thinking of their situation, he lifted up his eyes toward a familiar berg, for many months shrouded in darkness, and saw it sparkling in the sunlight. The King of Day was not yet above the intervening hills, but he had sent his sheen to proclaim his coming. Glad as a boy whom the full mid-winter moon invites to a coasting frolic, he started on a run, climbed the elevations, and bathed in his refreshing rays.

During the month of February, Petersen, Hans, and Godfrey had been sent out on the track of the Esquimo, but they returned and declared that Etah could not be reached. Their commander said, "Nay, it can!"

By the sixth of March the brig was again without fresh meat. The sick were once more suffering for it, and the well growing feeble. Hans, the resort in such emergencies, was given a light sledge, the two surviving dogs, and to him was committed the forlorn hope. His departure called forth from his commander a "God bless you!" and prayers followed him.

His story is simple and touching. He lodged the first night in the "wind-loved," forsaken, desolate, yet friendly hut of Anoatok. He slept as well as he could in a temperature fifty-three degrees below zero. The next night he slept in a friendly hut at Etah. The oft-tried feat was accomplished. But he found the Etahites lean and hungry. Hollow cheeks and sunken eyes spoke of famine. The skin of a young sea-unicorn, their last game, was all of food which remained to the settlement. They had even eaten their light and fire blubber, and were seated in darkness, gloomily waiting for the sun and the hunt. They had eaten, too, all but four of their ample supply of dogs.

They hailed the coming of Hans with a shout. He proposed to join them in a hunt, but they shook their heads. They had lost a harpoon and line in the attempt to take a walrus the day before. The ice was yet thick, and the huge monster in his struggles had broken the line over its sharp edge. Hans showed them his "boom," and bidding them come on, started for the hunting-grounds. Metek—Mr. Eider Duck—speared a fair-sized walrus, and Hans gave him five conical balls in quick succession from a Marston rifle, and he surrendered at discretion.

The return of the hunters caused great joy in the city of Etah, whose two huts poured out their inhabitants to greet their coming, and aid in rendering due honors to the game itself. As usual they laughed, feasted, and slept, to awake, laugh, eat, and sleep again. Hans and his boom were great in their eyes, but the Kablunah, whose representative he was, rose before their vision as the glorious sun which scatters the long winter darkness.

Hans obtained a hunter's share, and his appearance on the deck of the "Advance," heralded by the yelping of the dogs, sent a thrill of joy through every heart. As Dr. Kane grasped his hand on the deck, and began to listen to his story, he exclaimed: "Speak louder, Hans, that they may hear in the bunks!" The bunks did hear, and feel too, as the good news came home to their hunger-wasted bodies in refreshing food.

As the commander had requested, Hans brought Myouk with him to assist in hunting. The smart young hunter was delighted to be with the white men, though his itching fingers would secrete cups, spoons, and other valuables, which were made to come back to their proper places by sundry cuffs and kicks, which, though perhaps not altogether pleasant of themselves, caused him to cuddle down in his buffalo at his master's feet like a whipped spaniel, and their relations grew daily more enjoyable.

Hans and Myouk made soon after an unsuccessful hunt. This made the fresh meat question come up again with its emphatic importance. The fuel question, too, was becoming more and more a cause of concern. The manilla cable had been chopped up and burned, and such portions of the brig as could be spared, and not destroy her sea-going value, had gone in the same way. Now the nine feet of solid ice in which she was imbedded seemed to say that she would never float again, so she might as well yield her planks to the fire. But to see her thus used went to the hearts of her gallant men.

On the nineteenth of March Hans was dispatched to the Esquimo, well supplied with the first quality of cord for their harpoons, and such other prompters to, and helps in, the walrus hunt as occurred to his commander. He would bless thereby and please these starving people, hoping that the blessing would return in the form of fresh walrus to him and his suffering men.

During the absence of Hans there were unusual and painful developments at the brig. William Godfrey and John Blake had given Dr. Kane much trouble from the first. They were now evidently bent on mischief, and made constant watchfulness over them a necessity. Just as Hans left they feigned sickness, and were suspected of desiring rest and recruited strength for desertion. Their plan was believed to be to waylay Hans and get his sledge and dogs. Dr. Kane contrived so shrewdly to keep one of them at work under his eye, and the other in some other place, that they did not perceive his suspicions of them. One night Bill was heard to say that some time during the following day he should leave, and this was reported to the commander by a faithful listener. He was, of course watched, and at six o'clock was called to prepare breakfast. This he commenced doing uneasily, stealing whispers with John. Finally he seemed at his ease, and cooked and served the breakfast. Dr. Kane believed he meant to slip out the first opportunity, meet John on deck, and desert; he therefore armed himself, threw on his furs, made Bonsall and Morton acquainted with his plans, and crept out of the dark avenue and hid near its entrance. After an hour of cold waiting John crept out, grunting and limping, for he had been feigning lameness, looked quickly round, and seeing no one, mounted nimbly the stairs to the deck. Ten minutes later Godfrey came out, booted and fur-clad for a journey. As he emerged from the tossut his commander confronted him, pistol in hand. He was ordered back to the cabin, while Morton compelled John's return, and Bonsall guarded the door preventing any one passing out. In a few moments John came creeping into the cabin, awful lame and terribly exhausted in his effort to breathe a little fresh air on deck. He looked amazed as by the glare of the light he saw the situation.

The commander then explained to the company the offenses of the culprits, giving from the log-book the details of their plotting. He had prepared himself for the occasion, and Bill, the principal, was punished on the spot. He confessed his guiltiness, promised good behavior, and in view of the few men able to work, his hand-cuffs were removed and he was sent about his customary business. In an hour after he deserted. Dr. Kane was at the moment away hunting, and his escape was not noticed until he was beyond the reach of a rifle ball.

The next two weeks were weary, anxious weeks, though the ever-watchful Hand tendered in good time occasion for hope. Six sea-fowl and three hares were shot by Petersen, and gave indispensable refreshment to the sick.

On the second of April, just before noon, a man was seen, with a dog-sledge, lurking behind the hummocks near the brig. Dr. Kane went out armed to meet him. It proved to be Godfrey the deserter, who, seeing his old comrades, left the sledge and run. Leaving Bonsall with his rifle to make sure of the sledge, the doctor gave chase, and the fugitive, seeing but one following, stopped and turned around. He said he had made up his mind to spend the rest of his life with Kalutunah and the Esquimo, and that no persuasion nor force should prevent him. A loaded pistol presented at his head did, though, persuade him to return to the brig. When he reached the gangway he refused to budge another step. Petersen was away hunting, Bonsall and Dr. Kane were so weak that they could barely stand, and all the other men, thirteen, were prostrated with the scurvy, so that they could not compel him by physical force. As the doctor was desirous not to hurt him, he left him under the guardianship of Bonsall's weapons while he went below for irons. Just as he returned to the deck Godfrey turned and fled. Bonsall presented his pistol, which exploded the cap only. Kane seized a rifle, but being affected by the cold, it went off in the act of cocking. A second gun, fired in haste at a long range, missed its mark. So the rebel made good his retreat.

He had come back with Hans' sledge and dogs, and reported him sick at Etah from over exhaustion. But there was one consolation in the affair—the sledge was loaded with walrus-meat. The feast that followed revived the drooping men wonderfully. They ate, were thankful, and looked hopefully on the future.

Godfrey was suspected of having come back to get John. The desertion of two well men when so many were sick would imperil the lives of all. The commander felt that the safety of the whole required the faithfulness of each man, he therefore explained the situation to the men and declared his determination to punish desertion, or the attempt to desert, by the "sternest penalty."

Hans became now the subject of anxiety. Some unfair dealing toward him on the part of Godfrey was feared. It was thought but just that he should be sought, and, if in trouble, relieved. But who should go? Dr. Kane finally resolved to go after him himself. Besides, the question of more walrus was again pressing.

April tenth the doctor was off. The first eleven hours the dogs carried him sixty-four miles, a most remarkable speed for their short rations.

While thus speeding along, far out on the floe, he spied a black speck in-shore away to the south. Was it some cheat of refraction. He paused, took his gun, and sighted the object, a device of old Arctic travelers to baffle refraction. It is an animal—yes, a man! Away went the dogs, ten miles an hour, while the rider cheated them with the shout, "Nannook! nannook!"—a bear! a bear! In a few moments Hans and the doctor were in grateful, earnest talk. He had really been sick. He had been down five days, and, as he expressed it, still felt "a little weak." He took his commander's place on the sledge and both went to the friendly hut at Anoatok, where hot tea and rest prepared both for the return to the brig.

CHAPTER XXI.

CLOSING INCIDENTS OF THE IMPRISONMENT.

HANS had his story of adventure while at Etah. But the most important item in his estimation, and that which might prove far reaching in its results, was the fact that a young daughter of Sunghu appointed herself his nurse during his sickness, bestowing upon him care, sympathy, and bewitching smiles. She had evidently done what Godfrey tried in vain to do—she had entrapped him, at the expense, too, of a young Esquimo lady at Upernavik.

Hans had been successful in the hunt, and, besides what he had sent by Godfrey, had deposited some walrus at Littleton Island. He was at once sent after this, and intrusted at the same time with an important commission. Dr. Kane had been for some time meditating another trip toward the polar sea. To do this he desired more dogs. The Esquimo had been reducing their stock to keep away starvation, but Kalutunah had retained four. These, and such others as he could find, Hans was authorized to buy or hire, at almost any price. This northern trip made, the next move might be toward the abandonment of the "Advance." She could never float, it was plain, for now, late in April, the open water was eighty miles south.

While Hans was gone, the sick, yet numbering two thirds of the whole, and in a measure all of the other third, except the commander, were without fresh food, as they had been for several days. Yet the sunshine and the occasional supplies had put them all on the improving list. They could sit up, sew or job a little, making themselves useful, and keeping up good spirits. But, hark! what sound is that breaking on the still, clear air. It comes nearer. Bim, bim, bim, sounds upon the deck. It is Hans, whose coming is ever like the coming of the morning. A rabbit-stew and walrus liver follow his arrival, and over such royal dainties good cheer pervades the family circle.

Hans brought Metek with him, and Metek's young nephew, Paulik, a boy of fourteen. Metek and Hans spoke sadly of the condition of the Esquimo settlements. We have seen that the escaping party found those of the south flying northward from starvation. The report now was that they had huddled together at Northumberland Island until that yielded to the famine, and now they had come farther north. It was a sad sight to see men, women, and children fleeing over the icy desert before their relentless foe. Yet, says Hans, they sung as they went, careless of present want, and thoughtless of the morrow. Many had died, and thus year by year these few, scattered, improvident people decline, giving earnest that in a few years all will be gone.

Though light-hearted, death did bring its sorrows to these benighted heathen. Kalutunah lost a sister; her body was sewed up in skins, not in a sitting posture but extended, and her husband, unattended, carried it out to burial, and, with his own hand, placed upon it stone after stone, making at once a grave and a monument. A blubber lamp was burning outside the hut while he was gone, and when he returned his friends were waiting to listen to his rehearsal of the praises of the dead, and to hear the expressions of his sorrow, while they showed their grief by dismal chantings.

If sorrow did not keep the deceased in the memory of the living, imposed self-denials did. The Angekok, or medicine man, as our Indians would call him, determines the penance of the mourner, who is sometimes forbidden to eat the meat of a certain bird or beast, under the idea that the spirit of the departed has entered into it; at another time the mourner must not draw on his hood, but go with uncovered head; or he may be forbidden to go on the bear or walrus hunt. The length of time of these penances may be a few months or a year. The reader will recollect the widow with her birds, who appeared so often in the narrative of the escaping party.

Though thus mourning for the dead, these Esquimo do not hold life as a very sacred trust. The drones and the useless are sometimes harpooned in the back merely to get rid of them. Infants are put out of the way when they greatly annoy their parents. Hans, on one of his returns from Etah, had a story to tell illustrative of this. Awahtok, a young man of twenty-two, had a pretty wife —*pretty* as Esquimo beauty goes—sister of Kalutunah, and about eighteen years old. Dr. Kane had regarded this couple with some interest, and the husband "stuck to him as a plaster." Their first-born was a fine little girl. Well, Hans reported with becoming disgust and indignation that they had buried it alive under a pile of stones! When Dr. Kane next visited Etah he inquired of his friends Awahtok and his wife after the health of the baby, affecting not to have heard about its hard fate. They pointed with both hands earthward, but did not even shed the cheap, customary tear. The only reason reported for this murder was, that certain of its habits, common to all infants, were disagreeable to them!

Such is the mildest heathenism without Christianity. These and other similar gross sins were common among the South Greenland Esquimo, but have disappeared before the teachings of the Moravian missionaries.

Hans returned with the walrus he had deposited at Littleton Island, but he had made no progress in getting dogs, so Dr. Kane resolved to go to Etah for that purpose himself. Besides, having learned that Godfrey was playing a high game there and defying capture, and also fearing his influence over the friendly relations of the Esquimo, he resolved to bring him back to the brig. Metek was just starting for Etah, so he invited himself to return with him, while Paulik, his nephew, remained with Hans. This arrangement effected,

Dr. Kane was soon approaching Etah, perfectly disguised in the hood and jumper of Paulik, whose place on the sledge he occupied. The whole city ran out to meet their chief, among whom was the deserter, who shouted, and then threw up his arms with the most savage of them. He did not perceive his commander until a certain well understood summons entered his ear, and a significant pistol barrel gleamed in the sunlight near his eyes. He surrendered to this "boom" argument without discussion, and trotting or walking, he kept his assigned place ahead of the sledge through the eighty and more miles to the brig, halting only at Anoatok. We hear nothing of further attempt at desertion.

A little later Dr. Kane made another visit to Etah. The hunt had become successful, and the famine was broken; all was activity and good cheer. The women were preparing the green hides for domestic use. Great piles of walrus tushes were preserved for various useful purposes; some of these the children had selected as bats, and were engaged in merry sport. Their game was to knock a ball made of walrus bone up the slanting side of a hummock, and then, in turn, hit it as it rolled down, and so keep it from reaching the floe. They shouted and laughed as the game went on, much as our boys do over their sports.

Dr. Kane observed on this trip a way of taking walrus which has not, we think, been noted before. The monster at this early season sometimes finds the ice open near a berg only. He comes on the ice to sun himself; finds the change from the cold sea very agreeable, stays too long, the water freezes solid, and he cannot return. As he is unable to break the ice from above, he either waits for the current about the berg to open the ice again, or works himself clumsily to some already open place. In this helpless state the dogs scent him afar off, and the hunters, following their lead, make him an easy prey.

Hans came in on the twenty-fourth of April, accompanied by Kalutunah, Shanghee, and Tatterat, each of the Esquimo having sledges, and sixteen dogs in all. Hans had been sent to Cape Alexander, where Kalutunah was sojourning, to invite him to the brig in order to secure his aid in the proposed northern trip. He was fed well, and propitiated by a present of a knife and needles. He said, "Thank you," and added, "I love you well," which might uncharitably be taken to mean, "I love your presents well." The result of the presents, feasting, and flattery was a start north by the three Esquimo, with Dr. Kane and Hans, all the dog teams accompanying. The old route across Kennedy Channel to the west side, and so north-poleward, was attempted. First came a very fair progress; then came the hummocks, over which, by the aid of their dogs, they clambered until thirty miles from the brig had been made. Then Shanghee burrowed into a snow-bank and slept, the cold being thirty degrees below zero; the rest camped in the snow and lunched. Just as a fair start was again made, the party neared a huge male bear in the act of lunching on seal. In vain the doctor attempted to control either dogs or drivers. "Nannook! nannook!" shouted the Esquimo as they clung to their sledges, and the dogs flew over the ice in wild and reckless pursuit. After an exciting chase the bear was brought to a halt and to a fight, which the rifles and spears soon terminated against bruin. A feast by dogs and men, and a night's halt on the ice followed, to Dr. Kane, at least, both vexatious and comfortless.

The next day he would press on to the north. But bear tracks were every-where, and the savage chiefs preferred hunting to exploring; besides, they had, they said, their families to support, and there was no use trying to cross the channel so high up. The English of it was, we are "going in" for the bears, and you may help yourself. A day more was spent in a wild hunt among the bergs, and the party returned to the brig.

A little later still another attempt was made to unlock further the secrets of the extreme icy north, this time by only Kane and Morton with a six-dog sledge, the explorers walking. This, the last effort of the kind, ended in the usual way, excepting some additions to the surveys.

CHAPTER XXII.

HOMEWARD BOUND.

THE final escape from the brig must now be commenced. From the early fall its necessity had been thought of, and preparations for it commenced. Since the sick had begun to improve, the work in reference to it had been going on with system. Coverlets of eider down, beds, or furs which could be used as such, boots, moccasins, a full supply to meet emergencies, were prepared. Provision bags were made and filled with powder, ship-bread, pork-fat, and tallow melted down, and cooked concentrated bean soup. The flour and meat biscuit were put in double bags. Two boats had been made from the ship's beams twenty-six feet long, seven feet across, and three feet deep. Incredible toil by weak and sick men had been expended upon these boats. A neat "housing" of light canvas was raised over each of them. One other boat, the "Red Eric," was in readiness. There was no assurance that either of these boats would long float, yet all was done which the circumstances allowed to make them sea-worthy.

The three boats were mounted on sledges. The necessary outfit, so far as they could bear, was to be stowed away in them.

Every thing being in readiness, a vast amount of *thinking* having been employed by the commander in reference to all contingencies, a peremptory order of march was issued for the seventeenth of May. The men were given twenty-four hours to get ready eight pounds of such personal effects as they chose. From the date of starting the strictest discipline and subordination was to be observed, which came hard upon the long-indulged, improving sick ones. The perfectness of the preparations had a good effect, yet there were many moody doubters. Some insisted that the commander only meant to go further south, holding the brig to fall back upon; some thought he would get the sick nearer the hunting grounds; others believed that his purpose was to secure some point of look-out for the English explorers, or whaling vessels.

When the memorable day of departure came, the boats were in the cradle on the sledges, and the men, with straps over their shoulders and drag-ropes from these to the sledges, started for the ice-foot along which they were to travel. They had not yet received their loads, so they glided off easily, exciting a smile on some rueful countenances.

In twenty-four hours the boats were laden, on the elevated drive-way, covered with their canvas roof, and, with a jaunty flag flying, were ready for a final leave the next day. The exhausted men, for nearly all of them were yet invalids, returned to the vessel, ate the best supper the supplies afforded, "turned in," prepared for their first effort at dragging the boat-laden sledges.

But one sledge could be moved at once, with all hands attached; the first day they made two miles only with this one. For several days they made short distances and returned early to a hearty supper and warm beds in their old quarters, so that they marched back to the drag-ropes in the morning refreshed. The weather was, by the kind, overruling Hand, "superb."

The final leave-taking was somewhat ceremonious. All the men were assembled in the dismantled room which had been so long both a prison and providential home. It was Sunday; all listened to a chapter of the Bible, and prayers. Then, all silently standing, the commander read a prepared report of what had been done, and the reasons for the step about to be taken. He then addressed the company, honestly conceding the obstacles in the way of escape, but assuring them that energy and subordination would secure success. He reminded them of the solemn claims upon them of the sick and wounded; called to their minds the wonderful deliverance granted them thus far by the infinite Power, and exhorted them still confidently to commit all to the same Helper.

The response to this appeal was most cheering to Dr. Kane. The following engagement was drawn up by one of the officers and signed by every man:—

"The undersigned, being convinced of the impossibility of the liberation of the brig, and equally convinced of the impossibility of remaining in the ice a third winter, do fervently concur with the commander in his attempt to reach the south by means of boats.

"Knowing the trials and hardships which are before us, and feeling the necessity of union, harmony, and discipline, we have determined to abide faithfully by the expedition and our sick comrades, and to do all that we can, as true men, to advance the objects in view."

The party now went on deck, hoisted a flag and hauled it down again, and then marched once or twice around the vessel. The figure head—the fair Augusta—"the little blue girl with pink cheeks," was taken by the men and added to their load. She had been nipped and battered by the ice, and a common suffering made her dear to them. When Dr. Kane remonstrated against the additional burden, they said: "She is, at any rate, wood, and if we cannot carry her far we can burn her."

The final departure was too serious for cheers, and when the moment came they all hurried off to the boats and the drag-ropes.

Four men were sick, and had to be carried; and Dr. Kane was with the dog-team the common carrier and courier, as we shall see, so that there were but twelve men to the boats; these were organized into two companies, six each, for the two sledges; M'Gary having command of the "Faith," and Morton command of the "Hope."

Each party was separate in matters of baggage, sleeping, cooking, and eating; both were concentrated, in turns, upon each sledge under the command of Brooks. Both morning and evening of each day all gathered round, with uncovered heads, to listen to prayers. Every one had his assigned place at the track-line; each served in turn as cook, except the captains.

From an early day of the preparations, Dr. Kane had been at work refitting and furnishing the broken-down, forsaken hut at Anoatok. For this purpose many trips were made to it with the dog-team; it was made tight as possible; the filth carefully removed; cushions and blankets were spread upon the raised floor at the sides and a stove set up; blankets were hung up against the walls, and the whole made to look as cheerful as possible. While the sledges were approaching this place by short stages, Dr. Kane, with his team, brought to the hut the four sick men; they were Goodfellow, Wilson, Whipple, and Stephenson. Dr. Hayes, yet limping on his frozen foot, bravely adhered to the sledges. When the sick entered the hut none could wait upon the others, except Stephenson, who could barely light the lamp, to melt the snow and heat the water. But Dr. Kane made them frequent visits, supplying their wants, and reporting the daily progress toward them of their whole company. They grew better, and were able to creep out into the sunshine. Besides carrying the sick to Anoatok, Dr. Kane had, with his dogs, conveyed there and stocked near the hut most of the provisions for their march and voyage; eight hundred pounds out of fifteen were now there, and he proposed to convey the rest. This was done to relieve the overladen sledges.

The red boat—"Red Eric"—joined the party on the floe a few days after the start, increasing their burden, but assuring them of increased comfort and safety when they reached the open water.

One incident of this period will illustrate its hardships and the Christian courage with which they were met.

It was soon after the last sick man was borne to the hut that Dr. Kane, having, in one of his dog-team trips, camped on the floe, came upon the boat party early in the morning. They were at prayers at the moment, and, as they passed to the drag-ropes, he was pained at the evidence of increased scurvy and depression. Brooks's legs were sadly swollen, and Hayes ready to faint with exhaustion. They must have more generous meals, thought the noble-hearted commander. Taking Morton, he hastened back to the brig. As they entered a raven flew croaking away; he had already made his home there. Lighting the fires in the old cook-room, they melted pork, cooked a large batch of *light* bread without salt, saleratus, or shortening, gathered together some eatable, though damaged, dried apples and beans, and, the dogs having fed, hastened back to the men on the floe. Distributing a good supper to their comrades as they passed, and taking Godfrey along with them, they hastened to the hut. The poor fellows confined in it were rejoiced to see them. They had eaten all their supplies, their lamp had gone out, the snow had piled up at the door so that they could not close it, and the arctic wind and cold were making free in their never-too-warm abode. The poor fellows were cold, sick, and hungry. The coming of their commander was as the coming of an angel messenger of good tidings. He closed their door, made a fire of tarred rope, dried their clothes and bedding, cooked them a porridge of pea-soup and meat-biscuit, and set their lamp-wick ablaze with dripping pork fat. Then, after all had joined in prayer of thankfulness, a well relished meal was eaten. This was followed by a cheerful chat, and a long, refreshing forgetfulness in their sleeping-bags of all privations. When they awoke the gale had grown more tempestuous, with increasing snow. But they went on burning rope and fat until every icicle had disappeared, and every frost mark had faded out.

On their arrival at the hut the night before, Dr. Kane, seeing the condition of things, sent Godfrey forward to Etah for fresh supplies of game. After a time he returned with Metek, and the two sledges well laden with meat. A part of this was hurried off to the toilers at the drag-ropes.

Having blessed by his coming these weary voyagers, Dr. Kane, with Morton, Metek, and his sledge, went once more to the brig. They baked a hundred and fifty pounds of bread and sent it by Metek to Mr. Brooks, and the faithful messenger, having delivered it, returned immediately for another load. While he was gone, a hundred pounds of flour pudding was made, and two bagfuls of pork-fat tried out. This done, the three lay down upon the curled hair of the old mattresses, they having been ripped open and their contents drawn out to make the most comfortable bed the place afforded. They slept as soundly "as vagrants on a haystack."

The next day they set their faces toward the sledge company and Anoatok, both sledges having heavy loads, which included the last of the fifteen hundred pounds of provisions.

Dr. Kane had made one of his last trips to the brig: he would return for provisions only; but all his specimens of Natural History, collected with much toil, his books, and many of his well-tested instruments, he was compelled to leave. His six dogs had carried him, during the fortnight since the company left the brig, between seven and eight hundred miles, averaging about fifty-seven miles a day. But for their services the sick could scarcely have been saved, and the rest would have suffered more intensely.

Leaving, as usual, a part of the food with Mr. Brooks's party, they hastened on to replenish the stores and cheer the hearts of the lonely dwellers in the hut.

CHAPTER XXIII.

NARROW ESCAPES.

HAVING brought forward the provisions to Anoatok, Dr. Kane, with the help of Metek and his dogs, began to remove them still farther south, making one deposit near Cape Hatherton, and the other yet farther, near Littleton Island. But an immediate journey to Etah for walrus had become necessary. The hard-working men were improving on this greasy food, and they wanted it in abundance. Dr. Kane found the Etahites fat and full. He left his weary, well-worn dogs to recruit on their abundance, and returned with their only team, which was well fed and fresh. They made the trade without any grumbling.

When he came back the Brooks party were within three miles of Anoatok. They were getting along bravely and eating voraciously, and the old cry, "more provisions!" saluted the commander. Leaving the dogs to aid in transferring the stores to the southern stations, Dr. Kane and Irish Tom Hickey started afoot to the brig to do another baking. It was a sixteen hours' tramp. But ere they slept they converted nearly a barrel of flour, the last of the stock, into the staff of life. An old pickled-cabbage cask was used as a kneading trough, and sundry volumes of the "Penny Cyclopedia of Useful Knowledge" were burned during the achievement. Tom declared the work done to be worthy of his own country's bakers, and he had been one "of them same," so he deemed that praise enough. When the doctor lamented that the flour so used was the last of the stock, Tom exclaimed: "All the better, sir, since we'll have no more bread to make."

Godfrey came to the brig on the third day, with the dogs, to carry back the baking. But a howling storm delayed them all on board. It was Sunday, and the last time that Dr. Kane expected to be in the cabin with any of his men. He took down a Bible from one of the berths and went through the long-used religious service. The dreary place was less dreary, and their burdened hearts were no doubt made lighter by thus drawing near to God.

The commander and Tom left the next day with the sledge load, leaving Godfrey to come on after farther rest. But scarcely had the sledge party delivered their load of bread, and begun the sound sleep which follows hard work, when Godfrey came in out of breath with the hot haste of his journey. He reluctantly confessed the occasion of his sudden departure from the brig. He had lain down on the contents of the mattresses to sleep. Suddenly Wilson's guitar, left with other mementoes of two winters' imprisonment, sent forth music soft and sad. Bill was sure he heard aright, for he was awake and in his right mind. He fled on the instant, and scarcely looked behind until he reached his companions. He had never heard of the musical genius of Eolus, and it was not strange that the old forsaken, mutilated, ghostly, looking brig should excite the imagination of the lonely lodger.

The invalids of the huts were now doing well. Their housekeeping assumed a home-like appearance—after the fashion of Arctic homes—and they welcomed the doctor with a dish of tea, a lump of walrus flesh, and a warm place. The Brooks party were not afar off.

A storm which out-stormed all they had yet seen or felt of storms came down upon our explorers at this time.

When the storm had blown past, Morton was dispatched to Etah with the dogs, accompanied by two Etahites who had been storm-bound with the boat-parties. His mission was to demand aid of these allies on the ground of sacred treaty stipulations, and well-recognized Esquimo laws of mutual help. Dr. Kane took his place with the men on the floe. Sledging was now not only made by the storm and advancing season more laborious, but very dangerous; around the bergs black water appeared, and over many places there were to be seen pools of water. The boats were unladen, and their cargoes carried in parcels by sledges, yet serious accidents occurred. At one time a runner of the sledge carrying the "Hope" broke in, and the boat came near being lost; as it was, six men were plunged into the water. Sick and well men worked for dear life, and affairs were growing more than cloudy when the helping hand of the great Helper was seen as it had been so often. Morton returned from Etah, having been entirely successful in his appeal to the natives for aid. They came with every sound dog they possessed, and with sledges loaded with walrus. The dogs alone were equal to ten strong men added to the expedition. Dr. Kane took one of the teams, and with Metek made his last trip to the brig, and on his return commenced bringing down the invalids of the hut to the boats. As he came near the floe-party he found Ohlsen sitting on a lump of ice alone, some distance in their rear. He had prevented the "Hope's" sledge from breaking through the ice by taking for a moment its whole weight on a bar which he had slipped under it. He was a strong man, and the act was heroic, but he was evidently seriously injured. He was pale, but thought his only difficulty was "a little cramp in the small of his back," and that he should be better soon. Dr. Kane gave him Stephenson's seat on the sledge, carried him to the boat, and gave him its most comfortable place, and muffled him up in the best buffalo robes. Dr. Hayes gave him tender and constant attention all that night, but he declined rapidly.

Having stowed the sick away in the boats, the morning prayers being offered, the men on the sixth of June started anew at the drag-ropes. Two hours' drawing sufficed to show all hands their insufficiency for the task. Just then a spanking breeze started up. They hoisted the sails of the boats, and the wind increased to a gale and blew directly after them. Away the sledges sped toward the provision depot near Littleton Island. Ridges in the ice which would have delayed them at the drag-ropes for hours, but gave them the rise and fall as they glided over them of a ship on the waves. God, who "holds the wind in his fist," had unloosed it for their benefit. The foot-sore, weary men, who a few moments ago felt that an almost impossible task was theirs, were now jubilant, and broke out into song—the first sailor's chorus song they had sung for a year. They came to a halt at five o'clock P. M., having made under sail the distance of five drag-rope days.

While here they were joined by old Nessark, and by Sipsu, the surly chief who appears so conspicuously in the narrative of Dr. Hayes's escaping party. They came with their fresh dog-teams, and offered their services to the explorers. Nessark was sent after the last of the sick men at the hut.

The following five or six days were those of peril and discouragement. At one time a sledge had broken in, carrying with it several of the men, bringing affairs to a gloomy crisis. But the men scrambled out, and, to still further lift the burdens from the party, five sturdy Esquimo appeared, with two almost equally strong women. They laid hold of the drag-ropes with a will, and worked the rest of the day without demanding any reward. So there was always help in their time of need.

Nessark came in good time with Wilson and Whipple, the last of the sick; the old hut was now deserted, and all were with the boats except one. Hans had been missing for nearly two months. Early in April he came to his commander with a long face and a very plausible story; he had, he said, no boots; he wanted to go to one of the Esquimo settlements a little south to get a stock of walrus-hides. He did not want the dogs; he would walk, and be back in good time. But the hitherto faithful and trusted Hans had not returned. When inquiry was made of the people of Etah they said he certainly called there, and engaged of one of the women a pair of boots, and then pushed on to Peteravik, where Shanghee and his pretty daughter lived. The last information they had of him they gave with a shrug of the shoulders and a merry twinkle of the eye. He had been seen by one of their people once since he left Etah; he was then upon a native sledge, Shanghee's daughter at his side, bound south of Peteravik. He had forsaken the explorers for a wife!

The party were one day feeling their way along cautiously, pioneers going ahead and trying the soundness of the ice by thumping with boat hooks and narwhal horns. Suddenly a shout of distress was heard. The "Red Eric" had broken in! She contained the document box of the expedition, the loss of which would make their whole work profitless to the world even should the party be saved. She had on board too many provision bags. But, after great exposure and labor, all was saved in good condition, and the boat hauled upon the ice. Several of the men had narrow escapes. Stephenson was caught as he sunk by the sledge runner, and Morton was drawn out by the hair of his head as he was disappearing under the ice. A grateful shout went up from all hands that nothing serious resulted from the accident.

CHAPTER XXIV.

ESQUIMO KINDNESS.

THE company made slow and tiresome progress by Littleton Island, and were carrying their entire load forward in parcels to the mainland at the northern opening of Etah Bay, when the sad news was whispered to Dr. Kane, who was with the advanced party, that Ohlsen was dead. A gloom spread over the whole company. The fact was carefully concealed from the Esquimo, who were sent to Etah under the pretext of bringing back a supply of birds, the entire dog force being given them to hasten their departure.

The funeral service, though attended by sincere grief, was necessarily brief. The body was sewed up in Ohlsen's own blankets, the burial service read, the prayer offered, and it was borne by his comrades in solemn procession to a little gorge on the shore, and deposited in a trench made with extreme difficulty. A sheet of lead, on which his name and age was cut, was laid upon his breast; a monument of stones was erected over it, to preserve it from the beasts of prey, and to mark the spot. They named the land which overshadowed the spot Cape Ohlsen.

Having given two quiet hours, after the funeral service, to the solemn occasion, the work at the drag-ropes was continued. The Esquimo returned in full force, and with abundant provisions. They took their turn at the drag-ropes with a shout; they carried the sick on their sledges, and relieved the whole expedition from care concerning their supplies. They brought in one week eight dozen sea-fowl—little auks—caught in their hand-nets, and fed men and dogs. All ate, hunger was fully satisfied, care for the time departed, the men broke out into their old forecastle songs, and the sledges went merrily forward with laugh and jest.

Passing round Cape Alexander, down Etah Bay, a short distance toward the settlement, the expedition encamped. The long-sought, coveted open water was only three miles away; its roar saluted their ears, and its scent cheered their hearts. The difficult and delicate work of preparing the boats for the sea-voyage now commenced. In the mean time the people of Etah, men, women, and children, came and encamped in their midst, leaving only three persons—two old women and a blind old man—in the settlement. They slept in the "Red Eric," and fed on the stew cooked for them in the big camp-kettle. Each one had a keepsake of a file, a knife, a saw, or some such article of great value. The children had each that great medicine for Esquimo sickness, a piece of soap, for which they merrily shouted, "Thank you, thank you, big chief." There was joy in the Esquimo camp which knew but one sorrow—that of the speedy departure of the strangers. At the mention of this one woman stepped behind a tent screen and wept, wiping her teary face with a bird-skin.

Dr. Kane rode to Etah to bid the aged invalids good-bye. Then came the last distribution of presents. Every one had something, but the great gift of amputating knives went to the chief, Metek, and the patriarch, Nessark. The dogs were given to the community at large, excepting Toodla-mik and Whitey; these veterans of many well-fought battle-fields were reserved to share the homeward fortunes of their owners. Toodla was no common dog, but earned for himself a place in dog history. As we are to meet the dogs no more in our narrative, we will give Toodla's portrait to be set up with our pen sketches. He was purchased at Upernavik, and so he received the advantages of, at least, a partially civilized education. His head was more compact, his nose less pointed than most dogs of his kind, and his eye denoted affection and self-reliance, and his carriage was bold and defiant. Toodla, at the commencement of the cruise, appointed himself general-in-chief of all the dogs. Now it often happens, with dogs as well as with men, that to assume superiority is much easier than to maintain it. But Toodla's generalship was never successfully disputed. The position, however, cost him many a hard-fought battle, for the new comers naturally desired to test his title to rule. These he soundly whipped on their introduction to the pack. He even often left the brig's side, head erect, tail gracefully curled over his back, and moved toward a stranger dog with a proud, defiant air, as much as to say, "I am master here, sir!" If this was doubted, he vindicated his boasting on the spot. Such tyranny excited rebellions of course, and strong combinations were formed against him; but dogs which had been trounced individually make weak organizations, and the coalitions gave way before Toodla's prowess. It is but fair, however, to say that he had strong allies upon whom he fell back in great emergencies—the sailors. Toodla died in Philadelphia, and still lives—that is, his stuffed skin still exists in the museum of the Philadelphia Academy of Natural Sciences. His reputation is of the same sort as that of many of the heroes of history, and worth as much to the world.

Dr. Kane having distributed the presents and disposed of the dogs, there was nothing now but the farewell address to render the parting ceremony complete. Dr. Kane called the natives about him and spoke to them through Petersen as interpreter. He talked to them as those from whom kindness had been received, and to whom a return was to be made. He told them about the tribes of their countrymen farther south whom he knew, and from whom they were separated by the glaciers and the sea; he spoke of the longer daylight, the less cold, the more abundant game, the drift-wood, the fishing-nets, and kayaks of these relatives. He tried to explain to them that under bold and cautious guidance they might, in the course of a season or two, reach this happier region.

During this talk they crowded closer and closer to the speaker, and listened with breathless attention to his remarks, often looking at each other significantly.

Having thus parted with the natives, our exploring party hauled their boats to the margin of the ice. The "Red Eric" was launched, and three cheers were given for "Henry Grinnell and Homeward Bound." But the storm king said, "Not yet!" He sounded an alarm in their ears, and they drew the "Eric" from the water and retreated on the floe, which broke up in their rear with great rapidity. Back, back, they tramped, wearily and painfully, all that night, until the next day they found a sheltering berg near the land, where they made a halt. Here they rested until the wind had spent its wrath, and the sea had settled into a placid quiet. Their voyaging on the floe with drag-ropes and sledges was ended.

CHAPTER XXV.

MELVILLE BAY.

ON the nineteenth of June the boats were launched into the sea, now calm, the "Faith" leading under Kane, and the "Eric" under Bonsall, and the "Hope" under Brooks following. The sea birds screamed a welcome to the squadron, and flew about them as if to inquire why they came back in three vessels instead of one, as when they sailed northward two years before. But there was no leisure for converse with birds. They had just passed Hakluyt Island, when the "Eric" sunk. Her crew, Bonsall, Riley, and Godfrey, struggled to the other boats, and the "Faith" took the sunken craft in tow. Soon after Brooks shouted that the "Hope" was leaking badly, and threatening to sink. Fortunately the floe was not far off, and into one of its creek-like openings they run the boats, fastened them to the ice, and the weary men lay down in their bunks without drawing the boats from the water and slept.

The next day they drew their leaking crafts ashore, and calked them for another sea adventure. For several days they struggled with varying fortunes until they brought up, weary, disheartened, and worn down by work and an insufficient diet of bread-dust, and fastened to an old floe near the land. Scarcely were they anchored when a vast ice raft caught upon a tongue of the solid floe about a mile to the seaward of them, and began to swing round upon it as a pivot, and to close in upon our explorers. This was a new game of the ice-enemy. Nearer and nearer came the revolving icy platform, seeming to gather force with every whirl. At first the commotion that was made started the floe, to which they were fastened, on a run toward the shore as if to escape the danger. But it soon brought up against the rocks and was overtaken by its pursuer. In an instant the collision came. The men sprang, by force of discipline, to the boats and the stores, to bear them back to a place of safety, but wild and far-spread ruin was around them. The whole platform where they stood crumbled and crushed under the pressure, and was tossed about and piled up as if the ice-demon was in a frenzy of passion. Escape for the boats seemed for the moment impossible, and none expected it; and none could tell when they were let down into the water, nor hardly how, yet they found themselves whirling in the midst of the broken hummocks, now raised up and then shaken as if every joint in the helpless, trembling boats was to be dislocated. The noise would have drowned the uproar of contending armies as ice was hurled against ice, and, as it felt the awful pressure, it groaned harsh and terrific thunder. The men, though utterly powerless, grasped their boat-hooks as the boats were borne away in the tumultuous mass of broken ice and hurried on toward the shore. Slowly the tumult began to subside, and the fragments to clear away, until the almost bewildered men found themselves in a stretch of water making into the land, wide enough to enable them to row. They came against the wall of the ice-foot, and, grappling it, waited for the rising tide to lift them to its top. While here the storm was fearful, banging the boats against the ice-wall, and surging the waves into them, thus keeping the imperiled men at work for dear life in bailing out the water. They were at last lifted by the tide to the ice-foot, upon which they pulled their boats, all uniting on each boat. They had landed on the cliff at the mouth of a gorge in the rock; into this they dragged the boats, keeping them square on their keels. A sudden turn in the cave placed a wall between them and the storm, which was now raging furiously. While they were drawing in the last boat, a flock of eider ducks gladdened their hearts as they flew swiftly past. God had not only guided them to a sheltered haven, but had assured them of abundant food on the morrow. They were in the breeding home of the sea-fowl. Thus comforted they lay down to sleep, though wet and hungry. They named their providential harbor the "Weary Man's Rest," and remained in it three days, eating until hunger was appeased, and gathering eggs at the rate of twelve hundred a day, and laughing at the storms which roared without.

On the fourth of July, after as much of a patriotic celebration as their circumstances allowed, they again launched into the sea.

For some days they moved slowly south, but it was only by picking their way through the leads, for they found the sea nearly closed. As they approached Cape Dudley Digges their way was entirely closed. They pushed into an opening that led to the bottom of its precipitous cliff. Here they found a rocky shelf, overshadowed by the towering rocks, just large enough and in the right position at high tide to make a platform on which they could land their boats. Here they waited a whole week for the ice toward Cape York to give way. The sea-fowl were abundant and of a choice kind. The scurvy-killing cochlearia was at hand, which they ate with their eggs. It was indeed a "providential halt," for the fact was constantly forced upon them that they had come here, as they had to "Weary Man's Rest," by no skill or knowledge of their own.

It was the eighteenth of July before the condition of the ice was such as to make the renewal of their voyage possible. Two hundred and fifty choice fowl had been skinned, cut open, and dried on the rocks, besides a store of those thrown aboard as they were caught.

They now sailed along the coast, passing the "Crimson Cliffs" of Sir John Ross. The birds were abundant, their halting-places on the shore were clothed with green, and the fresh-water streams at which they filled their vessels were pouring down from the glaciers. They built great blazing fires of dry turf which cost nothing but the gathering. After a day's hard rowing the sportsmen brought in fresh fowl, and, gathered about their camp-fire, all ate, and then stretched themselves on the moss carpet and slept. They enjoyed thankfully this Arctic Eden all the more as they all knew that perils and privations were just before them.

They wisely provided during these favored days a large stock of provisions, amounting to six hundred and forty pounds, besides their dried birds. Turf fuel, too, was taken on board for the fires.

They reached Cape York on the twenty-first of July. From this place they were to try the dangers of Melville Bay, across which in their frail boats they must sail. It had smiled upon their northward voyage; would it favor their escape now? It certainly did not hold out to them flattering promises. The inshore ice was solid yet, and terribly hummocky. The open sea was far to the west, but along the margin of the floe were leads, and fortunately there was one beginning where they had halted. The boats were hauled up, examined, and as much as possible repaired. The "Red Eric" was stripped, her cargo taken out, and her hull held in reserve for fuel. A beacon was erected from which a red flannel skirt was thrown as a pennant to the wind to attract attention. Under this beacon records were left which told in brief the story of the expedition. This done, and the blessing of God implored, the voyagers entered the narrow opening in the ice.

For a while all went well, but one evening Dr. Kane was hastily called on deck. The huge icebergs had bewildered the helmsman in the leading boat, and he had missed the channel, and had turned directly toward the shore until the boat was stopped by the solid floe. The lead through which they had come had closed in their rear, and they were completely entangled in the ice!

Without telling the men what had happened, the commander, under the pretense of drying the clothes, ordered the boats drawn up, and a camp was made on the ice.

In the morning Kane and M'Gary climbed a berg some three hundred feet high. They were appalled by their situation; the water was far away, and huge bergs and ugly hummocks intervened. M'Gary, an old whaleman, familiar from early manhood with the hardships of Arctic voyaging, wept at the sight.

There was but one way out of this entanglement; the sledges must be taken from the sides of the boats, where they had been hung for such emergencies, the boats placed on them, and the old drag-rope practice must be tried until the expedition reached the edge of the floe. One sledge, that which bore the "Red Eric," had been used for fuel; so the "Red Eric" itself was knocked to pieces, and stowed away for the same use. About three days were consumed in thus toiling before they reached the lead which they had left, launched once more into waters, and sailed away before a fine breeze.

Thus far the boats had kept along the outer edge of the floe, following the openings through the ice. But as this was slow work, though much safer, they now ventured a while in the open sea farther west; but they were driven back to the floe by heavy fogs, and on trying to get the boats into a lead, one of those incidents occurred so often noticed, in which God's hand was clearly seen. All hands were drawing up the "Hope," and she had just reached a resting-place on the floe, when the "Faith," their best boat, with all their stores on board, went adrift. The sight produced an almost panic sensation among the men. The "Hope" could not possibly be launched in time to overtake her, for she was drifting rapidly. But before they could collect their thoughts to devise the means of her rescue, a cake of ice swung round, touched the floe where they stood, reaching at the same time nearly to the "Faith," thus bridging over the chasm. Instantly Kane and M'Gary sprung upon it, and from it into the escaping boat. She was saved.

CHAPTER XXVI.

SAVED.

MATTERS were getting into a serious condition. The delays had been so many that the stock of birds had been eaten, and the men had been for several days on short allowance, which showed itself in their failing strength. They were far out to sea, midway of the Melville Bay navigation, and the boats were receiving a rough handling, and required continual bailing to keep them from sinking.

It was just at this crisis that the ever timely aid came. A large seal was seen floating upon a small patch of ice, seeming to be asleep. A signal was given for the "Hope" to fall astern, while the "Faith" approached noiselessly upon him, with stockings drawn over the oars. Petersen lay in the bow with a large English rifle, and as they drew near, the men were so excited that they could scarcely row; the safety of the whole company seemed staked upon the capture of that seal. When within three hundred yards, the oars were taken in, and the boat moved silently on by a scull-oar at the stern. The seal was not asleep, for when just beyond the reach of the ball he raised his head. The thin, care-worn, almost despairing faces of the men showed their deep concern as he appeared about to make his escape. Dr. Kane gave the signal to fire; but poor Petersen, almost paralyzed by anxiety, was trying nervously to get a rest for his gun on the edge of the bow. The seal rose on his fore-flipper, looked curiously around, and coiled himself up for a plunge. The rifle cracked at the instant, and the seal at the same moment drooped his head one side, and stretched his full length on the ice at the brink of his hole. With a frantic yell the men urged the boats to the floe, seized the seal, and bore him to a safer place. They brandished their knives, cut long strips of the seal, and went dancing about the floe, eating and sucking their bloody fingers in wild delight. The seal was large and fat, but not an ounce of him was wasted. A fire was built that night on the floe, and the joyous feast went on until hunger was appeased; they had driven away its gnawings, and, happily, it returned no more.

On the first of August they had passed the terrible bay, and sighted land on its southern side. Familiar landmarks of the whalers came in sight. They passed the Duck Islands and Cape Shackelton, and coasted along by the hills, seeking a cove in which to land. One was soon found, the boats drawn up, a little time spent in thanksgiving and congratulations, and then they lay down on the dry land and slept.

They continued to coast near the shore, dodging about among the islands, and dropping into the bays, and landing for rest at night. It was at one of these sleeping-halts on the rocks that Petersen saw one of the natives, whom he recognized as an old acquaintance; he was in his kayak seeking eider-down among the rocks. Petersen hailed him, but the man played shy. "Paul Zacharias," shouted Petersen, "don't you know me? I am Carl Petersen!"

"No," replied the man; "his wife says he's dead."

The native stared at the weather-beaten, long-bearded man for a moment as he loomed up through the fog, and then turned the bow of his boat, and paddled away as if a phantom was pursuing him.

Two days after this the explorers were rowing leisurely along in a fog, which had just began to lift and dimly reveal the objects on shore. At this moment a familiar sound came to them over the water. It was the "huk" of the Esquimo, for which they had often taken the bark of a fox or the startling screech of the gulls; but this "huk! huk!" died away in the home-thrilling "halloo!"

"Listen, Petersen! what is it?"

Petersen listened quietly for a moment, and then, trembling with emotion, said, in an undertone, "Dannemarkers!"

Then the whole company stood up and peered into the distant nooks, in breathless silence to catch the sound again. The sound came again, and all was a moment silent. It was the first Christian voice they had heard beyond their own party for two years. But they saw nothing. Was it not a cheat after all of their nervous, excited feelings? The men sat down again and bent to their oars, and their boats swept in for the cape from which the sound proceeded. They scanned narrowly every nook and green spot where the strangers might be found. A full half hour passed in this exciting search. At last the single mast of a small shallop was seen. Petersen, who had kept himself during the search very still and sober, burst into a fit of crying, relieved by broken exclamations of English and Danish, gulping down his words at intervals, and wringing his hands all the while. "'Tis the Upernavik oil-boat!" "The Mariane has come! and Carlie Mossyn—"

Petersen had hit the facts. The annual ship, Mariane, had arrived at Proven, and Carlie Mossyn had come up to get the year's supply of blubber from Kinqatok.

Here our explorers listened while Carlie, in answer to their questions, gave them a hint of what had been going on in the civilized world during their long absence. The Crimean war had been begun and was in bloody progress, but "Sebastopol wasn't taken!" "Where and what is Sebastopol?" they queried. "But what of America?" Carlie didn't know much about that country, for no whale ships were on the coast, but said "a steamer and a bark passed up a fortnight ago seeking your party."

"What of Sir John Franklin?" they next inquired. Carlie said the priest had a German newspaper which said traces of his boats and dead had been found! Yes, found a thousand miles away from the region where our explorers had been looking for them!

One more row into the fog and one more halting on the rocks. They all washed clean in the fresh water of the basins, and brushed up their ragged furs and woolens. The next morning they neared the settlement of Upernavik, of which Petersen had been foreman, and they heard the yelling of the dogs as its snowy hill-top showed itself through the mist, and the tolling of the workmen's bells calling them to their daily labor came as sweet music to their ears. They rowed into the big harbor, landed by an old Brewhouse, and hauled their boats up for the last time. A crowd of merry children came round them with cheerful faces and curious eyes. In the crowd were the wife and children of Petersen. Our explorers were safe; their perils were over!

Having lived in the open air for eighty-four days, they felt a sense of suffocation within the walls of a house. But divided among many kind, hospitable homes, they drank their coffee and listened to hymns of welcome sung by many voices.

The people of Upernavik fitted up a loft for the reception of the wayfarers, and showed them great kindness. They remained until the sixth of September, and then embarked on the Danish vessel "Mariane," whose captain was to leave them at the nearest English port on his way to Denmark.

The boat "Faith" was taken on board, as a relic of their perilous adventure; the document box containing their precious records, and the furs on their backs—these were all that were saved of the heroic brig "Advance."

The "Mariane" made a short stay at Godhavn. The searching company under Captain Hartstene had left there for the icy north on the twenty-first of July, since which nothing was known of them.

The "Mariane" was on the eve of leaving with our explorers when the lookout shouted from the hill-top that a steamer was in the distance. It drew near with a bark in tow, both flying the stars and stripes. The "Faith" was lowered for the last time, and, with Brooks at the helm, Dr. Kane went out to meet them. As they came alongside Captain Hartstene hailed: "Is that Dr. Kane?" "Yes!" Instantly the men sprung into the rigging and gave cheers of welcome; and the whole country, on the arrival of the long-lost explorers, repeated the glad shout of welcome; and the Christian world echoed, "Welcome!"

CHAPTER XXVII.

OFF AGAIN.

DR. KANE'S party came home, as we have seen, in the fall of 1855. Dr. Hayes, with whom we have become acquainted as one of that number, began immediately to present the desirableness of further exploration in the same direction to the scientific men of the country, and to the public generally. His object was to sail to the west side of Smith's Sound, instead of the east, as in the last voyage, and to gather additional facts concerning the currents, the aurora, the glaciers, the directions and intensity of "the magnetic force," and so to aid in settling many interesting scientific questions. He aimed also, of course, to further peer into the mysteries of the open Polar Sea.

These efforts resulted in the fitting out for this purpose, in the summer of 1860, the schooner "United States," and the appointment of Dr. Hayes as commander. She left Boston July sixth, manned by fourteen persons all told. The vessel was small, but made for arctic warfare, and as she turned her prow North Poleward, she bore a defiant spirit, and, like all inexperienced warriors, reckoned the victory already hers. But if the vessel was "green" her commander was not. He was well able to help her in the coming battle with icebergs and floes.

Among her men were only two besides the doctor who had seen arctic service, one of whom was Professor August Sontag, who had been of Kane's party, and had also been of the number who accompanied Dr. Hayes in the attempt to escape. Of the rest of the crew were two young men nearly of an age, about eighteen, who are represented as joining the expedition because they would, and in love of adventure. Their names were George F. Knorr, commander's clerk, and Collins C. Starr. Both pressed their desire to go upon Dr. Hayes, and Starr told him that he would go in *any* capacity. The commander told him he might go in the forecastle with the common sailors, and the next day, to the surprise of the doctor, he found him on board, manfully at work with the roughest of the men, having doffed his silk hat, fine broadcloth, and shining boots of the elegant young man of the day before. The commander was so pleased with his spirit that he promoted him on the spot, sending him off to be sailing-master's mate.

In a little less than four weeks of prosperous sailing, the "United States" was at the Danish port of Proven, Greenland. It was the intention of the commander to get a supply here of the indispensable dog-teams, but disease had raged among them, and none could be bought. The vessel was delayed, in order that the chief trader, Mr. Hansen, who was daily expected from Upernavik, might be consulted in the matter. When he arrived he gave a gloomy account of the dog-market, but kindly *gave* the expedition his own teams. The couriers which had been sent out to scour the country for others, returned with four old dogs and a less number of good ones.

On the evening of the twelfth of August the explorers arrived at Upernavik. The Danish brig "Thialfe" lay at anchor in the harbor, about to sail for Copenhagen with a cargo of skins and oil, so the first letters to the dear ones at home were hastily written to send by her. They bore sad news to at least one family circle. Mr. Gibson Caruther retired to his berth well on the evening of their arrival, and in the morning was found dead. He had escaped the perils of the first Grinnell Expedition under Capt. De Haven to die thus suddenly ere those of his second voyage had begun. He was beloved, able, and intelligent, and his death was a great loss to the enterprise. His companions laid him away in the mission burial-ground, the missionary, Mr. Anton, officiating.

Before leaving Upernavik, Dr. Hayes secured the services of an Esquimo interpreter, one Peter Jensen, who brought on board with him one of the best dog-teams of the country; and soon after he came, two more Esquimo hunters and dog-drivers were enlisted; and a still better addition to the expedition were two Danish sailors, one of whom is our old friend whom we left here some five years ago rejoicing in re-union with wife and children—Carl

Christian Petersen. Petersen enlisted as carpenter as well as sailor.

With these six persons added to her company, making it twenty in all, the "United States" left Upernavik to enter upon the earnest work of the expedition. The settlement had scarcely faded in the distance, when the ice-bergs were seen marshaling their forces to give the little voyager battle. A long line of them was formed just across her course, some more than two hundred feet high and a mile long. They were numberless, and at a distance seemed to make a solid, jagged ice-wall. When the schooner was fairly in among them, the sunlight was shut out as it is from the traveler in a dense forest. She felt the wind in a "cat's-paw" now and then, and so the helm lost its control of her, and she went banging against first one berg and then another. The bergs themselves minded not the little breeze which was blowing, but swept majestically along by the under current. The navigators were kept on the alert to keep the vessel from fatal collision with its huge, cold, defiant enemies, as the surface current drove it helplessly onward. Sometimes, as they approached one, the boats were lowered, and the vessel was towed away from danger; at another crisis, as it neared one berg, an anchor was planted in another in an opposite direction, and she was warped into a place of security. Occasionally they tied up to a berg and waited for a chance for progress.

While thus beset with dangers, there were occasions of some pleasant excitement. The birds were abundant and of many varieties, affording sport for the hunters and fresh food for the table; the seals sported in the clear water, and were shot for the larder of the dogs; and Dr. Hayes and Professor Sontag found employment with their scientific instruments.

Such had been the state of things for four days, when one morning the vessel was borne toward a large berg, of a kind the sailors called "touch-me-nots." It was an old voyager, whose jagged sides, high towers, deep valleys and swelling hills, showed that time, the sun, and the tides, had laid their hands upon it. Such bergs are about as good neighbors as an avalanche on a mountain side, just ready for a run into the valley below. Warps and tow-boats, instantly and vigorously used, failed to stop the schooner's headway. She touched the 'berg, and down dropped fragments of it larger than the vessel, followed by a shower of smaller pieces; but they went clear of the vessel. Now the berg began to revolve, turning toward the explorers, and as its towering sides settled slowly over them, fragments poured upon the deck—a fearful hail-storm. There was no safety for the men except in the forecastle, and there appeared to be no escape for the schooner. But just in time an immense section of the base of the berg, which seemed to be far below the water line, broke off, and rose to the surface with a sudden rush, which threw the sea into violent commotion. The balance of the berg was changed; it paused, and then began, slowly at first but with increasing rapidity, to turn in the opposite direction. If this was intended as a retreat of the bergy foe, it defended well its rear. At its base, from which the piece had just been broken, was an icy projection toward the vessel; as the berg revolved, this tongue came up and struck the keel. It seemed intent upon tossing the vessel into the air, or rolling her over and leaving her bottom side up upon the sea. The men seized their poles and pushed vigorously to launch the vessel from the perilous position, but in vain. Just in time again the unseen Hand interfered for their deliverance. Deafening reports, like a park of artillery, saluted their ears, and a misty smoke arose above the berg. Its opposite side was breaking up, and launching its towering peaks into the sea. The berg paused again and began to roll back, and thus for the moment released the vessel. The boat had in the meantime fastened an anchor in a grounded berg, and the welcome shout came, "Haul in!" Steadily and with a will the men drew upon the rope, and the vessel moved slowly from the scene of danger, not, however, before the returning top of the berg had launched upon her deck a shower of ice-fragments, in fearful assurance that its whole side would soon follow and bury them as the shepherd's hut is buried by a mountain slide. A few moments later and the side came down with a tremendous crash, sending its spray over the escaped vessel, and tossing it as the drift-wood is tossed in the eddies beneath a water-fall.

All that day the roar of the icy cannon was continued, as if a naval battle was in progress for the empire of the north, and berg after berg went down, strewing the sea with their shattered fragments, while misty clouds floated over the field of conflict.

CHAPTER XXVIII.

COLLIDING FLOES.

AFTER this ice encounter the expedition put into a little port called Tessuissak, to complete their outfit of dogs. An impatient tarry of two days enabled them to count, on the deck of the little vessel, thirty first-class, howling dogs, whose amiable tempers found expression in biting each other, and making both day and night hideous with their noise.

This port was left on the twenty-third of August, and, much to the joy of all, the dreaded Melville Bay was clear of the ice-pack; the icebergs, however, kept their watch over its storm-tossed waters. Through these waters driven before a fierce wind, and buried often in a fog so dense that the length of the vessel could not be seen, the "United States" sped. Its anxious commander was on deck night and day, not knowing the moment when an icy wall, as fatal to the vessel as one of granite, might arrest its course and send it instantly to the bottom of the sea. Once they passed so near a berg just crossing their track that the fore-yard grazed its side, and the spray from its surf-beaten wall was thrown upon the deck. A berg at one time hove in sight with an arch through it large enough for a passage-way for the schooner. The explorers declined, however, the novel adventure. The passage of Melville Bay was made, with sails only, in fifty-five hours. The pack which had invariably troubled explorers seemed to have been enjoying a summer vacation, and the bergs were off duty. The expedition had reached the North Water and lay off Cape York.

The ocean current which sweeps past this cape, and opens the way to the other side of Baffin Bay, is wonderful. It is the great Polar current which comes rushing down through Spitzbergen Sea, along the eastern coast of Greenland, laden with ice, and taking the waters of its rivers with their freight of drift-wood as it passes. Leaving most of the wood along its shore, a welcome gift to the people, it sweeps around Cape Farewell, courses near the western shore in its run north until it has passed Melville Bay. When it has crossed over to the American shore near Jones Strait, it joins the current from the Arctic Sea, turns south, and makes the long journey until it reaches our own coast, dropping its ice freight as it goes, and sending its cooling air through the heat-oppressed atmosphere of our summer.

As our explorers approached the shore of Cape York they looked carefully for the natives. Soon a company of Esquimo were seen making their wild gesticulations to attract attention. A boat was lowered, and Dr. Hayes and Professor Sontag went ashore, and as they approached the landing-place one of the Esquimo called them by name.

It was our old friend Hans, of the Kane voyage, who, the reader will recollect, left his white friends for an Esquimo wife. The group consisted, besides Hans, of his wife and baby, his wife's mother, an old woman having marked talking ability, and her son, a bright-eyed boy of twelve years. Hans had found his self-imposed banishment among the savages of this extreme north rather tedious. He had removed his family to this lookout for the whale ships, and had watched and waited. It was the dreariest of places, and his hut, pitched on a bleak spot the better to command a view of the sea, was the most miserable of abodes. It had plainly cost him dear to break his faith with his confiding commander and the friends of his early Christian home.

Dr. Hayes asked Hans if he would go with the expedition. He answered promptly, "Yes."

"Would you take your wife and baby?"

"Yes."

"Would you go without them?"

"Yes."

He was taken on board with his wife and baby. The mother and her boy cried to go, but the schooner was already overcrowded.

Leaving Cape York, the vessel spread her sails before a "ten-knot" breeze, and dodging the icebergs with something of a reckless daring, seemed bent on reaching the Polar Sea before winter set in. At one time what appeared to be two icebergs a short distance apart lay in the course of the vessel. The helmsman was ordered to steer between them, for to go round involved quite a circuit. On dashed the brave little craft for the narrow passage. When she was almost abreast of them the officer on the lookout shuddered to see that the seeming bergs were but one, and that the connecting ice appeared to be only a few feet below the surface. It was too late to stop the headway of the vessel, or to turn her to the right or left. She rushed onward, but the water of the opening proved to be deeper than it appeared, and her keel but touched once or twice, just to show how narrow was the escape.

Hans was delighted with his return to ship life. His wife seemed pleased and half bewildered by the strange surroundings. The baby crowed, laughed, and cried, and ate and slept—like other babies.

The sailors put the new comers through a soap-and-water ordeal, to which was added the use of scissors and combs. Esquimo do not bathe, nor practice the arts of the barber, and consequently they keep numerous boarders on their persons. When this necessary cleansing and cropping was done, they donned red shirts and other luxuries of civilization. With the new dresses they were delighted, and they were never tired of strutting about in them. But the soap and water was not so agreeable. At first it was taken as a rough joke, but the wife soon began to cry. She inquired of her husband if it was a religious ceremony of the white men.

The vessel made good time until she came

within three miles of Cape Alexander. It was now August twenty-eighth, and so it was time these Arctic regions should begin to show their peculiar temper. A storm came down upon them, pouring the vials of its wrath upon the shivering vessel for about three days. During a lull in the storm the schooner was hauled under the shelter of the highlands of Cape Alexander and anchored. She rocked and plunged fearfully. At one time when these gymnastics were going on, the old Swedish cook came to the commander in the cabin with refreshments, but he was hardly able to keep his "sea legs." He remarks as he comes in, "I falls down once, but de commander sees I keeps de coffee. It's good an' hot, and very strong, and go right down into de boots."

"Bad night on deck, cook," remarks the captain.

"O, it's awful, sar! I never see it blow so hard in all my life, an' I's followed de sea morn'n forty years. An' den it's so cold! My galley is full of ice, and de water, it freeze on my stove."

"Here, cook, is a guernsey for you. It will keep you warm."

"Tank you, sar!" says the cook, starting off with his prize. But encouraged by the kind bearing of his captain, he stops and asks, "Would the commander be so kind as to tell me where we is? De gentlemen fool me."

"Certainly, cook. The land over there is Greenland; the big cape is Cape Alexander; beyond that is Smith's Sound, and we are only about eight hundred miles from the North Pole."

16

"De Nort Pole! vere's dat?"

The commander explains as well as he can.

"Tank you, sar. Vat for we come—to fish?"

"No, not to fish, cook; for science."

"O, dat it! Dey tell me we come to fish. Tank you, sar."

The old cook pulls his greasy cap over his bald head and thinks. "Science!" "De Nort Pole!" He dont get the meaning of these through his cap, and he "tumbles up" the companion-ladder, and goes to the galley to enjoy his guernsey.

Dr. Hayes and Knorr went ashore and climbed to the top of the cliffs, twelve hundred feet. The wind was fearfully breezy, and Knorr's cap left and went sailing like a feather out to sea. The view was full of arctic grandeur, but not flattering to the storm-bound navigators. Ice was evidently king a little farther north.

Soon after the explorer's return to the vessel the storm gathered fresh power, and the anchors began to drag. Soon one hawser parted, and away went the schooner, with fearful velocity, and brought up against a berg. The crash was appalling, and the stern boat flew into splinters. The spars were either bent or carried away; and, as they attempted to hoist the mainsail, it went to pieces. The crippled craft was with difficulty worked back into the projecting covert of Cape Alexander. Her decks were covered with ice, and the dogs were perishing with wet and cold, three having died.

Having repaired damages as well as they could,

they again pushed into the pack of Smith's Sound, which lay between them and open water, visible far to the north. Entering a lead under full sail, they made good progress for awhile ; but suddenly a solid floe shot across the channel, and the vessel, with full head-way, struck it like a battering ram. The cut-water flew into splinters, and the iron sheathing of the bows was torn off as if it had been paper.

Pushing off from the floe, and passing through a narrow lead, they emerged into an area of open water. But the floe was on the alert. This began to close up, and, taking a hint of foul play, the explorers steered toward the shore. But the ice battalions moved with celerity, piled up across the vessel's bow, and closed in on every side. In an hour they held her as in a vice, while the reserve force was called up to crush her to atoms. The foe was jubilant, for the power at his command was kindred to that of the earthquake. An ice-field of millions of tons, moved by combined wind and current, rushed upon the solid ice-field which rested against the immovable rocks of the shore. Between these was the schooner—less than an egg-shell between colliding, heavily laden freight trains. As the pressure came steadily, in well assured strength, she groaned and shrieked like a thing of conscious pain, writhing and twisting as if striving to escape her pitiless adversary. Her deck timbers bowed, and the seams of the deck-planks opened, while her sides seemed ready to yield.

Thus far the closing forces were permitted to strike severely on the side of the helpless vessel, to show that they could crush her as rotten fruit is crushed in a strong man's hand. Then He, without whose permission no force in nature moves, and at whose word they are instantly stayed, directed the floe under the strongly timbered "bilge" of the hull, and, with a jerk which sent the men reeling about the deck, lifted the vessel out of the water. The floes now fought their battle out beneath her, as if they disdained, like the lion with the mouse in his paw, to crush so small a thing. Great ridges were piled up about her, and one underneath lifted her high into the air. Eight hours she remained in this situation, while the lives of all on board seemed suspended on the slenderest thread.

Then came the yielding and breaking up of the floes. Once, at the commencing of the giving way, an ice prop of the bows suddenly yielded, let the forward end of the vessel down while the stern was high in the air. But finally the battered craft settled squarely into the water.

She was leaking badly, and the pumps were kept moving with vigor. The rudder was split, and two of its bolts broken; the stern-post started, and fragments of the cut-water and keel were floating away. But, strange to say, no essential injury was done. She was slowly navigated into Hartstene or *Etah* Bay, where we have been so often, anchored safely, and repairs immediately commenced.

CHAPTER XXIX.

THE WINTER HOME.

ONE more effort, after the repairs were finished, was made to push through the ice-floe of Smith's Sound. This resulting in failure, it was plainly impossible to get farther north. The vessel was brought into Etah Bay again, a harbor found eight miles north-east of Cape Alexander, and eighty by the coast from the harbor of the "Advance," though only twenty in a straight line, and preparations were at once begun for winter. Peter, the Esquimo dog-driver, and Hans were appointed a hunting party. Sontag, the astronomer, with three assistants, was mainly engaged in scientific observations and experiments. There was work for all the rest. Some were engaged in unloading the cargo and lifting it by a derrick to a terrace on the shore, far above the highest tide, where a storehouse was made for it. The hold of the schooner was cleared, scrubbed, and white-washed, a stove set up, and made a home for the sailors. The sails and yards were "sent down," the upper deck roofed in, making a house eight feet high at the ridge, and six and a half at the sides.

The crew moved into their new quarters on the first of October. The event was celebrated by a holiday dinner. There was joy on shipboard; thankful for escapes granted by the great Protector, trustful for the future, and, greatly encouraged by present blessings, none were unhappy. The hunters were very successful, bringing in every day game of the best kind, and in great abundance. A dozen reindeer were suspended from the shrouds, and clusters of rabbits and foxes were hung in the rigging; besides these, deposits of reindeer were made in various directions. The hard-working men ate heartily of the relishing fresh food, and laughed to scorn the scurvy. They called the place of their winter quarters Port Foulke.

When the floe became frozen, the sledges were put in readiness for the dog-teams. The dogs having been well fed, were in fine condition.

Blocks of ice were used to make a wall about the vessel, from the floe to the deck, between which and her sides the snow was crowded, making a solid defense against the cold.

On the fifteenth of October the sun bade them farewell for four months, and they anticipated the coming darkness under circumstances certainly much better than had been often granted to arctic sojourners.

As there was yet a long twilight, dog-trips were very exhilarating. Dr. Hayes once rode behind his dogs twelve measured miles in an hour and one minute, without a moment's halt. Sontag and the captain raced their teams, the captain beating, as was becoming, by four minutes.

The dogs were made to know their masters—a knowledge quite necessary for the good of all. Jensen observed that one of his team was getting rebellious. "You see dat beast," he said. "I takes a piece out of his ear." The long lash unrolls, the sinewy snapper on its tip touches the tip of the dog's ear, and takes out a piece as neatly as a sharp knife would have done.

The same day Jensen's skill at dog driving was put to a severe test. A fox crossed their path. Up went their tails, curling over their backs, their short ears pricked forward, and away they went in full chase. In such a case woe be to the driver who cannot take a piece of flesh out of any dog in the team at each snap of his merciless whip. Jensen was usually master of such a situation, but it so happened that a strong wind blew directly in the face of the team and carried the lash back before it reached its victim. Missing its terrible bite, the dogs became for a while unmanageable and raced after the fox at full speed. To make matters worse, treacherous ice lay just ahead. The dogs were already on the heels of the fox, and about to make a meal of him, when Jensen regained full control of his whip. It stung severely, now this one and then that. Their tails dropped, their ears drooped, and they paused and obeyed their master. But they were greatly provoked at the loss of the game, and at the harsh subjection, and, with characteristic amiability, they commenced to snap at and bite each other. Jensen jumped from the sledge and laid the whip-stock on them, knocking them to the right and left, until, it is presumed, made very loving by the process, they went about their assigned business.

Parties of the explorers were out nearly every day, hunting, or pursuing the scientific inquiries.

Knorr, the secretary of the commander, was off with Hans. He had his adventure to talk about on his return. He wounded in the valley a reindeer, which hobbled on three legs up a steep hill. The young hunter followed, and, getting within easy range, brought it down by a well-aimed shot. The deer being in a line with Knorr, came sliding down the hill, and, knocking against him, both went tumbling down together. Fortunately he carried no broken bones, but only bruises to the vessel as mementoes of his deer hunt.

Sontag, on the same day, had his perilous incident. He had climbed to the top of a glacier by cutting steps in the ice. Across the ice was a crack, bridged over with thin ice, but entirely concealed by it. Stepping on this he broke through and fell into the chasm; fortunately it was a narrow one, and the barometer which he carried, crossing the creek, broke the fall and probably saved his life. On what a slender thread hangs this mortal existence!

During this sledging season Dr. Hayes visited the homes of our old acquaintance at Etah, which was only four miles from the schooner; but they were deserted. Near the huts was a splendid buck, busily engaged in pawing up and eating the moss from under the snow. He seemed so unsuspecting, and withal so honestly engaged, that the doctor, though he had crept on the leeward side, within easy range, was reluctant to fire. Twice he aimed, and twice dropped his gun from its level. Bringing it to sight the third time he fired, and the ball went crashing through the noble animal. We hear nothing of compunction in eating him on the part of any on shipboard, and probably the pitying reader would have had none.

Our old friend Hans does not appear so favorably in the present narrative as he did in that of Dr. Kane. His five years of chosen exile among his purely heathen countrymen does not seem to have left many traces of his Christian education. Some allowance, however, must be made for a difference of estimate of his character by his former and present commander. In Dr. Hayes's judgment, "he is a type of the worst phase of the Esquimo character."

Hans's domestic relations are represented as not of the most happy kind. His wife's name is Merkut, but is known to the sailors as "Mrs. Hans." She passes for a "beauty," as Esquimo beauty goes; has a flush of red on rather a fair cheek when, exceptionally, she uses soap and water enough for it to be seen through the usual coating of dirt. Their baby, ten months' old, bears the pleasant name of Pingasuk—"Pretty One." Hans has a household of his own. He pitched a tent, when the schooner went into winter-quarters, under the roof of the upper deck. The Esquimo Marcus and Jacob make a part of his family.

Here, wrapped in their furs, where they choose to be, they huddle together, warm "as fleas in a rug," though the temperature is seldom higher than about the freezing point. Little "Pretty One" creeps out of the tent about the deck, having for covering only the ten months' accumulation of grease and dirt, not unfrequently accompanied by its mother, who on such occasion is guiltless of "costly array," or much of any whatever.

Hans's gentlemen lodgers were taken on board as dog-drivers, but they seemed to have been of no possible use except to give occasion for the mirthful jokes of the sailors.

Peter, chief dog manager, a converted Esquimo, brother to Jacob, gave his commander excellent satisfaction and stood high in his esteem. He was skillful, industrious, and trustworthy. Between him and Hans an intense jealousy existed. Hans had, under Dr. Kane, no rival in his sphere. Peter was now, at least, a peer, and so the glory of his exaltation from Esquimo hut-life was greatly eclipsed. His master even preferred Peter before him; but Prof. Sontag clung, with a little of the Dr. Kane partiality, to the favorite of the former voyage.

Hans had no reason, however, to complain of the consideration shown him by his chief. At one time he gave him, to quiet his jealousy, a new suit of clothes, with the very reddest of flannel shirts. In these he appeared at the Sunday inspection and religious service, quite as elated at his personal adornment, though probably not more so, as the "fine gents" of our home Sabbath assemblies.

CHAPTER XXX.

GLACIERS.

THE glacier is one of the wonderful things of the northern regions. We will visit one with Dr. Hayes, and, on our return to the vessel, listen to some curious and interesting facts concerning it. Although there was no sunshine at the time of the first glacier excursion, the twilight was long and clear; it was October twenty-first. The run was made to the foot of the glacier from the vessel, with the dogs, in forty minutes. It appeared here as a great ice-wall, one hundred feet high and a mile broad. The glacier in descending the valley extended in breadth not quite to the slope of the hills, so it left between them and each of its sides a gorge. It is very curious that the ice should not lean against the hills as it slips along and thus fill up all the valley as water would.

Our party first stopped and examined the front face of the glacier. It was nearly perpendicular, but bulging out a little in the middle. It was worn in places by the summer streams which run over it, and marred in other parts by the fall of great fragments into the valley below. While our visitors were gazing at it a crystal block came down as an angry hint for them to stand from under. Wisely heeding the warning, they turned up one of the gorges between the glacier side and the hill. Here was rough traveling, and, we should think, dangerous too. There were strewed along in their path ice fragments from the glacier on one side, and rocks and earth which had slid down the hill on the other. If the glacier was as evil disposed as its children, the icebergs, it might let loose some of its projecting crags on their heads.

Finding a favorable place, they began to cut steps in the side of the glacier in order to mount to its surface. Having reached the top they cautiously walked to the center of the icy stream, drove two stakes on a line in it, and then two half way between these and the sides of the glacier. Then they measured the distance of these stakes from each other, and sighted from their tops fixed objects on the hills. They purposed to come in the spring and examine the distance apart of the stakes, and sight from them the fixed objects, so as to determine how fast the frozen river was moving down the valley. Having set the stakes they scampered back to the vessel.

After a little rest another journey to the glacier was made, this time without the dogs, the sledges, having a light outfit, being drawn by the men. These were young Knorr, the sailor M'Donald, Mr. Heywood, a landsman from the west—an amateur explorer—the Dane, Petersen, and the Esquimo, Peter. When they arrived at the gorge, the way was so rough that they were compelled to carry the sledge loads in parcels on their backs.

It was rough work, and they sought an early camp; but with the frowning ice-cliffs on one side and hill-crags on the other, both evil-minded in the use of their icy and rocky missiles, and with also the uneven bed of rocks beneath them, no wonder they did not sleep. They were soon astir, pushed farther up the gorge, and finding a favorable place, began to cut steps up the glacier. The first one who attempted to mount reached some distance, then slipped, and in sliding down carried with him his companions who were following, and the whole company were promiscuously tumbled into the gorge. The one going ahead had better luck the next trial, carrying a rope by which the sledge was drawn up, and all mounted in safety.

They now started off up this ice-river toward the great sea of ice from whence it flowed. The surface was at first rough, and of course slightly descending toward its front edge. Dr. Hayes walked in advance of the sledge party, carrying a pole over his head grasped by both hands, being fearful of the treacherous cracks hidden by their ice. Soon down he went into one, but the pole reached across the chasm and he scrambled out. The depth of the chasm remains a mystery to this day. The ice grew smoother as they proceeded, and they made about five miles, pitched their canvas tents, cooked with their lamp a good supper, made coffee, ate and drank like weary men, crept into their fur sleeping bags, and slept soundly though the thermometer was about fifteen degrees below zero. The next day they traveled thirty miles, and came upon an even plain where the surface of the ice-sea was covered with many feet of snow, the crust of which broke through at every step. This made very hard traveling, yet the following day they tramped twenty-five miles more. Now came the ever-at-hand Arctic storm. They camped, but lower and lower fell the temperature, and fiercer and fiercer blew the wind. They could not sleep, so they decided to turn their faces homeward. The frost nipped their fingers, and assailed their faces as they hastily packed up and started. They were five thousand feet above the level of the sea, and seventy miles from the coast, and were standing in the midst of a vast icy desert. There was neither mountain nor hill in sight. As in mid-ocean the sailor beholds the sea bounded only by the sky, so here they beheld only ice, which stretched away to the horizon on every side—truly a sea of ice. Clouds of snow whirled along its surface, at times rising and disappearing in the cold air, or drifted across the face of the setting moon—beautiful clouds of fleecy whiteness to the eye, but "burning" the flesh as they pelted the retreating explorers, like the fiery sand-clouds of the Great Sahara. They scud before the wind, which they dared not for a moment face, nor halted until they had traveled forty miles and descended two thousand feet. They then pitched their tents, the cold and wind having lessened though yet severe. They arrived at the ship the next evening, not seriously the worse for their daring "sea-voyage" on foot.

Having been refreshed by food and rest, no doubt our explorers discussed the great glacier problem, and pleasantly chased away many an hour in talk about what they had seen and what they had read on this interesting subject. We think their conversation included some of the following facts:—

The ice upon which they had been voyaging is a part of a great ocean of ice covering the central line of Greenland from Cape Farewell on the south to the farthest known northern boundary, a distance of at least twelve hundred miles. Instead of being formed of drops of water like more southern oceans, it is made up of crystallized dew-drops and snow-flakes, which have been falling for ages, and which in these cold regions have no summer long enough, nor of sufficient heat, to convert them into water again.

But if the crystal dews and snows continue to fall for ages, and never melt, what prevents them from piling up to the sky, and sinking the very continent? The all-wise Director of the universe has made a very curious arrangement to prevent such a result. This ice-ocean runs off into the sea in great ice-rivers which find their way to the shore on both sides of the continent, just as the water does which falls from the clouds on the top of the Andes of South America. There we see the mighty Amazon, one of its rivers, almost an ocean of itself, as it sweeps along its banks between mountains, and through immense forests. Greenland has its Amazons in vastness and grandeur, as well as its smaller rivers and little streams. It has also its lakes and sublime Niagaras, its falls and cascades. But they are ice instead of water; that is all the difference between this Arctic circulation and that of warmer regions.

But of course this ice is not like that which many of the readers see every winter. It is a half-solid, pasty kind of substance. It holds together, yet slides along from the higher land where it accumulates, filling up the valleys, breaking through the openings in the mountain and hilly ridges, and pouring over the precipices; slowly, silently, but with mighty force, ever pressing onward until it reaches the sea.

These ice rivers move very slowly. It will be remembered that Dr. Hayes drove some stakes down in the one he visited in October. In the following July he visited the glacier again, and compared the relation of these to the landmarks he had noted. He thus found that this ice-river moved over one hundred feet a year. It had come down the valley ten miles. Two more miles would bring it to the sea. Some glacier streams which they visited were yet many miles from the shore, one as far away as sixty miles. The Great Glacier of Humboldt, farther north, was several times visited by Dr. Kane and parties of his explorers. Its face is a solid, glassy wall three hundred feet above the water-level, and extending from Cape Agassiz, a measured distance north, of sixty miles, and then disappearing in the unknown polar regions. Surely this must be the mouth of the Amazon of glacier rivers.

But the history of these rivers does not end when they reach the sea. When their broad and high glassy front touches the water it does not melt away nor fall to pieces, but goes down to the bottom, and if it be a shallow bay or arm of the sea, pushes the water back and fills up the whole space, it may be for many miles. When it reaches water so deep that more than seven eighths of its front is below the surface, it begins to feel an upward pressure, just as a piece of wood when forced below its natural water-line will spring back. So after a while this upward pressure breaks off the massive front, perhaps miles in extent, and many hundred feet in height. As this is launched into the sea its thunder crash is heard for miles, and the water boils like a caldron, while the disengaged mass rolls and plunges until, finding its equilibrium, it sails away a majestic ICEBERG. Hereafter the snow will at times cover it with a mantle of pure whiteness; the fierce storms will beat upon its defiant brow; the beams of the rising and setting sun will display their sparkling glories on its craggy top, or, falling upon the misty cloud which envelopes it, will encircle it with all the varying hues of the rainbow. As it voyages in stately dignity southward, anchored, it may be, at times for months, it will pass in sullen silence the drear, long, dark Arctic night, and emerge into the brief summer to be enlivened as the home of innumerable sea-fowl, who will rear their young upon its cold breast. Ultimately it will go back to the drops of water from which it came, to make a part of the great ocean, and possibly to sail away in clouds over the frozen regions, and to drop again upon its glassy plain in sparkling crystals.

CHAPTER XXXI.

A STRANGE DREAM AND ITS FULFILLMENT.

THE winter was fully settled down upon Port Foulke, but the dwellers in the schooner "United States" knew nothing of the anxieties and suffering from cold and hunger which most of the arctic voyagers have known. There was one foe, however, which they, in common with all who had gone before them, had to fight; namely, depression of mind produced by the weeks of inactivity and darkness. We have seen how many means were used by earlier as well as later explorers to meet and vanquish this foe. Dr. Hayes availed himself of the hints given by his predecessors, and had some devices peculiarly his own. To the "school of navigation," dramatic performances, and the publishing of a weekly "newspaper," was added the pleasant stimulus of a celebration of the birthday of every man on board. Such occasions were attended by special dinners, the passing of complimentary notes of invitations to the intended guests, which included all, and by fun-making, at which all laughed as a matter of course.

On Sunday all assembled in their clean and best suits. Brief religious service was performed in the presence of all, and the day was spent in reading or conversation, save the performance of the necessary routine work.

During the favoring light of the moon some excursions were attempted. One was made by Professor Sontag, accompanied by Hans and Jensen with two dog sledges. The object was to reach the harbor where Dr. Kane's "Advance" had been left, and ascertain if possible her fate. He started early in November, but returned in a few days, baffled by the hummocks and wide intervening, treacherous ice-cracks. The party had an encounter with and captured a bear and her cub. The mother fought with maternal fury for her child, tossed the dogs one after another until some of the stoutest and bravest retired bleeding and yelping from the field, and at times charged upon and scattered the whole pack, while the cub itself behaved bravely in its own defense. When the men came up they threw in, of course, the fatal odds of rifle balls. Once Hans, his gun having failed to go off, seized an Esquimo lance and ran at the beast. Accepting the challenge of a hand-to-hand fight, she made at him with such spirit that he dropped the lance and ran, and nothing saved the cub from supping on Esquimo meat but two well-directed balls, which whizzed at the right moment from the guns of Sontag and Jensen. The bears made a splendid resistance to the unprovoked attack upon them in the peaceable pursuit of an honest calling, that of getting a living, but were conquered and eaten.

Among the sad events of the winter was a fatal

disease among the dogs. They all died but nine by the middle of December. This was alarming, for upon them depended mainly the spring excursions North Poleward. Such being the situation, Sontag took at this time the surviving dogs, and, on a sledge with Hans as a driver, started south in pursuit of Esquimo. If they could be brought with their dogs into the vicinity of the ship and fed, there would be a fair chance of having dog-sledges when they were wanted. The nearest known Esquimo family was at Northumberland Island, a hundred miles off, and others were at the south side of Whale Sound, fifty miles farther —perhaps all had gone to the most distant point. They departed in fine spirits, and well equipped. Hans cracked his whip, and the dogs, well fed and eager for a run, caused the sledge to glide over the ice with the velocity of a locomotive. Their companions sent after them a "hip! hip, hurrah!" and a "tiger." The moon shed her serene light on their path, and all seemed to promise a speedy and successful return.

The second night after their departure the solicitous commander had a strange, disquieting dream. He says in the journal of the following morning: "I stood with Sontag far out upon the frozen sea, when suddenly a crash was heard through the darkness, and in an instant a crack opened in the ice between us. It came so suddenly and widened so rapidly that he could not spring over it to where I stood, and he sailed away on the dark waters of a troubled sea. I last saw him standing firmly upon the crystal raft, his erect form cutting sharply against a streak of light which lay upon the distant horizon."

Christmas came and was duly regarded. Stores of nice things, the gifts of friends far away, were brought out from secret corners where they had been hid. The tables were loaded with that which satisfied the appetite and gratified the eye, while the rooms of officers and men blazed with cheerful lights. Outside a feeble aurora seemed to be trying to exhibit an inspiring illumination, which contrasted strongly with its cloudy background.

January, 1861, came, and half its days passed, yet no tidings came from Sontag. The twilight had returned, and already the coming sun was heralded along the golden horizon. The commander was becoming uneasy concerning the missing ones, and began to devise ways of knowing what had become of them. Mr. Dodge was sent to follow their tracks, which he did as far as Cape Alexander, where he lost them and returned. A party was instantly put in readiness for farther search, and was about to start on the morning of January twenty-seventh, when a violent storm arose, detaining it two days. As it was on the instant of starting again, two Esquimo suddenly appeared at the vessel's side. One of them was Ootiniah, who appears so creditably in the narrative of Dr. Hayes's boat voyage. They were bearers of sad news. Professor Sontag was dead. Hans was on his way to the vessel with his wife, father and mother, and their son, a lad who was left behind with mother when Hans was first taken on board of the schooner. Some of the dogs had died, and the family were necessarily moving slowly.

Two days later Hans came in with the boy only, having left the dogs and the old people near Cape Alexander and come on for help. He was very cold and much exhausted, and both were sent below for food, warmth, and rest, before being questioned concerning the disastrous journey. The large sledge, drawn by fresh men, was sent for those left behind. The old people were found coiled up in an excavation made in a snow bank, and the dogs huddled together near them, neither dogs nor Esquimo being able to stir, and so all were bundled in a heap on the sledge and drawn to the schooner. The hardy savages soon revived under the influence of good quarters and good eating, but the dogs, five in number, the remnant of the strong force of thirty-six, lay on the deck unable to stir, and not disposed to eat.

Hans's story was this :—

They made a good run the first day, passing Cape Alexander, and camped in a snow hut on Sunderland Island. The next day they reached an Esquimo settlement, but found its huts forsaken. Resting and eating here, they started for Northumberland Island, and having traveled about five miles, Sontag, becoming chilled, sprang from the sledge and ran ahead of the dogs for warmth by exercise. Hans having occasion to halt the team to disentangle a trace fell some distance behind. He was urging forward his team to overtake his master when he saw him sinking. He had come upon thin ice covering a recently open crack, and had broken through. Hans hastened up and helped him from the water. A light wind was blowing, which disposed Sontag not to attempt to change his wet clothes—the fatal error. They hastened back to the hut in which they had spent the night. At first the professor ran, but after a while jumped on the sledge, and when he reached the hut he was stiff and speechless. Hans lifted him into the hut, drew off his wet clothes, and placed him into his sleeping bag. Having tightly closed the hut, he set the lamp ablaze, and administered to him a portion of brandy from a flask found on the sledge. But the cold had done its fatal work; he remained speechless and unconscious for nearly twenty-four hours, and died.

Hans closed up the hut to prevent beasts of prey from disturbing the body, continued south, and on the second night came upon a village where he was rejoiced to find several native families, who were living in the midst of abundance. Here Hans rested until two Esquimo boys, whom he hired with the Sontag presents, could go to Cape York after his wife's parents and their son. They over-drove or starved four of the dogs, which were left by the way.

The natives whom he found were ready on the moment of his arrival to return to the vessel with him, and Ootiniah and his companion were the first to show their good-will by starting with Hans on his return.

A few weeks later the body of Sontag was brought to the vessel, a neat coffin was made for it, and the whole ship's company followed it, mourning, to its last resting-place. The burial service was read, and it was carefully secured from molestation. At a later period a mound was raised over it, and a chiseled stone slab, with his name and age, marked the head.

August Sontag was only twenty-eight years of age when thus suddenly cut off. His loss to the expedition was very great.

Hans's parents and brother were added to his own family on deck, and proved to be much more efficient helpers in domestic affairs than Mrs. Hans. The boy was washed and scrubbed and combed by the sailors, with whom he became a great favorite, filling much the place on board as a pet monkey, and proved to be full as annoying to the old cook, who, in his extreme vexation at his mischievous tricks, threatened to "kill him—*a le-e-t-le.*" The old folks getting tired of the close quarters on board, built after a while a snow hut on the floe, and set up housekeeping for themselves.

CHAPTER XXXII.

THE CROWNING SLEDGE JOURNEY.

"THE glorious sun" reappeared February eighteenth, tarrying only a moment, but giving a sure prophecy of a coming to stay. Scarcely less welcome was the appearance soon after of Kalutunah, Tattarat, and Myouk, all old acquaintance whom the reader will not fail to recognize. Kalutunah was Angekok and Nalegak—priest and chief. His gruff old rival, who advised the starvation policy toward the escaping party in the miserable old hut, had been harpooned in the back and buried alive under a heap of stones. These comers brought the much-desired dogs, and they were followed by other old friends from Northumberland Island with additional dog-teams. These natives were treated with consideration—they were made content with abundant food and flattered with presents, all of which told favorably upon the success of the enterprise of the generous donors.

In the middle of March the northward excursions commenced. The first consisted of a party of three, Dr. Hayes and Kalutunah driving a team of six dogs, and Jensen with a sledge of nine. It was to be a trial trip, and the experiment began rather roughly. A few miles only had been made when Jensen, whose team was ahead, broke through the ice, and dogs and man went floundering together into a cold bath. The other team, fortunately, was just at hand, so they were drawn out, and all returned to the vessel for a fresh and warm start. The next trial they were gone four days, and traversed the Greenland shore to Cape Agassiz and to the commencement of the Great Glacier. The cold at one time was sixty-eight and a half degrees below zero. Yet the sun's rays through even such an atmosphere blistered the skin! The grains of snow became like gravel, and the sledge runners grated over it as if running on the summer sand of our own sea-shore. Kalutunah had an ingenious remedy for this. He dissolved snow in his mouth, and pouring the water into his hand coated the runners with it. It instantly freezing, made something like a glass plating for them.

Kalutunah was greatly puzzled in attempting to understand why this journey was made. But his perplexity took the form of disgust when the fresh tracks were seen of a bear and cub, and the white chief forbade the chase. He argued in the interest of Dr. Hayes, who might thereby have a new fur coat, pointed to the hungry dogs, and finally pleaded for his own family, who were longing for bear meat. But all in vain. The circumstances had changed since, in the same spot nearly, he had urged the dogs after a bear in spite of Dr. Kane, and thus defeated the purpose of his long trip.

On their return they turned into Van Rensselaer Harbor, the place made so famous by Dr. Kane's expedition. Every thing there was changed. Instead of smooth ice, over which Dr. Kane's party came and went so often, there were hummocks piled up every-where in the wildest confusion. Where the "Advance" was left when her men took a last look at her was an ice-pile towering as high as were her mast-heads. Old localities were undiscernible from the snow and icy aggressions. A small piece of a deck-plank picked up near Butler Island was all that could be found of the "Advance." The Esquimo told nearly as many diverse stories of her history after the white men left her as there were persons to testify, and some individuals, apparently to increase the chance of saying some item of truth, told many different stories. According to these witnesses she drifted out to sea and sunk, (the most probable statement,) she was knocked to pieces so far as possible and carried off by the Esquimo, and she was accidentally set on fire and burned. The graves of Baker and Pierre remained undisturbed, but the beacon built over them was broken down and scattered.

The result of this experimental trip was the decision of the commander not to attempt to reach the Open Polar Sea by the Greenland shore, but to cross Smith Sound at Cairn Point, a few miles north of the schooner. To this point provisions were immediately carried on the sledges for the summer journey beyond.

On the third of April the grand effort to reach the North Pole commenced. The party consisted of twelve persons, who were early at their assigned positions alongside of the schooner. Jensen was at the head of the line of march, on the sledge "Hope," to which were harnessed eight dogs; Knorr came next, "the whip" of the "Perseverance," with six dogs. Then came a metallic life-boat with which the Polar Sea was to be navigated, mounted on a sledge and drawn by men each with shoulder strap and trace. Flags fluttered from boat and sledges, all was enthusiasm, and at the word "march" the dogs dashed away, the men bent bravely to their earnest work, the "swivel" on deck thundered its good-bye, and the party were soon far away.

The very first day's exposure nearly proved fatal to several of the party. One settled himself down in the snow muttering, "I'm freezing," and would have proved in a half hour his declaration had not two more hardy men taken him in charge. The spirits of the men ran low, and they were two hours in building a snow-hut in which to hide from the pitiless wind. A rest at Cairn Point and increased experience gave them more energy, and the next snow-hut was made in less than one hour. They proved the snow-shovel a fine heat generator. On the fifth night out they were overtaken by a storm, and were detained two days in their hut. This was a pit in the snow eighteen feet long, eight wide, and four deep. Across its top were placed the boat-oars; across these the sledge was laid; over the sledge was thrown the boat's sails; and over the sails snow was shoveled. They crawled into this hut through a hole which they filled up after them with a block of snow. Over the floor

—a leveled snow floor—they spread an India-rubber cloth; on this was laid a carpet of buffalo-skins, and over this another of equal size. Between these they crept to sleep, the outside man of the row having no little difficulty in preventing his companions from "pulling the clothes off." The wind without blew its mightiest blow, and piled the snow up over the poor dogs, which were huddled together for mutual warmth, and were kept restless in poking their noses above the drift. The cooks were obliged to call to their help the commander in order to keep the lamp from being puffed out, and two hours were consumed in getting a steaming pot of coffee. But after a while the bread and coffee, and dried meat and potato hash, were abundantly and regularly served, and the men contrived to pass in talk and song and sleep the hours of the really dreary imprisonment.

Before the storm had fully subsided, the party went on the back track to bring up to this point a part of the provisions they had been obliged to deposit. This done, they put their faces to the opposite, or American side of the sound. But the difficulties were truly fearful. The ice, like great bowlders, was scattered over the entire surface, now piled in ridges ten, twenty, and even a hundred feet high, and then scattered over a level area with only a narrow and ever-twisting way between them. Over these ridges the sledges had to be lifted, the load often taken off and carried up in small parcels, and the sledges and boat drawn up and let down again. Frequently in the midst of this toil a man would fall into a chasm up to his waist; another would go out of sight in one. These terrible traps were so covered with a crust of snow that they could not be discerned. The boat was, of course, capsized often, and much battered. When a ridge had been scaled, and the party had picked their way for a time through the winding path among the ice-bowlders, they would come to a sudden impassable barrier, and be obliged to retrace their steps. A whole day of gigantic exertion, and of many miles of zigzag travel, would sometimes advance them only a rifle-shot in a straight line.

Of course it was simply impossible to carry the boat, and it was abandoned. They were yet only about thirty miles from Cairn Point, but had traveled perhaps five times that distance.

For several days after this the heroic explorers struggled on. A fresh snow with a half-frozen crust was added to their other obstacles. Hummocks and ridges and pitfalls grew worse and worse. The sledges broke, the limbs of the men were bruised and sprained, their strength exhausted, and at last their spirits failed. They had toiled twenty-five days, advanced half way across the sound, and brought along about eight hundred pounds of food.

On the twenty-eighth of April the main party were sent homeward. Dr. Hayes, Knorr, M'Donald, and Jensen, pushed on toward the American shore. Their way was, as one of the party remarked, like a trip through New York over the tops of the houses. They progressed a mile and a half, and traveled at least twelve, carrying their provisions over the ground by repeating the journey many times. Such was the daily experience, varied by many exciting incidents. Jensen sprained a leg which had been once broken ; the dogs were savage as the wildest wolves with hunger, though having a fair amount of food ; once Knorr in feeding them stumbled and fell into the midst of the pack, and would have doubtless been devoured as a generous morsel of food tossed to them, had not M'Donald pounced upon them at the moment with lusty blows from a whip-stock. All four of the explorers held out bravely in this fearful strain on mind and body, even young Knorr never shrinking from the hardest work, nor the longest continued exertions.

On the eleventh of May the party encamped under the shadow of Cape Hawkes, on Grinnell Land, off the American coast. The distance from Cairn Point, in a straight line northwest, was eighty miles. They had been traveling thirty-one days, and made a twisting and clambering route of five hundred miles.

The travel up the coast had the usual variety of dangers, hair-breadth escapes, and exhausting toil. A little flag-staff, planted by Dr. Hayes during the Kane expedition, was found bravely looking out upon the drear field it was set to designate, but the flag it bore had been blown away. Remains of Esquimo settlements long deserted were found. A raven coaked a welcome to the strangers, or it may be a warning, and followed them several days.

On the fourth day up the coast Jensen, the hardiest of the vessel's company, utterly failed. He had strained his back as well as leg, and groaned with pain. What could be done? The party could not proceed with a sick man, nor would they for a moment think of leaving him alone. So the following course was adopted by the commander: M'Donald was left in the snow-hut with Jensen, with five days' food and five dogs, with orders to remain five days, and then, if Hayes and Knorr, who were to continue on, had not returned, to make his best way with Jensen back to the vessel.

The journey of Dr. Hayes and Knorr was continued two full days. On the morning of the third day they had proceeded but a few miles when they came to a stand. They had on their left the abrupt, rocky, ice-covered clifts of the shore; on their right were high ridges of ice, through which the waters of an open sea broke here and there into bays and inlets which washed the shore. Farther progress north by land or ice was impossible. They climbed a cliff which towered eight hundred feet above the sea, whose dark waters were lost in the distance toward the north-east. North, standing against the sky, was a noble headland, the most northern known land, and only about four hundred and fifty miles from the North Pole. The spot on which our explorers stood was about one degree farther north than that occupied by Morton, of Kane's Expedition, yet on the shore of the same open water. Now, if they only had the boat they were obliged to leave among the hummocks in Smith Sound, with the provisions and men they had *hoped* to bring to this point, how soon would they solve the mystery locked up from the beginning, and in the keeping of his Frosty Majesty of the Pole itself! But, alas! there were neither boat nor provisions, and the movement of the treacherous floes warned the daring strangers that the bridge of ice over which they had come to this side might soon be torn away, and make a return impossible. They built a monument of stones, raised on it a flag of triumph, deposited beneath it a record of their visit placed in a bottle, and turned their faces homeward.

CHAPTER XXXIII.

LAST INCIDENTS OF THE EXPEDITION.

DR. HAYES and Knorr were buffeted by a fierce storm soon after starting. They were over fifty miles from M'Donald and Jensen, only ten of which were traversed before they were obliged to encamp. But the storm howled, and tossed the snow-clouds about them, making it impossible to build a snow hut. After a brief halt, and feeding the dogs with the last morsel of food which remained, they pushed on. The snow was deep, often nearly burying the dogs as they plunged along; the hummocks and rocks over which they climbed lay across their path, and the wind blew with unabated fury; yet they halted not until the remaining forty or more miles were accomplished, and they tumbled into the hut of their companions. The dogs rolled themselves together on the snow the moment they were left, utterly exhausted. The weary men slept a long, sound sleep. When they awoke a steaming pot of coffee and an abundant breakfast awaited them. They had fasted thirty-four hours, and traveled in the last twenty-two over forty miles, which the hummocks and deep snow made equal to double that distance of smooth sledging. The last few miles were made in a state of partial bewilderment, so their final safety was another of their many marked deliverances. The remaining run to the vessel had its daily perils and escapes. As they were approaching the American shore they stepped across a crack on the ice. They had traveled but a short distance when they perceived that there was an impassable channel between them and the land ice. They ran back to recross the crack, and that had become twenty yards wide. They were, in fact, on an ice-raft, and were sweeping helplessly out to sea! They had hardly collected their thoughts after this terrifying surprise before one of the shore corners of their raft struck a small grounded iceberg, and on this, as on a pivot, the outer edge swung toward the shore, struck its margin, allowed them to scamper off, and then immediately swung again into the open water, and shot out to sea.

The poor dogs, being insufficiently fed, and necessarily overworked, now began to fail. Jensen's lameness compelling him to ride, increased their burden. One died just before the party left the hummocks, and two soon after. A fourth having failed, the commander, thinking to shorten his misery, shot him. The ball only wounding him, he set up a terrible cry, at which his companions flew at him, tore him in pieces, and, almost before his last howl had died away in the dreary waste, they had eaten the flesh from his bones.

They arrived at the schooner safely after two months' absence, during which they had traveled thirteen hundred miles.

The commander was cheered to learn that the party who returned under M'Cormick had reached Port Foulke in safety. The whole ship's company were in good health. The vessel was immediately thoroughly examined and put in sailing order. As the summer came on, the birds, the green mosses, hardy little flowers, several species of moths and spiders, and even a yellow winged butterfly, appeared to greet its coming. The open water was daily coming nearer the schooner. While awaiting the loosening of its icy fetters, a boat's crew had an exciting walrus hunt. Dr. Hayes had been on a hill-top which overlooked the bay, when the hoarse bellowing of distant walrus saluted his ears. Drifting ice-rafts were coming down the sound, on which great numbers of these monsters could be seen. He hurried to the vessel, and called for volunteers. Soon a whale-boat was manned, and the men, armed with three rifles and a harpoon and line, dragged it to the open water, launched it, and rowed into the midst of the drift-ice. The first cake of ice which they approached contained a freight of twenty-four walruses, pretty well covering it. The lubberly, ugly looking sea-hogs appeared as content as their very distant relatives of our sties, while they huddled together and twisted for the sunniest spot, and bellowed in one another's ears. Our hunters were all eager for the fight as they approached with muffled oars, but on coming near to the floe, it was apparent that the hunt was not to be all fun, nor the fighting on one side only. The hides of the monsters looked like an iron plating, and were, in fact, an inch thick, smooth, hairless, and tough, suggesting a good defensive ability; while their great tusks, projecting from a jaw of elephantine strength, hinted unpleasantly to the invaders that their antagonists were prepared for assault as well as defense. Very likely if one could have seen at that moment the countenances of our boat's crew, they would have shown more of a wish to be in the vessel's cabin than they would have cared to confess with their lips. But there was no flinching. There were two male walruses in the herd—huge, fierce-looking fellows, which roused up a moment to scan the strangers, and then, giving each other a punch in the face with their tusks, stretched out again upon the ice to sleep.

In this walrus party there were, besides the two fathers, mothers with children of various ages, from the "little ones" of four hundred pounds, to the "young folks." Of course they were a loving, happy group. The boat came within a few times its length of the ice-raft. Miller, an old whaleman, was in the bow of the boat with a harpoon. Hayes, Knorr, and Jensen stood in the stern with their rifles leveled each at his selected victim, while the oarsmen bent forward to their oars. At the word the rifles cracked, and the oarsmen at the same moment shot the boat into the midst of the startled walrus. Jensen hit one of the males in the neck, not probably doing him much harm; Hayes's ball struck the other bull in the head, at which he roared lustily. Knorr killed a baby walrus dead, but he disappeared from the raft with the rest, probably pushed off by his mamma. When the old fellow which was wounded by the commander rolled into the water, Miller planted his harpoon in him with unerring skill, and the line attached spun out over the gunwale with fearful velocity. There were a few moments of suspense, and then up came the herd, a few yards from the boat, the wounded bull with the harpoon among them. They uttered one wild, united shriek, and answering shrieks from thousands of startled walruses, on the walrus laden ice-rafts for miles around, filled the air. It was an agonized cry for help, and the answering cry was, "we come!" There was a simultaneous splash from the ice-rafts, and the hosts, as if by the bugle call, came rushing on, heads erect, and uttering the defiant "huk, huk, huk!" They came directly at the boat, surrounding it, and blackening the waters with their numbers. The wounded bull, attached still to Miller's line, led the attack. The hunters had aroused foemen worthy of their steel, and they must now fight or die. It seemed to be the purpose of the walruses to get their tusks over the side of the boat, and so easily tear it to pieces or sink it, and then, having its audacious crew in the water, make short work of them. As they came on, Miller, in the bow, pricked them in the face with his lance, the rowers pushed them back with their oars, while Hayes, Jensen, and Knorr sent, as fast as they could load and fire, rifle-balls crashing through their heads. At one time a huge leader had come within a few feet of the boat. Hayes and Jensen had just fired, and were loading, but Knorr was just in time to salute him with a ball. The men were becoming weary, while the walrus assaulting column was constantly supplied with fresh troops. The situation was now critical, when, as if to crush his enemy and end the conflict in victory on his side, a walrus Goliath, with tusks three feet long, led on a solid column of undismayed warriors. Two guns had just been fired, as before. His terrible weapons were fearfully near the gunwale, when Knorr's gun came to the rescue; its muzzle was so near his open mouth that the ball killed him instantly, and he sunk like lead. This sent consternation through the walrus ranks. They all dove at once, and when they came up they were a considerable distance off, their tails to their foes, and retreating with a wild shriek. The battle was ended, and the saucy explorers were victors. The sea in places was red with blood. The harpooned bull and one other were carried as trophies to the vessel.

On the twelfth of July the schooner floated, after an ice imprisonment of ten months. The Esquimo seeing that the white friends were about to leave them, gathered on the shore in sorrowful interest. They had been the receivers of gifts great in their estimation, and they had rendered the strangers no small favors, especially in the use of their dogs, without which no excursions of importance could have been made. Kalutunah actually wept on parting with Dr. Hayes. He had enjoyed under his patronage the Esquimo paradise—"plenty to eat, plenty sleep, no work, no hunt." He spoke feelingly of the fading away of his people. "Come back," he said, "and save us; come soon or we shall be all gone."

He had reason to express these fears concerning his people. Since Dr. Kane left thirty-four had died, and there had been in the same time only nineteen births. There seemed to be in all the settlements, from Cape York to Etah, only a hundred!

The explorers bid adieu to Port Foulke on the fourteenth, and sailed away to the west side of Smith Sound, and reached a point about ten miles south of Cape Isabella. The hope was entertained by the commander that he might work his way with the vessel north through the now loosening ice over which he had just been traveling with sledges, get through even Kennedy Channel, to the open sea on the shore of which he had so lately stood, and then sail away to the North Pole. What a stimulating thought! But he found the schooner ice-battered, and, weakened by the "nips" she had experienced, was unequal to the required fight with the defiant pack which every-where filled the sound. So the explorers turned homeward. They arrived at Upernavik on the twelfth of August after many exciting incidents but no accident. Here they learned the startling news of the commencement of the great Rebellion. During their absence President Lincoln had been inaugurated, the black cloud of war had settled heavily over the whole country, and the bloody battle of Bull Run had been fought. They were now to return home and transfer their interest in fighting ice-packs, bergs, and Polar bears, to the conflicts of civil war.

CHAPTER XXXIV.

SOMETHING NEW.

WHILE the civilized world were awaiting with deep interest the results of the search for Sir John Franklin, and while learned geographers and practical navigators to the regions of cold were devising new methods of search for him, a young engraver was working out a problem in reference to this great enterprise peculiarly his own. Without special educational advantages, without the resources of wealth or influential friends, but with the inspiration of one feeling, "a divine call" to the undertaking, he matured his plans and began to publish them abroad. He seems to have at once imparted his own enthusiasm to others. The mayor of his own city, Cincinnati, the governor and senator of his own State, Ohio, the latter the eminent Salmon P. Chase, late Chief-Justice of the United States, became his patrons. Coming east, many of the great and wise men of our large cities gave him an attentive hearing, and not a few encouraged his project. The princely merchant, Henry Grinnell, who had already done so much in the Franklin search, took him at once into kindly sympathy.

From New York he went to New London. From the old whalemen, at least from individuals of them of marked character and large experience in Arctic navigation, he obtained encouraging words.

His plan of search which thus so readily commended itself was this: He would go into the region where it was now known that Franklin and some of his men had died; he would live with the Esquimo, learn their language, adopt their habits of life, and thus learn all that they knew of the history of the ill-fated expedition. He assumed that many of its men might yet be alive, and if they were, the natives would know it, know where they were, and could guide him to them.

To prepare himself for this work he became conversant with Arctic literature, learning all that the books on the subject taught; he applied himself closely to the study of the practical science bearing on his enterprise, learning the use of its instruments. He sought interviews and correspondence with returned explorers and whalemen. In fact, his heart was in the work with a downright enthusiasm.

The marked features of his plan seemed to be two—it was inexpensive and new. As to the manning of his expedition, he proposed to go alone; as to vessels, he asked none. He only asked to be conveyed to the proposed Esquimo country, and to be left with its natives. We might name a third attractive feature of this plan, one which always inspires interest—it was bold, bordering on the audacious!

We need hardly say to our readers that the

name of this new candidate for Arctic perils and honors was Charles Francis Hall—a name now greatly honored and lamented.*

Mr. Hall was born in Rochester, New Hampshire, in 1821, where he worked a while at the blacksmith's trade, but left both the trade and his native place in early life for the Queen City of the West. The result of Mr. Hall's enthusiastic appeals was an offer by the firm of Williams & Haven, whale-ship owners of New London, to convey him and his outfit in their bark "George Henry" to his point of operations, and if ever desired, to give him the same free passage home in any of their ships. The "George Henry" was going, of course, after whales, and proposed thus to convey him as an obliging incident of the trip.

This proposal was made in the early spring of 1860. On the twenty-ninth of May he sailed. His outfit was simple, and had the appearance of a private, romantic excursion. It consisted of a good sized, staunch whaleboat built for his special use, a sledge, a few scientific instruments, a rifle, six double-barreled shot-guns, a Colt's revolver, and the ammunition supposed to be necessary for a long separation from the source of supply. A start was given him in a small store of provisions; beyond that he was to supply himself. A tolerable supply of trinkets were added as a basis of trade with the natives. What funds this miniature exploring expedition required was given largely by Mr. Grinnell.

* See Frontispiece.

The "George Henry" was accompanied by *a tender*, a small schooner named the "Rescue," having already an Arctic fame. The officers and crew of both vessels numbered twenty-nine, under command of Captain S. O. Buddington.

We have spoken of Mr. Hall as the only man of his exhibition; he had after all one companion. The previous year Captain Buddington had brought home an Esquimo by the name of Kudlago, who was now returning to his fatherland and to his wife and children. Upon him Mr. Hall largely depended as an interpreter, a friend, and guide, in his work.

The run of the "George Henry" to the Greenland coast was made with but one marked incident. That was to Mr. Hall a very sad one, giving him the first emphatic lesson in the uncertainty of his most carefully devised schemes. It was the death and burial at sea of Kudlago. He had left New London in good health, taken cold in the fogs of Newfoundland, and declined rapidly. He prayed fervently to be permitted to see his wife and children—only that, and he would die content. He inquired daily while confined to his berth if any ice was in sight. His last words were, "*Teiko seko? teiko seko?*"—Do you see ice? do you see ice? The Greenland shore was just in sight when he departed, and his home and family were three hundred miles away.

The "George Henry" and her tender, the "Rescue," sailed north, along the Greenland coast, as far as Holsteinberg, where Mr. Hall purchased six

Esquimo dogs. The vessel then stood southwest across Davis Strait and made, August eighth, a snug harbor, which Mr. Hall called Grinnell Bay, a little north of what is known as Frobisher Strait. Here Mr. Hall was to land and commence his Esquimo life, alone and far away from a Christian home, while the vessel went about its business capturing whales. His feelings on the voyage are indicated by the following extract from his diary:

"A good run with a fair breeze yesterday. Approaching the north axis of the earth! Aye, nearing the goal of my fondest wishes. Every thing relating to the arctic zone is deeply interesting to me. I love the snows, the ices, the icebergs, the fauna and the flora of the North. I love the circling sun, the long day, *the arctic night, when the soul can commune with God in silent and reverential awe!* I am on a mission of love. I feel to be in the performance of a duty I owe to mankind, myself, and God! Thus feeling I am strong at heart, full of faith, ready to do or die in the cause I have espoused." How he felt when actually engaged in his "mission of love," we shall see.

We must not, however, think of Mr. Hall in a region comparable to that which included the winter-quarters of Kane and Hayes in the expeditions we have just described. They were at least twelve degrees farther north, Mr. Hall being south of the arctic circle, so that his winter nights were shorter and milder. His present field of operation was on a coast visited by the whale-ships, and where they at times wintered. Besides, natives had been for many years in contact with white men, and were in *some* respect more agreeable companions. He will therefore, as we follow him, lead us into new scenes of peculiar interest, and show us novel features in the character of the Esquimo.

The whale-ship "Black Eagle," Captain Allen, lay in Grinnell Bay on the arrival of our voyagers, and the captain soon appeared on the deck of the "George Henry," with several Esquimo. One of these natives, named Ugarng, especially attracted Mr. Hall's attention. He was intelligent, possessing strong lines of character, and a marked physical development. He had spent a year on a visit to the United States. Speaking of New York, he said with a sailor's emphasis: "No good! too much horse! too much house! too much white people! Women? Ah! women great many—good!" Ugarng will become a familiar acquaintance.

Mr. Hall had giving special attention on the voyage across Davis Strait to his dogs, and they were now to become a chief dependence. He fed them on *capelin*, or dried fish. One day he called them all around him, each in his assigned place, to receive in turn his fish. Now there was one young, shrewd dog, Barbekark, who had not heard, or had never cared to heed the proverb that "honesty is the best policy." He said to himself, "If I can get *two* of the fish while the other dogs get but one, it will be a nice thing to do;" so, taking his place near the head of the row, he was served with his capelin. Then, slipping out, he crowded between the dogs farther down, and with a very innocent look awaited his turn. His master thought this so sharp in young Barbekark that he pretended not to see the trick, and dealed him a fish as if he had received none. On going the round again his master found him near the head of the row and then at the foot, so the rogue obtained Benjamin's portion. Seeing his success, he winked his knowing eye as much as to say, "Ain't I the smartest dog in the pack!" But Barbekark had entered on a rough road with many turns, as all rogues do. After going round several times, during which the trick was a success, Mr. Hall *skipped* the trickster altogether. It mattered not what place he crowded into, there was no more fish for him. The upshot was that he received many less than did his companions. Never did a dog look more ashamed. From that time he kept his place when fish were distributed.

Mr. Hall, making the vessel his home, made frequent visits ashore, and received many Esquimo visitors on board, and was thus becoming acquainted with the people. An early visitor was Kokerjabin, wife of Kudlago, accompanied by her son. She had learned in her tent that her anxiously awaited husband had been left in the deep sea. She entered the cabin and looked at her husband's white friends, and at the chest which contained his personal goods, with deep emotion; but when Captain Buddington opened the chest, the tears flowed freely; and when she, in taking out things, came to those Kudlago had obtained in the States for herself and her little girl, she sat down, buried her face in her hands, and wept with deep grief. She soon after went ashore with her son to weep alone.

Another very marked character was Paulooyer, or, as the white men called him, Blind George. He was now about forty years of age and had been blind nearly ten years, from the effects of a severe sickness. To this blindness was added domestic sorrow. His wife Nikujar was very kind to him for five years after his loss of sight, sharing their consequent poverty. But Ugarng, who had already several wives, offered her a place in his tent as his "household wife"—the place of honor in Esquimo esteem. The offer was tempting, for Ugarng was "a mighty hunter," and rich at all times in blubber, in furs and skin tents and snow huts. So she left poor George, taking with her their little daughter, called Kookooyer. This child became a pet with Ugarng, as she was with her blind father.

CHAPTER XXXV.

A FEARFUL STORM.

WHILE the "George Henry" lay at Grinnell Bay, Mr. Hall talked much with the masters of the whale-ships and with the most intelligent of the natives concerning his proposed journey to King William's Land. This was a far-away region, where the remains of the Franklin expedition had been found. He proposed to secure the company of one or more Esquimo and make an attempt to reach it with a dog-sledge, and to take up his abode with its natives in search of information of the lost ones. But both his white and Esquimo advisers agreed that it was too late in the season to begin such a journey. Mr. Hall would then take the whale-boat built for him, man it with natives, and make the attempt by water. But this was deemed impracticable until spring. So he decided to make his home on board the vessel so long as she remained on the coast, and pursue his study of the Esquimo language and his survey of the region of country, with this home as a base of operations.

On his return from one of his inland excursions with Kudlago's son, whom the whites called *captain*, he saw his widow, apart from all the people, weeping for her great bereavement. Her son ran to her and tried to comfort her, but she would not be comforted. When Mr. Hall approached she pointed to the spot where their tent was pitched when Kudlago left for the United States. She also showed him the bones of a whale which he had assisted in capturing.

Soon after this the widow visited the vessel with her daughter, Kimmiloo, who had been the idol of her father. She looked sad on the mention of her father's name, but, child-like, her eyes gleamed with joy on seeing the fine things his chest contained for her. Captain B.'s wife had sent her a pretty red dress, necktie, mittens, belt, and other like valuables of little white girls. But Mr. Hall suggested that Kimmiloo's introduction to the dress of civilization should be preceded by soap and water. The process of arriving at the little girl through layers of dirt was very slow. When this was done, her kind friend Hall took a *very coarse* comb, and commenced combing her hair. This had never been done before, and of course the comb "pulled" in spite of the care of the operator, but Kimmiloo bore it bravely. Her locks were filled with moss, greasy bits of seal, and disgusting reindeer hairs, besides other things both *active* and numerous. A full hour was spent on the hair, but when the comb went through it easily, then the little girl run her fingers into it and braided quickly a tag on each side of her head; she then drew these through brass rings which Mr. Hall had given her. Her Esquimo fur trowsers and coat were thrown off, and the now clean and really beautiful girl put on the red dress. Her happiness would have been complete had her father been there to share her joy.

Mr. Hall's kindly nature led him to study the natives in these incidents, and to record them in his journals. Ugarng was one time in the cabin when Mr. Hall had put a few small balls of mercury on a sheet of white paper. It was a new article to the Esquimo, and he tried to pick it up with his thumb and finger, but it escaped his grasp. His efforts would scatter it over the sheet in small globules, and then as he lifted the corners of the paper it would run together, and Ugarng would commence catching it with new vigor. He continued his efforts for a full half hour. Amused at first, but finally losing his temper, he gave it up, exclaiming petulantly that there was an evil spirit in it.

Blind George became a constant visitor. At one time Mr. Hall gave him a much worn coat, showing one of the several holes in it. George immediately took a needle, and, bringing his tongue to the aid of his hands, threaded it, and mended *all* of the rents very neatly. At another time Mr. Hall put into George's hand a piece of steel with a magnet attached. The way the steel flew from his hand to the magnet amazed him. At first he seemed to think it was not really so; but when he clearly felt the steel leap from his fingers, he threw both steel and magnet violently upon the floor. But feeling he was not hurt, and that some little girls laughed at him, he tried it again more deliberately, and was better satisfied. Mr. Hall next gave him a paper of needles, desiring him to bring the magnet near them. He did so, and when the needles flew from his hand by the attraction he sprung to his feet as if an electric current had touched him, and the needles were scattered in every direction over the floor. He declared that Mr. Hall was an "Angekok."

On the fourteenth of August another whaling vessel belonging to the owners of the "George Henry" arrived at Grinnell Bay. Her name was the "Georgiana," Captain Tyson; so there were now four vessels near each other—the "Rescue" and "Black Eagle," besides those just named. There were social, merry times. But Captain Buddington, having built a hut here that some of his men might remain to fish, took his vessels farther south, for winter-quarters, into a bay separated from Frobisher Bay on the south by only a narrow strip of land. This Mr. Hall named Field Bay. Here, snugly hid in an inlet of its upper waters, the vessels proposed to winter. The Esquimo were not long in finding the new anchorage of the whites, and in a few days a fleet of kayaks containing seven families appeared. Among them was Kudlago's oldest daughter, now married to a native the sailors called Johnny Bull. She had not heard of her father's death, and stepped on deck elated at the thought of meeting him. "Where is my father?" she inquired of Ugarng's wife. When she was tenderly told the sad story of his death she wept freely.

Mr. Hall was at once busy visiting the "tupics," summer tents made of skins, pitched by the natives near the shore. He also rowed to the islands in various directions, generally accompanied by one or more Esquimo. On one of these visits to an island with a boy he had a narrow escape. After several hours' ramble they returned to the landing, where they had left their boat fastened to a rock. The tide had risen and the boat was dancing on the waves out of reach. Here was a "fix!" They were far away from the vessel, the night, cold and dark, was coming on, and they were without shelter. But necessity sharpens one's wits. After some delay and perplexity, Mr. Hall hit upon this plan: He took the seal-skin strings from his boots, and the strings by which various scientific instruments were attached to his person, tied them together, and thus made quite a long and strong line. To this he tied a moderate sized stone. Holding one end of the line in his hand, he tossed the stone into the boat and gently drew it to him, jumped into it, and was soon at the vessel. If Mr. Hall had not been a *green* boatman he would not have fastened his boat below high-water mark when the tide was coming in! He probably did not again.

One day the crew of the "Henry" captured a whale in the bay, and the Esquimo joined with others in towing the monster to the ship. In one of the boats was an Esquimo woman with a babe; she laid her child in the bow of the boat and pulled an oar with the strongest of the white men.

Before they reached the vessel the wind blew a gale, the sea ran high, and at times the spray shot into the air and came down in plentiful showers into the boat. The mother cast anxious glances at her child, and, as if it was for its life, rowed with giant strength. At last the prize was safely moored to the "Henry," and the natives were rewarded with generous strips of its black skin, which they ate voraciously, raw and warm from the animal. They carried portions of it to their tupics on shore for future use. This skin is about three fourths of an inch thick, and, in even Mr. Hall's estimation, is "good eating" when raw, "but better soused in vinegar."

Soon after this, Captain Tyson brought the "Georgiana" round into Field Bay, and the crews of the two vessels were often together when a whale made its appearance, a circumstance sometimes the occasion of strife when he is captured. One day Smith, an officer of the "Henry," fastened a harpoon in a whale, and was devising means to secure his prey. Captain Tyson, who was near in his boat, killed the monster with his lances, and without a word, left Smith to enjoy the pleasure of taking it to his vessel. The generous act was appreciated on board the "Henry."

On the twenty-sixth of December a terrible storm commenced, causing the boats which were cruising for whales to scud home. The three vessels—the "Henry," "Rescue," and "Georgiana"—were anchored near each other, and near an island toward which the wind was blowing. It was about noon when the storm began, and as the day declined the wind increased, bringing on its wings a cloud of snow. When the night came on it was intensely dark, and the waves rose higher and higher as, driven by the tempest, they rolled swiftly by and dashed upon the rocky shore. The vessels labored heavily in the billows and strained at their anchors, now dipping their bows deep in the water, then rising upon the top of a crested wave, and leaping again into the trough of the sea, as if impatient of restraint and eager to rush upon the rocks to their own destruction. The roar of the sea and the howling of the winds through the shrouds were appalling to all on board, while they awaited with breathless interest the integrity of the anchors, on which their lives depended.

As the night wore on the watch on deck, peering through the darkness, saw the dim outlines of the "Rescue" steadily and slowly moving toward the shore. "She drags her anchors!" were the fearful words which passed in whispers through the "George Henry." But all breathed easier to hear the report from the watch soon after that she had come to a pause nearly abreast of the "Henry."

About midnight the storm put forth all the fury of its power, and the small anchor of the "Georgiana" gave way, and the others went plowing along their ocean beds, and, as the vessel neared the island, her destruction and the loss of all on board seemed certain. The endangered craft worried round a point of rocks, pounding against them as she went, and reached smoother and safer waters, where her anchors remained firm. The ghostly-looking forms of her men were soon after seen on the island, to which they had escaped! In the mean time the men on the "Henry" were in constant fear that their vessel would be dashed upon rocks.

Just as the morning was breaking the "Rescue" broke away and went broadside upon the island. With a crash the breakers hurled her against the rocks, and seemed to bury her in their white foam. She was at once a hopeless wreck, but her crew still clung bravely to her. When the morning light had fully come, at the first lull in the storm, while yet the waves rolled with unabated fury, a whaleboat was lowered into the sea from the stern of the "Henry" with a strong line attached, and mate Rogers and a seaman stepped into it. Cautiously and skillfully it was guided to the stern of the "Rescue." Into it her men were taken, and drawn safely to the "Henry." All were saved! A shout of joy mingled with the tumult of the elements!

The "Henry" safely outrode the storm. The "Georgiana" was not seriously injured, and her men returned to her and sailed away for other winter-quarters. The "Rescue" was a complete wreck, and, what was a stunning blow to the enterprise of Mr. Hall, his expedition boat, in which, with an Esquimo crew, he had hoped to reach the far-away land of his lone sojourn and search for the Franklin men, was totally wrecked too! What now should he do? That was to him the question of questions. One thing he resolved *not* to do—he would not abandon his mission. Captain Buddington thought at first that he might spare him one of the ship's boats in which to reach King William's Land; but, on careful inquiry, he found that the only one he could part with was rotten and untrustworthy. So waiting and watching became his present duty.

CHAPTER XXXVI.

THE AURORA.

MR. HALL had an eye for the beautiful in nature. The aurora deeply impressed him, inspiring feelings of awe and reverence. It will be noticed that explorers in the low latitude of Frobisher Bay are treated to displays of the aurora on a scale of magnificence and beauty never seen in the high latitudes of the winter-quarters of Dr. Kane and Hayes. Night after night through the months of October, November, and December Mr. Hall's sensitive nature was in raptures at the wonderful sights. The heavens were aglow. The forms of brightness, and colors of every hue, changed with the rapidity of fleecy clouds driven before the wind. Before the mind had comprehended the grandeur of one scene, it had changed into another of seeming greater beauty of form, color, and brightness. Thousands of such changes occurred while he gazed. No wonder he exclaims: "Who but God could conceive such infinite scenes of glory! Who but God execute them, painting the heavens in such gorgeous display!"

Again he exclaims: "It seemeth to me as if the very doors of heaven have opened to-night, so *mighty* and *beauteous* and *marvelous* were the waves of golden light which swept across the azure deep, breaking forth anon into floods of wondrous glory. God made his wonderful works to be remembered."

Mr. Hall had been on deck several times, witnessing the enrapturing display, and had returned into the cabin to go to bed, when the captain shouted down the companion-way: "Come above, Hall, at once! *The world is on fire!*" Mr. Hall hastened on deck. He says: "There was no sun, no moon, yet the heavens were flooded with light. Even ordinary print could be read on deck. Yes, flooded with *rivers* of light!—and *such* light! light all but inconceivable! The golden hues predominated; but in rapid succession prismatic colors leaped forth.

"We looked, we saw, and we trembled; for even as we gazed the whole belt of aurora began to be alive with flashes. Then each pile or bank of light became myriads; some now dropping down the great pathway or belt, others springing up, others leaping with lightning flash from one side, while more as quickly passed into the vacated space; some, twisting themselves into folds, entwining with others like enormous serpents, and all these movements as quick as the eye could follow. It seemed as though there was a struggle with these heavenly lights to reach and occupy the dome above our heads. Then the whole arch above became crowded. Down, down it came! nearer and nearer it approached us! Sheets of golden flames, coruscating while leaping from the auroral belt, seemed as if met in their course by some mighty agency that turned them into the colors of the rainbow.

"While the auroral fires seemed to be descending upon us, one of our number exclaimed, 'Hark! hark!' Such a display, as if a warfare were going on among the beauteous lights, seemed impossible without noise. But all was silent."

After the watchers, amazed at what they saw, retired to the cabin, they very naturally commenced a lively conversation on what they had witnessed. Captain Buddington declared that, though he had spent most of his time for eleven years in the northern regions, he had never witnessed so grand and beautiful a scene. And he added in an earnest tone: "To tell you the truth, friend Hall, I do not care to see the like again!"

In November Mr. Hall became acquainted with two remarkable Esquimo whom we shall often meet. Their names were Ebierbing and his wife Tookoolito, but were known among the white people as Joe and Hannah. They had been taken to England in 1853, and lionized there for two years. They had visited the great and good of that land at their homes, and had aptly learned many of the refinements of civilization. Queen Victoria had honored them with an audience, and they had dined with Prince Albert. Joe declared that the queen was "pretty—yes, quite pretty;" and the prince was "good—very good." They made their visit on shipboard in a full-blown English dress, but when Mr. Hall returned their visit in their *tupic* on shore they were in the Esquimo costume. Yet Tookoolito busied herself with her *knitting* during his call. She said, as they conversed: "I feel very sorry to say that many of the whaling people are bad, making the Innuits bad too; they swear very much, and make our people swear. I wish they would not do so. Americans swear a great deal—more and worse than the English. I wish no one would swear. It is a very bad practice I believe."

Tookoolito's spirit and example had done much to improve her people, especially the women; these, many of them, had adopted her habit of dressing her hair, and of cleanliness of person and abode. In her and her husband, whom we shall meet often, we shall see the Esquimo as modified by a partial Christian civilization.

Mr. Hall made frequent visits to the Esquimo village on shore, mingling with the people, conforming to their habits, and studying their character. Their summer, skin-covered huts—tupics—had now given way to the *igloos*, the snow-house, essentially like those we have before seen. We will accompany Mr. Hall in a visit made in October. He found on creeping into a hut a friend whom he knew as a pilot and boatman; his name was Koojesse. He was sitting in the midst of a group of women drinking with a gusto hot seal blood. Our white visitor joined them, and pronounced the dish excellent. On going out he was met by blind George. "Mitter Hall! Mitter Hall!" shouted the blind man on hearing Mr. Hall's voice. There was a pensive earnestness in the call which arrested his attention. "Ugarng come to-day!" continued George. "He come to-day. My little Kookooyer way go! She here now. Speak-um, Ugarng! My little pickaninny way go! Speak-um."

The facts were these: Ugarng, who, as we have stated, had married George's wife, and taken with the mother his little daughter, was at the village attended by the latter. George, who was very fond of the child, desired her company for a while. Mr. Hall did of course "speak-um." Ugarng and the darling Kookooyer were soon seen in happy intimacy with her father.

Mr. Hall's attention was attracted by an excited crowd, who were listening to the harangue of a young man. He was evidently master of the situation, for at one moment his audience clenched their fists and raved like madmen, and then, under another touch of his power, they were calm and thoughtful, or melted to tears. He was an *Angekok*, and was going through a series of *ankootings*, or incantations. His howlings and gesticulations were not unlike those of the heathen priests of the East, and of the medicine men of our Indians. On seeing Mr. Hall the Angekok left his snow-platform, from which he had been speaking, and ran to him with the blandest smiles and honied words. He put his arm in his and invited him into his tent, or place of worship, as it might be called; others ran ahead, and it was well filled with worshipers. Koojesse, who was passing at the time with water for the ship, on a wave of the

Angekok's hand set his pail down and followed. All faithful Esquimo in this region obey the Angekok. If he sees one smoking, and signifies that he wishes the pipe, the smoker deposits it in the Angekok's pocket.

When in the tent the Angekok placed Koojesse on one side, and Mr. Hall facing him on the other side. Now commenced the service. The Angekok began a rapid clapping of his hands, lifting them at times above his head, then passing them round in every direction, and thrusting them into the faces of the people, muttering the while wild, incoherent expressions. The clapping of his hands was intermitted by a violent clapping of the chest on which he sat, first on the top, then on the sides and end. At times he would cease, and sit statue-like for some moments, during which the silence of death pervaded the audience. Then the clapping and gesticulations broke forth with increased violence. Now and then he paused, and stared into the farthest recess of the tent with the fiery eyes and the hideous countenance of a demon. At the right time, to heighten the effect, the wizard, by a quick sign or sharp word, ordered Koojesse to fix his eyes on this point of the tent, then on that, intimating in mysterious undertones that in such places *Kudlago's spirit shook the skin covering!* Koojesse, though one of the most muscular and intelligent of the natives, obeyed with trembling promptness, while the profuse sweat stood in drops upon his nose, (Esquimo perspire freely *only* on the nose,) and his countenance beamed with intense excitement. The climax was at hand. The Angekok's words began to be plain enough for Mr. Hall's ears. Kudlago's spirit was troubled. Would the white man please give it rest? One of his double-barreled guns would do it! White man! white man! give Kudlago's spirit rest! Give the double-barreled gun!

The cunning wizard! But Mr. Hall, who, though brimful of laugh, had been a sober-looking listener, was not to be caught with this chaff, *except in his own interest.* He whispers to Koojesse, "Would the Angekok be a good man to go with me in the spring to King William's Land?"

"Yes," was the reply.

Then Mr. Hall turned to the Angekok and said aloud, "If you go with me next spring on my explorations you shall have one of my best guns."

Thinking the gift was to be given immediately, his crafty reverence shouted, thanked Mr. Hall, threw his arms about his neck, and danced with an air of triumph about the tent, seeming to say as he looked upon his amazed followers, "I have charmed a kablunah"—white man.

Mr. Hall tried to set him right about the terms of the gift—that it was to be when he had served him in the spring. But he would understand it as he would have it. His joy found a fullness of expression when, pointing to his two wives, he said to Mr. Hall, "One shall be yours; take your choice." He was disgusted when the white man told him that he had a wife, and that kabluna wanted but one wife.

CHAPTER XXXVII.

THE DYING ESQUIMO.

CHRISTMAS and New Year's (1861) were not forgotten as holidays by the sojourners in the regions of cold and ice. Mr. Hall gave his friend Tookoolito a Bible as a memento of December twenty-fifth. She was much pleased, and at once spelled out on the title-page, *Holy Bible.*

Mr. Hall having heard that an Esquimo named Nukerton was seriously sick, invited Tookoolito to visit her with him. Sitting down with the sick one, with Tookoolito as an interpreter, Mr. Hall spoke to her of Jesus and the resurrection, while many of her friends stood listening with intense interest. Tookoolito bent over her sick friend weeping, and continued the talk about God, Christ, and heaven, after Mr. Hall had ceased.

Mr. Hall visited the sick one daily, administering to her bodily and spiritual wants. Going to see her on the fourth of January, he found that a new snow-hut had been built for the dying one, and her female friends had carried her into it, opening, to pass her in, a hole on the back side. It was at once her dying chamber and her tomb. For this purpose it was built in conformity to the Esquimo usage. He found Nukerton in her new quarters of stainless snow, on a bed of snow covered with skins, happy at the change though she knew that she had been brought there to die, *and to die alone*, as was the custom of her people. Mr. Hall proposed to carry her to die on board the ship. But even Tookoolito objected to this. It was better she should die alone; such was the custom of their fathers. Mr. Hall remained to watch alone with the dying one, but, on his leaving her igloo to do an errand at a neighboring tent, her friends sealed up its entrance. He threw back the blocks of snow piled against it and crept in. Nukerton was not dead; she breathed feebly; the lamp burned dimly, and the cold was intense; the solemn stillness of the midnight hour had come; sound of footsteps were heard, and a rustling at the entrance. Busy hands were fastening it up, not knowing, perhaps, that Mr. Hall was within. "Stop! stop!" he shouted, and all was silent as the grave. "Come in!" he again said. Koodloo, Nukerton's cousin, and a woman came in. They remained a few moments and left. Mr. Hall was alone again, and remained until the spirit of the dying woman departed. He gently closed her eyes, laid out the body as if for Christian burial, closed up the igloo, and departed.

Mr. Hall knew cases, later in his stay with this people, in which the dying were for some time alone before the vital spark was extinguished. The only attendance that the sick have is the howling and mummery of the Angekoks, who are sometimes women. They give no medicine.

Mr. Hall made several sledge excursions with his Innuit friends. One to Cornelius Grinnell Bay was full of thrilling incidents, of storms, of perils by the breaking up suddenly of the ice on which he had encamped, and one showing the wolfish rapacity of Esquimo dogs. He also had a bear chase and capture. But these, though full of exciting interest, are similar to those of other explorers, already related. The Esquimo themselves, with all their knowledge of the ice and storms, have many desperate adventures. A party of them was once busily engaged in spearing walrus, when the floe broke up and they went out to sea, and remained three months on their ice-raft! The walrus were plenty, and they had a good time of it, and returned safely.

We have given our readers an incident relating to Mr. Hall's dog, Barbekark—a not very creditable incident, it will be remembered, so far as that dog's discernment of moral right is concerned. But then we must remember that heathen dogs are not supposed to know much in that respect. Barbe, as we will call him for shortness, appears again in our story in a way which shows that he was very knowing about some matters at least.

One day, at nine in the morning, a party of the ship's company, attended by the native Koojesse, started for an excursion into Frobisher Bay. When well out of sight of the vessel a blinding storm arose, making farther progress both difficult and dangerous. Koojesse counseled an immediate construction of a snow-hut, and a halt until the storm subsided, which was the right thing to do. But the white leader ordered a return march. The dogs, as they generally will with a fierce wind blowing in their face, floundered about in reckless insubordination. Their leader, a strong animal, finally assumed his leadership, and dragged them for a while toward some islands just appearing in sight. But Barbe set back in his harness, pricked up his ears, and took a deliberate survey of the situation. To be sure he could *see* only a few rods in any direction, but his mind was made up. He turned his head away from the islands, and drew with such vigor and decision that all, both men and dogs, yielded to his guidance. Through the drifts, and in the face of bewildering clouds of snow which darkened their path, he brought the party straight to the ship! A few hours more of exposure and all would have perished.

Young Barbe was a brave hunter as well as skillful guide. On a bright morning in March, the lookout on the deck of the "Henry" shouted down the gangway that a herd of deer were in sight. Immediately the excitement of men and dogs was at fever-heat. The dogs, however, did not get the news until Koojesse had crept out, and from behind an island had fired upon the deer. His ball brought down no game, but the report of the gun called out Barbe with the whole pack of wolfish dogs at his heels, in full pursuit of the flying, frightened deer. The fugitives made tortuous tracks, darting behind the islands, now this way, and then off in another direction. But Barbe struck across their windings along the straight line toward the point at which they were aiming, while the rest of the dogs followed their tracks, and so fell behind. Koojesse returned to the vessel, the hope which just now was indulged of a venison dinner was given up, and the affair was nearly forgotten, except that some anxiety was felt lest the dogs should come to harm in their long and reckless pursuit.

About noon Barbe came on board having his mouth and body besmeared with blood. He ran to this one, and then to that, looking beseechingly into their faces, and then running to the gangway stairs, where he stopped and looked back, as much as to say, "An't you coming? Do come, I'll show you something worth seeing!" His strange movements were reported to Mr. Hall in the cabin, but being busy writing he took no notice of it. One of the men having occasion to go toward the shore Barbe followed him, but finding that he did not go in the right direction he whined his disappointment, and started out upon the floe, and then turned and said as plainly as a dog could speak, "Come on; this is the way!"

A party from the ship determined now to follow. Barbe led them a mile northward, then, leaving them to follow his foot-prints in the snow, he scampered off two miles in a western direction. This brought the men to an island, under the shelter of which they found the dogs. Barbe was sitting at the head of a slaughtered deer, and his companions squatting round as watchful sentinels. The deer's throat had been cut with Barbe's teeth, the jugular vein being severed as with a knife. The roots of the tongue, with bits of the windpipe, had been eaten, the blood sipped up, but nothing more. Several crows were pecking away at the carcass unforbidden by Barbe, who petted crows as his inferiors.

Barbe wagged his tail and shook his head as the men came up, and said in expressive dog-language, "See here, now! didn't I tell you so!"

The disturbed and blood-stained snow around showed that the deer had fought bravely. One of his legs was somewhat broken in the bloody conflict, which incident might have determined Barbe's victory.

The men skinned the deer, and bore the skin and dissected parts to the vessel.

CHAPTER XXXVIII.

CUNNING HUNTERS.

OUR sketch of Mr. Hall's Esquimo life brings us to the early summer of 1861. He had made many excursions in and about Frobisher and Field Bays which we have not noted. Their results were mainly valuable for the relics obtained of the visits here of the famous old explorer Frobisher, nearly three hundred years ago. There were, too, he ascertained, traditions among the natives of these visits, as well as that of Parry, nearly fifty years before, which so well accorded with the known facts as to show the reliability of such traditions.

An incident occurred during one of these excursions which illustrates the deceitful effect of refraction in the northern atmosphere. He landed on a headland in Frobisher Bay, and secured an enchanting view of land and sea. Points of historic interest were under his eye, and nature was clothed with a wild Arctic beauty. But an object of still more thrilling interest comes in view. A steamer! Yes, there is her hull and smoke-pipe, all very unmistakable! See, she tacks, now this way, then that, working her way no doubt toward the land on which he stands.

Mr. Hall ran to the camp, and told the good

news to Koojesse and Ebierbing, his companions. His mind was fairly bewitched with visions of news from civilization, from his country, and perhaps letters from his dear ones of the family circle. Each shouldered his loaded gun, and walked round to the point on the shore toward which the steamer was coming. They would make a loud report with their guns, and *compel* those on board to notice them. When they reached the spot there was no steamer. The Esquimo looked with blank amazement, and turned inquiringly toward Mr. Hall. Had she sailed away? No, that was impossible. It was only that rock yonder, half buried in snow! There, it does even now look like a steamer! Wait a while. No, it no more looks like a steamer than it looks like a cow! It is a cruel "sell!"

It will be recollected that the "George Henry" had made her winter-quarters in a little nook in Field Bay called Rescue Harbor. From his home in her cabin Mr. Hall was going forth on his explorations. But the whalers had made a "whaling depot" on a cape of Frobisher Bay, which commanded a view of its waters and of the waters of Davis Strait. Here they watched for whales, or made excursions after them. To this depot Mr. Hall made an excursion with Koojesse about the middle of June. On their way over the ice, Koojesse gave illustrations of two Esquimo methods of taking seal that were very peculiar. The dogs scented the seal and broke into a furious run, making the sledge "spin" over the ice. Soon Koojesse perceived him lying with his head near his hole. On the instant the dogs and their driver set up a vociferous, startling yell. The seal lifted up his head, frightened almost out of his wits, so that the dogs were within a few rods of him before he so far recovered his senses as to plunge into his hole and escape.

Koojesse said that only young seals are so caught. In this case fright had nearly cost the poor seal his life.

At another time Koojesse saw a seal sunning himself, and lying, as is their habit, near his hole. The hunter stopped the sledge, took his gun, and, keeping back the dogs, lay down and drew himself along upon his breast, making at the same time a peculiar, plaintive sound, varied in intonation. To this "seal talk," as the Esquimo term it, the animal listens, and is charmed into a pleasant persuasion that some loving friend is near. He looks, listens, and then lays his head languidly upon the ice. So the wily hunter approaches within easy range, the rifle cracks, and the fatal ball goes through the vitals of the confiding seal. Thus seals, like men, sometimes die of alarm, and are sometimes taken in the flatterer's snare.

Mr. Hall found the whale depot a busy place. Numerous tents of the white men and Esquimo were grouped together, in the midst of which, on a substantial flag-staff, the stars and stripes were waving. The Esquimo and dogs proclaimed their welcome in their peculiar way, and the officers and crew made the visitor feel at home.

The question soon discussed concerned a boat for Mr. Hall's journey to King William's Land. Captain Buddington said seriously that the question had been much on his mind, and had been anxiously considered, and his painful conclusion was that he had no whale-boat adequate for the undertaking. The boat made on purpose for that service, which had been lost when the "Rescue" was wrecked, was the only one brought into those waters which could convey him safely. To go in any other would be to throw away his life. So Mr. Hall said heroically: "I will make the best of my stay here, in explorations and study of the Esquimo traits and language. Do you return to the States, get another suitable boat, and, God willing, I will yet go to King William's Land."

Touching incidents of Innuit life were constantly passing before Mr. Hall. Here is one. There was a young man, Etu, about twenty-five years of age, whom our old acquaintance, Ugarng, had taken into his favor. Etu had the misfortune to be born spotted all over his body, precisely like the snow-white and black spotting of the skin of one species of seal. His heathen parents seemed on this account to have loathed their child, for, after enduring his presence a few years in the family, the father carried him to an unfrequented barren island to die. But God, who cared for the child Ishmael and the little Moses, watched over Etu. He caught the sea-birds which flocked to the land *with his hands*—an extraordinary exploit. The summer thus passed and winter came, and the boy yet lived. It so happened—shall we not the rather say, God so ordered—that a kayak of natives rowed that way. They were surprised when they saw a boy alone on a drear island, and the child was frightened at their presence. But when they made friendly signs he rushed into their arms.

The boy returned to his people, but being shunned and slighted he became discouraged and indolent. Such was his situation when Ugarng took him into his family. One day Mr. Hall entered the tent of Ebierbing and found there a girl thirteen years of age, Ookoodlear, weeping as though her heart would break. She also was of Ugarng's family, but had been staying with the kind Tookolito, wife of Ebierbing. Her trouble was that Ugarng was coming to take her away and make her the wife of Etu! Marry a seal-spotted man! the thought was awful! Then, she was so young!

Ebierbing took with him a friend, and called upon Etu and told him the dislike felt toward him of the girl. Poor Etu! Then Tookoolito agreed with Ugarng to take charge of Ookoodlear, so the marriage was prevented.

Marriage contracts among the Esquimo are made by the parents or other friends, often in the childhood of the parties. Those immediately concerned seldom have any thing to do or say in the matter. Among the Esquimo of Whale Sound the proposed bridegroom was sometimes required to be able to carry off to his igloo, in spite of herself, his intended bride. The resistance in such cases on the part of the woman is supposed to depend upon circumstances.

There is no marriage ceremony. In these Esquimo communities the two great events, marriage and death, transpire without special note. Among the natives of the region we are now visiting the new-born child generally first sees the light alone with its mother, and in an igloo built expressly for her.

Late in July the ice broke up and liberated the "George Henry" from her icy prison. The sailors returned on board, and she sailed away on a whaling cruise. Mr. Hall was left alone with his Innuit friends. He had planned a voyage of exploration in his whale-boat with a crew of them, to be absent about two months. On his return, if he found the whalers in those regions he would go to the States in one of them; if not, he would remain in Esquimo life until their return.

Ebierbing and Tookoolito were of course to be of his party. But Ebierbing was taken seriously sick and so was prevented from accompanying him, much to his regret. His crew, as finally selected, were Koojesse and wife, Charley (his Esquimo name is too long to write) and his wife, Koodloo, and a widow, Suzhi, remarkable for her great size and strength, weighing two hundred,

The party were off the ninth of August. They passed through Lupton Channel, a narrow run of water connecting Field Bay with Frobisher Bay. A white whale preceded them, leisurely keeping the lead, as if conscious that there were no harpoons in the boat; perhaps he assumed his safety from the presence of the women. The sea-fowl were abundant. The Esquimo, to save ammunition, adopted one of their own amusing yet cruel ways of capturing them. They rowed softly and swiftly to a cluster of them in the water. Just as the birds were about to fly the whole crew set up a most terrific yell, at the same time stamping and throwing their arms about with wild gesticulations. Down go the frightened birds, diving, instead of flying, to escape the enemy. The crew now seize their oars, and the steerer guides the boat by the disturbed surface of the water to the spot where they come up. The moment they show their heads the uproar is renewed. Down go the birds again without taking breath. This course, though exciting sport to the hunters, is soon death to the poor birds, which, exhausted and finally drowned, are picked from the surface of the water. One of the ducks taken in this way was a mother with a fledgeling. As the parent gasped in its dying agony, the child would put its little bill in her mouth for food, and then nestle down under her for protection.

The explorers having entered Frobisher Bay, sailed west along its northern shore. They camped at night on the land, and made slow progress by day. The Esquimo were in no hurry, while Mr. Hall would make good time to the extreme west of the bay and survey that line of coast, as the waters had hitherto been deemed a strait. But his free and easy companions were more disposed to have a good time than to add to geographical knowledge. At one time Koojesse, taking up Mr. Hall's glass, saw a bear some miles away on an island. Fresh duck was plenty on board, and a chase after "*ninoo*" at the expense of time was unnecessary. But it would be *fun;* that settled the matter. Away sped the rickety old whale-boat, impelled by strong hands. Bruin soon snuffed the strangers, stood and looked, then comprehending the danger, turned and ran over to the other side of the island. Soon the boat was in sight of him, and he plunged into the water. The Esquimo now adopted a part of the game they had played so successfully on the ducks. They occasionally made a sudden and deafening uproar. Ninoo would stop and turn round to see what was the matter, and so time was gained by his pursuers. But he made good speed for the main land, and after a while began so far to comprehend the situation that no noise arrested his course. On he went for dear life. The balls soon reached him and dyed his coat in crimson, yet he halted not until one struck his head. This enraged him; he deemed the play decidedly foul. He turned, showed his teeth, and this brought the boat to a stand-still. The hunters did not care for a hand-to-paw fight. The rifle settled the unequal conflict, and ninoo's body was towed ashore.

The bladder of the bear was inflated, and with some other *charms*, put on a staff to be elevated on the top of the tupic when the party encamped, and in the bow of the boat when sailing. This insured good luck according to Esquimo notions.

The explorers were, while in camp at one time, in want of oil for their lamp. Koodloo found some strips of sea-blubber and carried it to Suzhi, who was "in tuktoo"—that is, in bed. She sat up, rested upon her elbows, put a dish before her, took the blubber, bit off pieces, chewed it and sucked the oil out, and then spirted it out into the dish. In this way she "milled" oil enough to fill two large lamps. This done she lay down again and slept, with unwashen hands and face. There were no white sheets to be soiled.

CHAPTER XXXIX.

ROUND FROBISHER BAY.

THE explorers found occasionally during their voyage encampments of natives. In these many incidents occurred illustrating Esquimo habits. At one place the women were busily employed on seal-skins, making women's boots. One of them was diligently sewing while her big boy *stood* at her breast nursing!

Before reaching the head of the bay Mr. Hall's party was joined by a boat load of Esquimo, and several women canoes. A beautiful river emptied into the bay here which abounded with salmon, which proved most excellent eating. Vegetation was abundant. The women brought Mr. Hall a good supply of berries, resembling, in size and color, blueberries. They were deemed a great luxury. Wolves barked and howled about the camp. The aurora danced and raced across the heavens in strange grandeur. The deer roamed about the rocky coast undisturbed except by the occasional visits of the Innuits.

Mr. Hall, having pretty thoroughly explored the head of the bay, purposed to return on the side opposite that on which he came. Here were hills covered with snow. It had no attractions for his Esquimo companions, and they muttered their discontent at the route. Ascending one of these hills, Mr. Hall planted on it, with much enthusiasm, a flag-staff from which floated the stripes and stars. On returning to the encampment he found his tent occupied by several Esquimo busily engaged in various items of work. One of the women having done him a favor he gave her some beads, asking her at the same time what she had done with those he had given her on a former occasion. She said she had given them to the Angekok for his services in her sickness. Mr. Hall went to a tin box and took out a copy of the Bible and held it up before the woman, saying, "This talks to me of heaven!" Instantly, as though a light from heaven had flashed upon them all, both men and women left their work, and springing to their feet looked at Mr. Hall. At first they seemed terrified; then a smile of joy came over their faces, and they said, "Tell us what it talks of heaven."

As well as he was able, with but a slight knowledge of their language, he unfolded to them the great truths of Revelation. When he paused one of his hearers pointed downward, inquiring if it talked of the grave, or perhaps meaning the place of the wicked. When he answered "Yes," they looked at each other with solemnity and surprise.

But an incident which occurred soon after showed that these Esquimo did not feel the presence of eternal things. A white whale had been seen and chased by the men and women. He escaped, and the men returned in bad humor.

As one of the women was helping to unload the boat her husband threw a seal-hook at her with great force. She parried the blow, and it caught in her jacket. She calmly removed it, and continued at her work as if nothing had happened.

Esquimo men are generally the mildest, if not the most affectionate, of savages in their relation of husbands; yet in their fits of passion they throw any thing that is at hand at their wives, a hatchet, stone, knife, or spear, as they would at a dog.

At one time the Esquimo men all left Mr. Hall's boat on a hunt. He continued his voyage with the three women rowers. The boat was pleasantly gliding along, when in passing an island it fell into a current which rushed over a bed of slightly covered rocks with the rapidity of a mill-race, seething and whirling in its course. The women, though frightened, rowed with great vigor, Suzhi showing herself more than an ordinary man in the emergency. For some time the struggle was fearful and uncertain. To go with the current was certain death; to get out of it seemed impossible. At last slowly, steadily, they gained on the rushing current, and then the boat shot into a little cove in tranquil waters. They landed and rested six hours.

Mr. Hall had now, September twelfth, been out thirty-five days, and he determined to return to Rescue Harbor, hoping to find that the "George Henry" had returned from her whaling trip. This pleased the Esquimo, but they did not like his south-side route. Koojesse would, in spite of Mr. Hall, steer the boat toward the opposite side, and the rowers enjoyed the joke. At one time our explorer wished to stop and make further examination of a certain locality, but Koojesse was heading the boat northward. His captain urged him to stop, and he replied with savage sharpness, "You stop; I go!" Even the women rowers when alone with Mr. Hall set up an independent authority at one time, and it was only after considerable urging that they yielded to the white man. Once when Koojesse was acting contrary to orders, Mr. Hall turned upon him with tones of authority and a show of determination. He yielded, and five minutes afterward the whole Esquimo crew were as jovial as if nothing had occurred. Yet it was not quite certain that this was a safe course. The life of the lone white man was in their hands.

During this voyage Mr. Hall was treated without stint to the delights of one Esquimo practice. We have spoken of the wild songs of their incantations, rising often into a dismal howl. One of the crew, a woman, had a gift in this way, and when she *ankooted* the rest accompanied, or came in on the chorus. In this way they often made the night of their encampment hideous. One day the boat was gliding smoothly along under the steady strokes of the rowers. The unemployed were nestling down in their furs, dreamily musing, while the dreary expanse of sky and sea was profoundly still, save the distant screech of the sea-fowl, and the occasional bark of the seal. Suddenly the female enchanter commenced her mystical song. Her voice was shrill as a night-bird's, and varied by sharp and sudden cracks, like fourth-of-July fire-crackers. The Esquimo crew came in on the chorus, and the rowers put forth at the same time a frantic energy, their eyes glaring and countenances fearfully distorted. The whole scene was intensely demoniac. The enchanters seemed intoxicated with their howlings, and continued them through the night and most of the two following days.

Only one incident more of a noticeable character occurred on this excursion. When one of their nightly encampments had just commenced *a gold fever* seized the Esquimo, and shook the little community as if they had been white folks. A huge lump of gold had been found! It was precisely the article for which the sovereign of England and her savans had sent here, three hundred years before, the sturdy Frobisher, with a fleet of empty ships. It was emphatically *fool's gold.*

Friday, September twenty-seventh, 1861, the explorers arrived at Rescue Harbor. The "George Henry" was already there. Her energetic officers and crew had toiled through all the season and taken nothing! The explorer and the ship's commander, after a warm supper, sat in the cabin talking over the incidents of their experience while separated until a late hour of the night. The whole community were jubilant at their return, as fears were indulged that the crazy craft had sunk with all its occupants.

Mr. Hall was not long in finding the tupic of his friends, Ebierbing and wife. When the wife of Tookoolito saw him she buried her face in her hands and burst into tears so great was her joy. While chatting with them, Mr. Hall heard the plaintive sound of an infant voice. Turning back the folds of Tookoolito's fur wrapper a little boy was seen only twenty-four days old, an only child.

October twentieth came, and the whalers had secured three whales — an encouraging success after a long failure. But her captain had not intended to stay another winter. His time was out, and so, nearly, were his provisions. But while Rescue Harbor was yet clear of ice, and he was getting ready to return, purposing to take with him the still enthusiastic explorer, the heavy "pack" was outside of the harbor in Davis Strait. It had come, an untimely, unwelcome voyager from the north. While the anxious whalemen were looking for a "lead" to open and permit them to sail homeward the Frosty King of the north waved his icy scepter, and Davis Strait was as unnavigable as the solid land. Another winter was spent in Rescue Harbor, and it was not until early in August, 1862, that the vessel was set free and spread her sails for home. This year, too, was diligently improved by Mr. Hall in explorations and the further study of the Esquimo language and character. He confidently expected to return, after a short stay in the United States, and carry out his proposed plan of explorations in King William's Land. He took home with him Ebierbing and Tookoolito, with their infant boy, Tuk-e-lik-e-ta. The dog Barbekark made one of the returning party.

They arrived in New London September thirteenth, 1862, after an absence of two years and three and a half months.

CHAPTER XL.

THE "POLARIS."

WE have seen that Mr. Hall's enthusiasm for arctic research was unabated when he returned from his first adventure. In 1864 he was off again. He sailed from New London in the whaler "Monticello," accompanied by his Esquimo friends, Ebierbing and Tookoolito. The "Monticello" entered Hudson Bay, landed the daring explorers on its northern shores, and left them to their fortunes. From thence they made the long, dreary journey to King William's Land, where the relics of Franklin's party had been found, some of whom Hall hoped to find alive. For five years he lived an Esquimo life, experiencing many thrilling adventures, and escaping many imminent dangers. At one time he saved his own life only by shooting an assailant who was leading against him a party who had conspired to murder him. The result of his long sojourn in this region of cold was a store of knowledge of the Esquimo habits and language, but nothing important relating to the fate of the Franklin expedition. Many sad confirmations were indeed found of the fact before generally accepted, that they had all miserably perished.

On his return, Mr. Hall, nothing daunted by

hardships and failures, commenced writing and lecturing on the theory of an open Polar Sea. As he had done before, so now he succeeded in impressing not only the popular mind but scientific men and statesmen with the plausibility of his theory and the practicability of his plans. Another North Pole expedition was proposed; Congress appropriated to it fifty thousand dollars, and Mr. Hall was appointed its commander. A craft of about four hundred tons, being larger than either of its predecessors on the same errand, was selected, and named the "Polaris." She was a screw-propeller, and rigged as a fore-topsail schooner. Her sides were covered with a six-inch white oak planking, nearly doubling their strength. Her bows were nearly solid white oak, made sharp, and sheathed with iron. One of her boilers was fitted for the use of whale or seal oil, by which steam could be raised if the coal was exhausted. She was supplied with five extraordinary boats. One of these must have been the last Yankee invention in the boat line. It is represented as having a capacity to carry twenty-five men, yet weighing only two hundred and fifty pounds; when not in use it could be folded up and packed snugly away. The "Polaris" was, of course, amply equipped and ably manned, and great and useful results were expected from her. President Grant is said to have entered with interest into this enterprise of Captain Hall, and the nation said, "God bless him and his perilous undertaking!" though many doubted the wisdom of any more Arctic expeditions. A few days before his departure Mr. Hall received from the hand of his friend, Henry Grinnell, a flag of historic note. It had fluttered in the wind near the South Pole with Lieutenant Wilkes, in 1838; had been borne by De Haven far northward; it had gone beyond De Haven's highest in the Kane voyage, and was planted still farther North Poleward by Hayes. "I believe," exclaimed Captain Hall, on receiving it, "that this flag, in the spring of 1872, will float over a new world, in which the North Pole star is its crowning jewel."

The "Polaris" left New York June 29, 1871, tarried for a few days at New London, and was last heard from as she was ready to steam northward, the last of August, from Tussuissak, the most northern of the Greenland outposts. At this place Captain Hall met our old acquaintance, Jensen, of the Hayes expedition. He was flourishing as "governor" of a few humble huts occupied by a few humbler people, and he put on consequential airs in the presence of his white brother. He would not be a dog-driver again to an Arctic exploration—not he! Hall says he had "a face of brass in charging for his dogs." But the full complement of sixty was made up here, and his stock of furs was increased.

As our voyagers are now about to enter upon the terribly earnest conflicts of North Pole explorers, and as their complement of men *and women* are complete, we will further introduce them to our readers.

The commander, Hall, they know; he is well-proportioned, muscular, of medium height, quiet, but completely enthusiastic in his chosen line of duty, believing thoroughly in himself and his enterprise, yet believing well too easily of others, especially of the rough men of his command, some of whom have grown up under the harsh discipline of the whale-ship or the naval service. The next in command is the sailing-master, Captain S. O. Buddington of our last narrative. Captain Tyson, commissioned as assistant navigator to the expedition, has been introduced to the reader at Frobisher Bay, while in command there of a whale-ship. We shall have occasion to become very intimate with him. Here is our old acquaintance, William Morton, whom we knew so favorably by his heroic deeds in the Dr. Kane expedition; he is second mate now.

Of course, Captain Hall's old friends of his first and second Arctic experience, Ebierbing and Tookoolito, his wife, are here. They are now known as Joe and Hannah, and although it does some violence to our taste to drop their Esquimo names, we will conform to the usage about us, and know them in this narrative by these English names. They are accompanied by an adopted daughter from among their people, about ten years old, whom they call Puney.

And here, too, is our old friend Hans, taken on board at Upernavik. Having been with Kane and Hayes, nothing daunted by the perils of their voyages, he is here to see, if possible, with Hall,

Captain Buddington.

the North Pole, though no doubt thinking much more of his twenty-five dollars a month as hunter and dog-driver than of the desired discoveries. His wife and their three children are with him, for, like a good husband and father, he would not be separated from his family. The children are Augustina, a girl about thirteen years, heavy built, and most as large as her mother; Tobias, a boy of perhaps eight, and a little girl, Succi, of four years. Think of such a group daring the known and unknown perils of Arctic ice and cold!

With the rest of the ship's company we shall form acquaintance as our narrative progresses.

On the twenty-fourth of August the "Polaris" left Tussuissak, and fairly began her Arctic fight in the ice, current, and wind encounters of Melville Bay. But on she steamed, passing in a few days through the Bay into the North Water, into Smith Sound, passing Hayes's winter-quarters, yet steaming on by Dr. Kane's winter-quarters, not even pausing to salute our old friends Kalutunah and Myouk, sailing up the west side of Kennedy Channel, the scene of Dr. Hayes's conflicts and heroic achievements, the "Polaris" finally brings up in the ice barriers of north latitude 82° 16′. The highest points of previous voyages in this direction are far south. That new world of which the North Pole star is "the crowning jewel," is less than six hundred miles farther. If that open sea located in this latitude by confident explorers was only a fact, how easily and how soon would the brave "Polaris" be there! But the ice-floe, strong and defiant, and the southern current, were facts, and the open sea nowhere visible. The "Polaris" was taken in hand by the ice and current in the historic, Arctic fashion, and set back about fifty miles. The Ice King had said, "Thus far and no farther," and pointed with his frosty fingers southward.

The "Polaris" early in September was glad to steam in under the land, anchor to an ice-berg, and make her winter-quarters. Captain Hall called the harbor "Thank-God Harbor," and the friendly anchorage "Providence Berg." He had a right here now, for a little farther north, at a place he called "Repulse Harbor," he went ashore, threw the stripes and stars to the breeze, and took possession of the land "in the name of God and the President of the United States." We shall not expect to hear that a territorial representative from this land enters the next Congress. If this part of our national domain has a representative in the life-time of our distinguished acquaintance, Kalutunah, we nominate him for the position, as one of the nearest known inhabitants.

Now commenced in earnest preparations for an Arctic winter. We have seen how this is done, and Hall and some, at least, of his officers knew how to do it. The hunters were abroad at once, and an early prize was a musk-ox weighing three hundred pounds. His meat was tender and good, having no musky odor. This was but the beginning of the good gunning afforded by this far northern region. Two seals were soon after shot.

The country was found to abound in these, and in geese, ducks, rabbits, wolves, foxes, partridges, and bears. The scurvy was not likely to venture near our explorers.

A pleasant incident occurred on shipboard about this time which the reader will better appreciate as our story progresses. It was September twenty-fourth. The Sabbath religious service of the preceding day had been conducted by Chaplain Bryant in his usual happy manner. At its close Commander Hall made some kind, earnest remarks to the men by which their rough natures were made tender, and they sent a letter from the forecastle to the cabin expressing to him their thanks. To this he replied in the following note:—

"SIRS: The reception of your letter of thanks to me of this date I acknowledge with a heart that deeply feels and fully appreciates the kindly feeling that has prompted you to this act. I need not assure you that your commander has, and ever will have, a lively interest in your welfare. You have left your homes, friends, and country; indeed, you have bid farewell for a time to the whole civilized world, for the purpose of aiding me in discovering the mysterious, hidden parts of the earth. I therefore must and shall care for you as a prudent father cares for his faithful children."

October tenth, after careful preparation, Captain Hall started northward on an experiment in the way of sledging. He purposed more extended sledge journeys in the spring, until the Pole itself should be reached. He took two sledges, drawn by seven dogs each. Captain Hall and Joe accompanied one, and Mr. Chester, the mate, and Hans, the other. Their experience on this trip was simply of the Arctic kind, of which we have seen so much. Deep snows, treacherous ice, which was in a state of change by the action of winds and currents, intense cold, and vexed and vicious dogs, all put in their appearance. But Captain Hall says, "These drawbacks are nothing new to an Arctic traveler. We laugh at them, and plod on determined to execute the service faithfully to the end." The sledge expedition was gone two weeks, and traveled north fifty miles. They discovered a lake and a river. They came to the southern cape of a bay which they had seen from the "Polaris" in her drift from above. They named the bay Newman Bay, and attached Senator Sumner's name to the cape. From the top of an ice-berg they surveyed the bay, and believed it extended inland thirty miles. Crossing the mouth of the bay they clambered up its high northern cape, which they called Brevoort. Here they looked westward over the waters up which a good distance past this point the "Polaris" had sailed, and which they had named Robeson Strait. They peered longingly into the misty distance, and fondly hoped to penetrate it with sledge or steamer in the spring. Joe, the architect of the journey, built here their sixth snow-hut. It was warmer than at Thank-God Harbor, and birds, musk-oxen, foxes, and rabbits, were seen, and bear and wolf tracks were in the vicinity. Captain Hall was joyous at the future prospect. He wrote a dispatch from this high latitude in which he says, "We have all been well up to this time." A copy of it was placed in a copper cylinder and buried under a pile of stones. The party turned their faces homeward; Captain Hall's Arctic explorations were ended.

CHAPTER XLI.

DISASTER.

ABOUT noon of October twenty-fourth Captain Hall and his party were seen in the distance approaching the ship. Captain Tyson, the assistant navigator, went out to meet them. Not even a dog had been lost, and Captain Hall was jubilant over his trip and the future of the expedition. While he was absent the work of banking up the "Polaris" with snow as an increased defense against the cold, the building of a house on shore for the stores, and their removal to it from the ship, had gone forward nearly to completion. He looked at the work, greeted all cheerfully, and entered the cabin. He obtained water, and washed and put on clean underclothes. The steward, Mr. Herron, asked him what he would have to eat, expressing at the same time a wish to get him "something nice." He thanked him, but said he wanted only a cup of coffee, and complained of the heat of the cabin. He drank a part of the cup of coffee and set it aside. Soon after he complained of sickness at the stomach, aud threw himself into his berth. Chester, the mate, and Morton, second mate, watched with him all night, during which he was at times delirious. It was thought he was partially paralyzed. The

Unloading Stores from the "Polaris."

surgeon, Dr. Bessel, was in constant attendance, but after temporary improvement he became wildly delirious, imagining some one had poisoned him, and accused first one, then another. He thought he saw blue gas coming from the mouths of persons about him. He refused clean stockings at the hand of Chester, thinking they were poisoned, and he made others taste the food tendered him before taking it himself, even that from sealed cans opened in his cabin. During the night of November seventh he was clear in his mind, and as Surgeon Bessel was putting him to bed and tucking him in, he said in his own kind tone, "Doctor, you have been very kind to me, and I am obliged to you." Early in the morning of November eighth he died, and with his death the American North Polar Expedition was ended.

The grave of their beloved commander was dug by the men under Captain Tyson, inland, southeast, about a half mile from the "Polaris." The frozen ground yielded reluctantly to the picks, and the grave was of necessity very shallow.

On the eleventh a mournful procession moved from the "Polaris" to the place of burial. Though not quite noon it was Arctic night. A weird, electric light filled the air, through which the stars shone brilliantly. Captain Tyson walked ahead with a lantern, followed by Commander Buddington and his officers, and then by the scientific corps, which included the chaplain, Mr. Bryan; the men followed, drawing the coffin on a sled, one of their number bearing another lantern. The fitting pall thrown over the coffin was the American flag. Following the sled were the Esquimo—last in the procession but not the least in the depth and genuineness of their sorrow. At the grave, Tyson held the light for the chaplain to read the burial service. As the solemn, yet comforting words were uttered, "I am the resurrection and the life, saith the Lord," all were subdued to tears. Only from the spirit of the Gospel, breathing its tender influence through these words, was there any cheerful inspiration. The day was cold and dismal, and the wind howled mournfully. Inland over a narrow snow-covered plain, and in the shadowy distance, were huge masses of slate-rock, the ghostly looking sentinels of the barren land beyond. Seaward was the extended ice of Polaris Bay, and the intervening shore strown with great ice-blocks in wild confusion. About five hundred paces away was the little hut called an observatory, and from its flag-staff drooped at half-mast the stars and stripes.

Far away were his loved family and friends, whose prayers had followed him during his adventures in the icy north, who even now hoped for his complete success and safe return; and far away the Christian burial place where it would have been to them mournfully pleasant to have laid him. But he who had declared that he loved the Arctic regions, and to whose ears there was music in its wailing winds, and to whose eyes there was beauty in its rugged, icy barrenness, had found his earthly resting-place where nature was clothed in its wildest

Arctic features. A board was erected over his grave in which was cut:—

"TO THE MEMORY OF

C. F. HALL,

Late Commander of the North Polar Expedition.

Died November 8, 1871,

Aged fifty years."

When the funeral procession had returned to the ship, all moved about in the performance of their duty in gloomy silence. It is sad to record that the great affliction caused by the death of Hall was rendered more intense by the moral condition of the surviving party. Two hideous specters had early in the expedition made their appearance on board the "Polaris." They were the spirits of Rum and Discord! Commander Hall had forbidden the admission of liquor on shipboard, but it had come *with* the medicines whether *of* them or not. It was put under the key of the locker, but it broke out—no, we will not do injustice even to this foulest of demons: *an officer*, selected to guard the safety and comfort of the ship's company, broke open the locker and let it out. This brought upon him a reprimand from Captain Hall, and later a letter of stricture upon his conduct. The doctor's alcohol could not be safely kept for professional purposes, which raised "altercations" on board. So Rum and Discord, always so closely allied, went stalking through the ship, with their horrid train. Insubordination, of course, was from the first in attendance. Hall had, it would seem, in part *persuaded* into submission this ghastly specter. Where, on shipboard, the lives of all depend upon submission to one will, rebellion becomes, in effect, murder. We have seen that Dr. Kane argued down this bloody intruder by a pistol in a steady hand leveled at the head of the chief rebel; and that Dr. Hayes saved his boat party by the same persuasive influence over Kalutunah. But Hall was not reared in the navy, and was cast in a gentle mold.

On the Sunday following the burial of Hall it was announced that from that time the Sunday service would be omitted. "Each one can pray for himself just as well," it was remarked. The faithful chaplain, however, seems to have held religious service afterward for such as pleased to attend. Hall had taken great pleasure in it, and it had, we think, attended every Arctic expedition through which we have carried the reader.

After such a purpose to dismiss public worship from the vessel we are not surprised to learn that "the men made night hideous by their carousings." Nature without had ceased to distinguish night from day, and our explorers did not follow the example of their predecessors in this region, and *make* day and night below decks by requiring the light to be put out at a stated hour. So the noise and card-playing had all hours for their own. Under these circumstances, as if to make the "Polaris" forecastle the counterpart of one of our city "hells," pistols were put into the hands of the men. Discord was now armed, and Alcohol was at the chief place of command.

The Christmas came, but no religious service with it. New-Year's day brought nothing special. The winter dragged along but not the wind, which roared in tempests, and rushed over the floe in currents traveling fifty-three miles an hour. It played wild and free with the little bark which had intruded upon its domains, breaking up the ice around it, and straining at its moorings attached to the friendly berg.

Spring came at last. Hunting became lively and successful. His majesty, the bear, became meat for the hunters after a plucky fight, in which two dogs had their zeal for bear combat fairly subdued. Musk-oxen stood in stupid groups to be shot. White foxes would not be hit at any rate. Birds, trusting to their spread wings, were brought low, plucked and eaten. Seals coming out of their holes, and stretching themselves on the ice to enjoy dreamily a little sunshine, to which they innocently thought they had a right as natives of the country, were suddenly startled by the crack of the rifles of Hans and Joe, and often under such circumstances died instantly of lead. It seemed hardly fair. In fact we are confident that the animals about Polaris Bay contracted a prejudice against the strangers, except the white foxes, who could not see what *hurt* these hunters did—at least to foxes—and they were of a mind that it was decided fun to be hunted by them.

The Esquimo have been in this high latitude in the not distant past, as a piece of one of their sledges was found.

Soon after Hall's death the chief officers had mutually pledged in writing that, "It is our honest intention to honor our flag, and to hoist it upon the most northern point of the earth." During the spring and summer some journeys northward were made, but were not extended beyond regions already visited. The eye which would have even now looked with hope and faith to the region of the star which is the "crowning jewel" of the central north, was dim in death. Captain Buddington, now in chief command, had faith and hope in the homeward voyage only.

On the twelfth of August, 1872, the "Polaris" was ready, with steam up, for the return trip. On that very day there was added to the family of Hans a son. All agreed to name him Charlie Polaris, thus prettily suggesting the name of the late commander and of the ship. Little Charlie was evidently disgusted with his native country, for he immediately turned his back upon it, the ship steaming away that afternoon. The "Polaris" had made a tolerably straight course up, but now made a zig-zag one back. On she went, steaming, drifting, banging against broken floes, through the waters over which we have voyaged with Kane and Hayes, until they came into the familiar regions of Hayes's winter-quarters. On the afternoon of the fifteenth of October the wind blew a terrific gale from the north-west. The floe, in

Perilous Situation of the "Polaris."

an angry mood, *nipped* the ship terribly. She groaned and shrieked, in pain but not in terror, for with her white oak coat of mail she still defied her icy foe, now rising out of his grasp, and then falling back and breaking for herself an easier position. The hawsers were attached to the floe, and the men stood waiting for the result of the combat on which their lives depended. At this moment the engineer rushed to the deck with the startling announcement that the "Polaris" had sprung a leak, and that the water was gaining on the pumps. "The captain threw up his arms, and yelled the order to throw every thing on the ice." No examination into the condition of the leak seems to have been made. A panic followed, and overboard went every thing in reckless confusion, many valuable articles falling near the vessel, and, of course, were drawn under by her restless throes and lost. Overboard went boats, provisions, ammunition, men, women, and children, nobody knew what nor who. It was night—an intensely dark, snowy, tempestuous night.

It was in this state of things, when the ship's stores and people were divided between the floe and her deck, that the anchors planted in the floe tore away, and the mooring lines snapped like pack-thread, and away went the "Polaris" in the darkness, striking against huge ice-cakes, and drifting none knew where. "Does God care for sparrows?" and will he not surely care for these imperiled explorers, both those in the drifting steamer, and those on the floe whom he alone can save, unhoused in an Arctic night on which no sun will rise for many weeks, exposed to the caprice of winds, currents, and the ever untrustworthy ice-raft on which they are cast?

We will leave the floe party awhile in His care, and follow the fortunes of the brave little vessel and her men.

CHAPTER XLII.

THE LAST OF THE "POLARIS."

THOSE left on board of the "Polaris" were oppressed with fears both for themselves and those on the floe. The leak in the ship was serious, and the water was gaining in the hold, and threatened to reach and put out the fires, and thus render the engine useless. Besides, the deck pumps were frozen up, and only two lower ones could be used. But "just before it was too late," hot water was procured from the boiler and poured in buckets-full into the deck-pumps, and they were thawed out. The men then worked at the pumps with an energy inspired by imminent danger of death. They had already been desperately at work for six unbroken hours, and ere long the fight for life was on the verge of failure. Just then came to the fainting men the shout "steam's up," and tireless steam came to the rescue of weary muscles.

As the dim light of the morning of October sixteenth dawned on the anxious watchers, they saw that they had been forced by the violent wind out of Baffin Bay into Smith Sound.

Not until now, since the hour of separation, had they counted their divided company. The assistant navigator, the meteorologist, all the Esquimo, and six seamen were missing; part of the dogs had also gone with the floe party. Fourteen men remained, including the commander and the mate, the surgeon, and the chaplain.

Men were sent to the mast-head to look for the missing ones, but the most careful gaze with the best glass failed to discern them. Hope of their safety was inspired by the fact that they had all the boats, even to the little scow; yet it was not certainly known that the boats had not been sunk or drifted off in the darkness, and thus lost to them. So all was tantalizing uncertainty.

An examination revealed the encouraging fact that a good supply of fuel and provisions remained on board. A breeze sprung up at noon by whose aid the "Polaris" was run eastward, through a fortunate lead, as near to the land as possible. Here lines were carried out on the floe and made fast to the hummocks, all the anchors having been lost. She lay near the shore, and grounded at low water. An examination showed that the vessel was so battered and leaky, that surprise was excited that she had not gone down before reaching the shore. It was decided at once that she could not be made to float longer. The steam-pumps were stopped, the water filled her hold, and decided her fate.

The sheltered place into which the "Polaris" had by Divine guidance entered was Life-Boat Cove, only a little north of Etah Bay, every mile of which we have surveyed in former visits. The famous city of Etah with its two huts was not far away, but out of it and its vicinity had come timely blessings to other winter-bound explorers.

Our party at once commenced to carry ashore the provisions, clothing, ammunition, and all such articles from the vessel as might make them comfortable. The spars, sails, and some of the heavy wood-work of the cabin, were used in erecting a house. When done their building was quite commodious, being twenty-two feet by fourteen. The sails aided in making the roof, which proved to be water-tight, and the snow thrown up against the sides made it warm. Within, it was one room for all, and for all purposes. "Bunks" were made against the sides for each of the fourteen men. A stove with cooking utensils was brought from the ship and set up; lamps were suspended about the room, and a table with other convenience from the cabin were put in order.

But before this was done a party of Esquimo with five sledges made their appearance. They stopped at a distance, and signified their friendly purpose by their customary wild gesticulations and antics. The white men at first took them for the floe party, and raised three rousing cheers of welcome. We doubt not, though it is not stated, that they were led on by our special friend, Kalutunah. The surly Sipsu, it will be remembered, had received what he had sought to give to another, a harpoon planted in the back, and was dead. So there was left none to rival Kalutunah. Myouk, the boy that was, in Kane's day, was reported as an old man now. Esquimo grow old rapidly. The whole party went to work with a will, having pleasant visions before them of a new stock of needles, knives, and other white-man treasures. They clambered over the hummocky floe, bringing loads of coal from the ship, and with their sleds brought fresh-water ice for the melting apparatus. Several families finally came, built their huts near the vessel, and spent the winter. The ship-wrecked whites had nearly worn out their fur suits, and their supply had been greatly reduced by the losses on the floe. So the Esquimo replenished their stock, and their women repaired the worn ones. Thus God makes the humblest and the weakest able at times to render essential help to the strong, and none need be useless.

The winter wore off. There was no starvation, nor even short rations. The coal burned cheerfully in the stove until February, and then fuel torn from the "Polaris" supplied its place. The friendly natives brought fresh walrus meat, and scurvy was kept away. For all their valuable services the Esquimo felt well repaid in the coveted treasures which were given them.

The time during the sunless days was passed in reading, writing, amusements, and discussions, according to the taste and inclination of each. Of course there were some daily domestic duties to be done. The scientific men pursued their inquiries so far as circumstances allowed.

The dismal story which has so often pained our ears concerning the Esquimo was true of them generally during the winter—they were suffering with cold and hunger, and three, one of whom was Myouk, died. The explorers returned the Esquimo kindness by sharing with them, in a measure, their own stock of provisions.

The spring came, and with it successful hunting. One deer was shot, and some hares caught. Chester, the mate, who seems to have been *the* Yankee of the party, planned, and assisted the carpenter in building two boats. The material was wrenched from the "Polaris." They were each twenty-five feet long and five feet wide, square fore and aft, capable of carrying, equally divided between them, the fourteen men, two months' provisions, and other indispensable articles. When these were done they made a smaller boat, and presented it to the Esquimo; it would aid them in getting eggs and young birds about the shore.

Clear water did not reach Life-Boat Cove until the last of May. On its appearance in the immediate vicinity the waiting explorers put every thing in readiness for their departure. The boats were laden, and each man assigned his place. Bags were made of the canvas sails in which to carry the provisions. What remained of the "Polaris" was given to the Esquimo chief—we guess to our friend Kalutunah—as an acknowledgment of favors received. On the third of June, in fine spirits and good health, the explorers launched their boats and sailed southward. At first the boats leaked badly, but they sailed and rowed easily, and proved very serviceable. It was continuous day, and the weather favorable. Seals could be had for the pains of hunting them, and the sea-fowl were so plenty that ten were at times brought down at a shot. On the downward trip old localities were touched, such as Etah, Hakluyt Island, and Northumberland Island. The average amount of Arctic storms were encountered, the drift ice behaved in its usual manner, though not as badly as it has been known to do. The little crafts had their hair-breadth escapes, and were battered not a little. Every night, when the toils of the day were over, the boats were drawn upon the floe, every thing taken out, and the only hot meal of the day was prepared. Each boat carried pieces of rope from the "Polaris," and a can of oil. With these a fire was made in the bottom of an iron pot. Over this fire they made their steaming pots of tea.

The party halted a while at Fitz Clarence Rock in Booth Bay, about sixteen miles south of Cape Parry, and within sight of the high, bleak plain on which Dr. Hayes's boat-party spent their fearful winter. On the tenth day of their voyaging they had reached Cape York. In comparison to Dr. Kane's trip over the same waters, theirs was as a summer holiday excursion. But Melville Bay was now before them with its defiant bergs, hummocks, currents, stormy winds, and blinding snows—a horrid crew! No wonder that the fear prevailed among them that if not rescued they could never reach any settlement. Chester, however, said, "We can, and will." But the rescuers were not afar off. For another ten days they were made to feel that their battle for life was to be a hard-fought one. On the twenty-third they saw, away in the distance, what appeared to be a whaler. Could it be! They dared scarcely trust their eyes, for the object was ten miles away. Yes, it was a steamer, and beset, too, so she could not get away. New courage was inspired, and they toiled on. But for this timely spur to their zeal they would have lost heart, for one of the boats in being lifted over the hummocks was badly stove, and their provisions were giving out, though they had calculated that they had two months' supply. Soon after they saw the steamer they were seen by the watch from the mast-head. They were taken for Esquimo, but a sharp lookout was kept upon their movement, which soon showed them to be white men. Signals of recognition were immediately given, and eighteen picked men were sent to their relief. Seeing this, Captain Buddington sent forward two men, and the rescuers soon met and returned with them. With even this addition to their strength, it took six hours to drag the boats the twelve miles which intervened between them and the whaler. They were received with a kind-hearted welcome by the noble Scotchman, Captain Allen, of the "Ravenscraig," of Dundee. Their toils were over, and their safety insured. We will return to those on the floe.

CHAPTER XLIII.

THE FEARFUL SITUATION.

ONE of the anchors of the "Polaris," in starting on the night of the separation, tore off a large piece of the floe with three men upon it. As the "Polaris" swept past them they cried out in agony, "What shall we do?" Captain Buddington shouted back, "We can do nothing for you. You have boats and provisions; you must shift for yourselves." This was the last word from the "Polaris."

Seeing the sad plight of these men, Captain Tyson, who from the first had been upon the floe, took "the donkey," a little scow which had been tossed upon the ice, and attempted to rescue them. But the donkey almost at once sunk, and he jumped back upon the floe and launched one of the boats. Some of the other men started in the other boat at the same time, and the three men were soon united to the rest of the floe party.

One of the last things Tyson drew out of the way of the vessel as its heel was grinding against the parting floe were some musk-ox skins. They lay across a widening crack, and in a moment more would have been sunk in the deep, or crushed between colliding hummocks. Rolled up in one of them, and cozily nestling together, were two of Hans's children! Does not God care for *children!*

Our darkness and storm-beset party did not dare to move about much, for they could not tell the size of the ice on which they stood, nor at what moment they might step off into the surging waters. So they rolled themselves up in the musk-ox skins and *slept!* Captain Tyson alone did not lie down, but walked cautiously about during the night. The morning came, and with it a revelation of their surroundings. Hugh bergs were in sight, which had in the storm and darkness charged upon the floe, and caused the breaking up of the preceding night. It had been a genuine Arctic assault. Their own raft was nearly round, and about four miles in circumference, and immovably locked between several grounded bergs. It was snow-covered, and full of hillocks and intervening ponds of water which the brief summer sun had melted from their sides. Those who had laid down were covered with snow, and looked like little mounds. When the party roused, the first thing they thought of was the ship. But she was nowhere to be seen. A lead opened to the shore inviting their escape to the land. Captain Tyson ordered the men to get the boats in immediate readiness, reminding them of the uncertainty of the continued opening of the water, and of the absolute necessity of instant escape from the floe in order to regain the ship and save their lives. But the men were in no hurry, and obedience to orders had long been out of their line. They were hungry and tired, and were determined to eat first; and they didn't want a cold meal, and so they made tea and chocolate, and cooked canned meat. This done they must change their wet clothes for dry ones.

In the mean time the drifting ice *was* in a hurry and had shut up in part the lead. But Tyson was determined to try to reach the shore though the difficulties had so greatly increased during the delay. The boats were laden and launched, but when they were about half way to the shore the lead closed, and they returned to the floe and hauled up the boats. Just then the "Polaris" was seen under both steam and sail. She was eight or ten miles away, but signals were set to attract her attention, and she was watched with a glass with intense interest until she disappeared behind an island. Soon after, Captain Tyson sent two men to a distant part of the floe to a house made of poles, which he had erected for the stores soon after they began to be thrown from the vessel. In going for these poles the steamer was again seen, apparently fast in the ice behind the island. She could not then come to the floe party, being beset and without boats, and so Tyson ordered the men to get the boats ready for another attempt to reach the land, and thus in time connect with the vessel. He lightened the boats of all articles not absolutely necessary, that they might be drawn to the water safely and with speed. He then went ahead to find the nearest and best route for embarking. The grounded bergs in the mean while, relaxed their grasp upon the explorers' ice-raft, and they began to drift southward. With malicious intent, on came a terrific snow-storm at the same time. Tyson hurried back to hasten up the men. They were in no hurry, but, with grumbling and trifling, finally made ready as they pretended, one boat crowded with every thing both needful and worthless. When at last it was dragged to the water's edge, it was ascertained that the larger part of the oars and the rudder had been left at the camp far in the rear. In this crippled condition the boat was launched. But not only oars and rudder, but *will* on the part of the men was wanting. So the boat was drawn upon the floe, and left with all its valuables near the water. The night was approaching, the storm was high, and the men were weary, so no attempt was made to return it to the old camp. All went back to the middle of the floe. Tyson, Mr. Meyers, one of the scientific corps, and the Esquimo, made a canvas shelter, using the poles as a frame, and the others camped near them. Captain Tyson, after eating a cold supper, rolled himself in a musk-ox skin, and lay down for the first sleep he had sought for forty-eight hours. His condition seemed to be a specially hard one. While, on the night of the great disaster, he was striving to save the general stores, the saving of which proved the salvation of the company, others were looking after their personal property, so they had their full supply of furs and fire-arms, while his were left in the ship. He, however, slept soundly until the morning, when he was startled by a shriek from the Esquimo. The floe had played them an Arctic trick; it had broken and set the whole party adrift on an ice-raft not more than one hundred and fifty yards square. What remained of their old floe of four miles' circumference contained the house made of poles, in which remained six bags of bread, and the loaded boat, in which were the greater part of their valuables. Here was a fearful state of things! Yet one boat remained with which they might have gone after the other one, but the men seemed infatuated and refused to go. Away the little raft sailed, crumbling as it went, assuring its passengers that they must all stow away in their one boat or soon be dropped in the sea. For four days they thus drifted, during which the Esquimo shot several seals. On the twenty-first Joe was using the spy-glass, and suddenly shouted for joy. He had spied the lost boat lodged on a part of the old floe which had swung against the little raft of our party. He and Captain Tyson, with a dog-team, instantly started for it, and after a hard pull returned with boat and cargo. Soon after, their old floe, in an accommodating mood, thrust itself against the one they were on, the boats were passed over, and every thing was again together—boats and provisions.

Let us now look around upon our party more critically. The whole number was twenty, including the ten weeks' old Charlie Polaris, who, of course, was somebody. As we have stated, *all* the Esquimo were of this party. Both the cook and steward were here. Much the larger number of the dogs belonging to the expedition were on the floe, but no sledges. Fortunately, in addition to the two boats, one of the kayaks had been saved. It might, in the skillful hands of a Joe, meet some emergency.

As there was only faint hope now of again seeing the "Polaris," and as their ice-boat seemed to sail farther and farther from the shore, they began to make the best winter-quarters their circumstances allowed. Under the direction of Joe, as architect and builder, several snow houses were put up. One was occupied by Captain Tyson and Mr. Myers; one by Joe and family; a larger one by the men; and one was used for the provisions, and one for a cook house. All these were united by an arched passage way. Hans and family located their house apart from the others, but near.

The huts erected, their next pressing need was sledges. The men, with great difficulty, dragged some lumber from the old store-house, and a passable one was made.

Though the quantity of provisions was quite large, yet with nineteen persons to consume it, (not to reckon little Charlie's mouth, who looked elsewhere for his supply,) and with possibly no addition for six months, it was alarmingly small. Besides, in their unprincipled greed, some of the party broke into the store-room and took more than a fair allowance. So the party agreed upon two meals a day, and a weighed allowance at each meal.

It was now the last of October. The sun had ceased to show his pleasant face, and the long night was setting in. To add to their discomfort, the question of light and fuel assumed a serious aspect. The men, either from want of skill or patience, or both, did not succeed well in using seal fat for these purposes, in the Esquimo fashion; so they began, with a reckless disregard to their future safety, to break up and burn one of the boats.

Hans, with a true Esquimo instinct, when the short allowance pinched him, began to kill and eat the dogs. He might be excused, however. Four children, with their faces growing haggard, looked to him for food.

Thus situated, our floe party drifted far away from the land—drifting on and on, whether they slept or woke—drifting they knew not to what end.

CHAPTER XLIV.

THE WONDERFUL DRIFT.

EARLY in November Captain Tyson saw through his glass, about twelve miles off to the southeast, the Cary Islands, so they were in the "North water" of Baffin Bay, and south-west from Cape Parry, where we have been so many times. From this cape, or a little south of it, it would not be a great sledge trip to where they last saw the "Polaris," and where they had reason to think she now was. So our party made one more effort to reach the shore. The boats being in readiness the night before, they started early in the morning. Of course their day was now only a noon twilight, and the *morning* was most mid-day. But the floe was not in a favoring mood. The hummocks were as hard in their usage of the boats and men as usual. The deceitful cracks in the ice at one time put the lives of the dogs and men in great peril; and, as if these obstacles were not enough, a storm brought up its forces against them. They had dragged the boats half way to the shore when they retreated "before superior forces."

Their huts being of perishable material, were reconstructed. A little later the men built a large snow hut as "a reserve." All were weak through insufficient food. Mr. Meyers was nearly prostrate, and went to live with the men; Captain Tyson, whose scanty clothing, added to care and short rations, caused him to suffer much, took up his quarters with Joe and Hannah, and their little Puney. Not the least of the trial in the Esquimo huts were the piteous cries of the children for food. Joe and Hans were out with their guns every day during the three hours' twilight, hunting seals. The first one captured was shot by Joe, November sixth. Nearly two weeks passed before any further success attended the hunters; then several were shot, and Captain Tyson, who was ready to perish, had one full meal—a meal of uncooked seal meat, skin, hair, and all, washed down with seal blood. *Some* others had not been so long without a full meal, as the bread continued to be stolen.

The *home* Thanksgiving Day came. A little extra amount of the canned meat was allowed each one, and all had a taste of mock-turtle soup and canned green corn, kept for this occasion, to which was added a few pieces of dried apple. How far it all fell short of the *home* feast may be judged by the fact that Captain Tyson, to satisfy the fierce hunger which remained after dinner, finished "with eating strips of frozen seals' entrails, and lastly seal skin, hair and all."

The hunters had seen tracks of bears, so they were on the lookout for them while they hunted seal. One day Joe and Hans went out as usual with their guns. They lost sight of each other and of the camp. Joe returned quite late, expecting to find Hans already in his hut. When he learned that he had not returned, he, as well as others, felt concerned about him. Accompanied by one of the men, he went in search of him. As the two, guns in hand, were stumbling over the hummocks, they saw in the very dim twilight, as they thought, a bear. Their guns were instantly leveled and brought to the sight, and their mouths almost tasted a bear-meat supper. "Hold on there! That's not a bear! what is it?" "Why, it's Hans!" Well, he *did* look in the darkness like a bear, as in his shaggy coat he clambered, on all-fours, over the ice-hills.

December came in with its continuous night. Seals could not be successfully hunted in the darkness, and where seals could not be seen bears would not make their appearance. The rations became smaller than ever, and ghastly, horrid starvation seemed encamped among our drifting, forlorn party. Under these circumstances a specter even *worse* than starvation appeared to Joe. To him, at least, it was a terrifying reality. It was the demon form of Cannibalism! He had looked into the eyes of the men in the big hut, and they spoke to him of an intention to save themselves by first killing and eating Hans and family, and then taking him and his. He and Hannah were greatly terrified, and he handed his pistol to Captain Tyson, which he was not willing to part with before. He was assured that the least child should not be touched for so horrid a purpose without such a defense as the pistol could give.

Christmas came. The last ham had been kept for this occasion, and it was divided among all, with a few other dainties, in addition to the usual morsel.

The shore occasionally appeared in the far away distance. They were drifting through Baffin Bay toward the *western* side, so that their craft evidently did not intend to land them at any of the familiar ports of Greenland. It seemed to have an ambition to drop them nearer home.

As the year was going out, and Joe's family were gnawing away at some *dried* seal skin, submitted, to be sure, to a process Hannah called cooking, a shout was heard from him. "Kayak! kayak!" he cried. He had shot a seal, and it was floating away. Fortunately the kayak was at hand, and the game was bagged. As usual, it was divided among all. The *eyes* were given to Charlie Polaris, and they were nice in his eyes, and mouth, too.

New Years came, and Captain Tyson dined on two feet of frozen seal entrails, and a little seal fat. There was now nothing to burn except what little seal blubber they could spare for that purpose. One boat had been burned, their only sled had gone the same way, and the reckless, desperate men could hardly be restrained from burning the only one now remaining, and thus cut off all good hope of final escape. To be sure, their provocation to this act was very great; the temperature was thirty-six below zero! In their strait, the desperate expedient was entertained of trying to get to land. The emaciated men would have to drag the loaded boat over the hummocky ice without a sledge. The women and children must be added to the load or abandoned. It would be a struggle for life against odds more fearful than that which now oppressed them. But what *should* they do! God knew! Hark! what shout is that! "Kayak! kayak!" The kayak was at hand, but it had to be carried a mile. Yet it paid, for a seal shot by Joe was secured just in time to keep the men from utter desperation. To this item of comfort another was added a few days later. The sun reappeared January nineteenth, after an absence of eighty-three days, and remained shining upon them two hours. He brought hope to fainting hearts. Through January there was a seal taken at long intervals, but one always came just before it was too late! The men continued to grumble and deceive themselves with the idea of soon getting to Disco, "where rum and tobacco were plenty." How sad that man can sink *below* the brute, which, however hungry, never cries out for "rum and tobacco!"

Leaving for a moment the white men, let us look into the Esquimo huts and see how the terrible condition of things affects them. The men are almost always out hunting, but just now, as we step into Joe's snow dwelling, he is at home. The only light or fire is that which comes from the scanty supply of seal oil. Captain Tyson is trying to write with a pencil in his journal, but he appears cold in his scanty covering of furs, and looks weak and hungry. Joe and Hannah are striving to pass away the weary hours by playing checkers on an old piece of canvas which the captain has marked into squares with his pencil. They are using buttons for men, and seem quite interested in the game. Little Puney is sitting by, wrapped in a musk-ox skin, uttering at intervals a low, plaintive cry for food. It is the most cheerful home "on board" the floe, but surely it is cheerless enough.

We shall not wish to tarry long in the hut of Hans, for besides the unavoidable misery of the place, Mr. and Mrs. Hans are noted for the boarders they keep—about their persons. Under the most favorable circumstances they regard bathing as one of the barbarous customs of civilization. The reader will recollect that the first experience Mrs. Hans had of a personal cleansing was on board Dr. Hayes's vessel, and she then thought it a joke imposed by the white people's religion, too grievous to be borne. On another exploring vessel she and her husband were cruelly required to put off their long-worn garments, wash and put on clean ones, and put the old "in a strong pickle," for an obvious reason. It is not certainly known that they were ever washed at any other times.

Mrs. Hans's hut is not in the most tidy order, but the circumstances must be taken into the account, and also the fact of the sad neglect of her early domestic education. We have just drifted from her native land—or, rather, *ice*—where she was married, in Dr. Kane's time, it being a runaway match, at least on the part of the husband.

Well, here they are, father, mother, and four children, on a voyage unparalleled in the history of navigation. Mr. and Mrs. Hans do not play any household games; they do not know what to do at home, except to eat, and feed the children, and make and mend skin clothing. We know full well to what sad disadvantage the eating is subjected at the time of our call, and we are authorized to say, to the credit of Mrs. Hans, that as to the making and mending, she has been of real service to the men on this voyage.

The children of Hans cannot fail to attract our attention and sympathy. Augustina, the first-born, usually fat and rugged if not ruddy, is thin and pale now, and sits chewing a bit of dried seal skin, or something of the sort, and trying to get from it a drop of nourishment; her brother, Tobias, has thrown his head into her lap as she sits on the ground. The poor little fellow has been sick, unable to eat even the small allowance of meat given him, and has lived, one hardly knows how, on a little dry bread. Succi, the four-year-old girl, squats on the ground—that is, the canvas-covered ice floor—hugging her fur skin about her, and in a low, moaning tone repeats, "I is *so* hungry!" Her mother is trying to pick from the lamp, for the children, a few bits of "tried-out" scraps of blubber. Little Charlie's head is just discernible in the fur hood which hangs from the mother's neck at her back. If he gets enough to eat, which we fear is not the case, he is sweetly ignorant of the perils of this, his first trip, in the voyage of life. We shall not want to stay longer in this sad place.

February was a dreadful month on board the floe. The huts were buried under the snow. It was with difficulty that Joe and Hans, almost the entire dependence of the party, could go abroad for game, and when they did they secured a few seals only, very small, and now and then a dovekie, a wee bit of a pensive sea-bird. Norwhal, the sea unicorn, were shot in several instances, but they sunk in every case and were lost. Hunger and fear seemed to possess the men in the large tent, and Joe and Hannah began to be again terrified by the thought that these hunger-mad men would kill and eat them.

Now, will not God appear to help those in so helpless a condition? Yes, his hand has ever been wonderfully apparent in all Arctic perils. On the second of March, just when the dark cloud of these drifting sufferers was never darker, it parted, and a flood of light burst upon their camp. Joe shot an *oogjook*, belonging to the largest species of seal. He was secured and dragged by all hands to the huts. He measured nine feet, weighed about seven hundred pounds, and contained, by estimation, thirty gallons of oil. There was a shout of seal in the camp! The warm blood was relished like new milk, and drank freely. All eat and slept, and woke to eat again, and hunger departed for the time from the miserable huts it had so long haunted. Joe and Hannah dismissed their horrid visions of cannibalism. God was the helper of these hungry ones, and they *were* helped.

CHAPTER XLV.

THE WONDERFUL ESCAPE.

OUR voyagers needed all the strength and courage which the timely capture of the great seal had given them. They had drifted into a warmer sea, and windy March was well upon them. Their floe began to herald its fast approaching dissolution. The weary and anxious drifters were startled by day, and awakened suddenly by night, by a rumbling, mingled with fearful grindings and crashes underneath them. Heavy ice-cakes, over-rode by the heavier floe, ground along its under surface, and when finding an opening of thin ice, rushed with a thundering sound to the upper surface. The din was at times so great that it seemed to combine all alarming sounds:—

> "Through all its scale the horrid discord ran;
> Now mocked the beast—now took the groan of man."

On the eleventh a storm commenced. Whole fleets of icebergs, having broken away from the icy bands in which the floe had held them, hovered round to charge upon the helpless campers. The vast area of ice on which they had been riding for so many months was lifted in places by mighty seas beneath, causing it to crack with a succession of loud reports and dismal sounds, some of which seemed to be directly under them. The wind drove before it a dense cloud of snow, so that one could scarcely see a yard. Night came with a darkness that could be felt. The icy foundation of their camp might separate at any moment, and tumble their huts about their ears, or plunge them in the sea. They gathered their few treasures together, and stood ready to fly—but where? Death seemed to guard every avenue of escape. Suddenly, soon after the night set in, the disruption came. Their floe was shattered, with a fearful uproar, into hundreds of pieces, and they went surging off among the fragments on a piece less than a hundred yards square. They were within twenty yards of its edge, but God had kindly forbid the separation to run through their camp and sever them from their boat or from each other.

After raging sixty hours the storm abated, and their little ice-ship drifted rapidly in the pack. A goodly number of seals were shot, and they began to breathe more freely. After a short time another *oogjook* was captured, so food was plenty.

March wore away, seals were plenty, and readily taken; and though the bergs ground together and made fierce onsets into the pack, our ice-ship held gallantly on her way. One night the inmates of Joe's hut were about retiring, when a noise was heard outside. "What is it, Joe? is the ice breaking up?" Joe does not stop to answer, but rushes out. But in ten seconds he comes back in a greater hurry, pale and breathless. "There's a bear close to my kayak," he exclaims in an excited tone. Now the situation was this: The kayak was within ten paces of the entrance to the hut, and the loaded guns, which can never be kept in an Esquimo hut on account of the moisture, were in and leaning against the kayak. If the bear should take a notion to put his nose at the hut door, and, liking the odor, knock down the snow wall with his strong paw, and commence a supper on one of its inmates, what was to hinder him? But bears, like many young people, often fail to improve their golden opportunities. He found some seal fat and skins in the kayak, and these he pulled out, and walked off with them a rod or two to enjoy the feast. Joe crept out of the hut, and ran to alarm the men. Captain Tyson followed, slipped softly up to the kayak and seized his gun, but in taking it he knocked down another one and alarmed the bear, who looked up and growled his objections to having his supper disturbed. Tyson leveled his rifle, snapped it, but it missed fire. He tried a second and third time, and it did not go—but *he* did, for his bearship was taking the offensive. Content to see his enemy flee, the bear returned to his supper. How many foolish bears have we seen on our explorations lose their lives by an untimely *eating;* but some men, more foolish, lose *more than life* BY DRINKING. The captain returned to the field with a new charge in his gun. This time it sent a ball *through* the bear; the ball entering the left shoulder and passing through the heart, came out at the other side. He staggered, but before he fell Joe had sent another ball into his vitals. He dropped dead instantly. This affair occurred when it was too dark to see many yards, and was much pleasanter in its results than in its duration.

The seal hunting was successful, and with bear meat and blubber, a full store, there was no hunger unappeased; but the wind blew a gale, and the sailless, rudderless, oarless little ice-ship, now banging against a berg, and now in danger of being run down by one, all the while growing alarmingly smaller, finally shot out into the open sea away from the floe. This would not do. So, feeling that they might soon be dropped into the sea, they loaded the boat with such things as was strictly necessary, and all hands getting aboard, sailed away. A part of their ammunition, their fresh meat, a full month's supply, and many other desirable things, were abandoned. The boat, only intended to carry eight persons, was so overloaded with its twenty, including children, that it was in danger of being swamped at any moment. The frightened children cried, and the men looked sober. They sailed about twenty miles west, and landed on the first tolerably safe piece of ice which they met. Hans and family nestled down in the boat, and the rest, spreading on the floe what skins they had, set up a tent, and all, after eating a dry supper of bread and pemmican, lay down to rest. Thus, boating by day, and camping on the ice at night for several days, they drew up on the fourth of April upon a solid looking floe. Snow-huts were built, seals were taken, and hope revived. But what is hope, resting on Arctic promises? The gale was abroad again, the sea boisterous, and their floe was thrown into a panic. Fearful noises were heard beneath and around them, and their icy foundations quaked with fear. Joe's snow-hut was shaken down. He built it again, and then lot and house fell off into the sea and disappeared. Thus warned, the camp was pushed farther back from the water. But they did not know where the crack and separation would next come. Thus they lived in anxious watchings through weary days, the gale unabated. Finally, one night, the feared separation came. All hands except Mr. Meyers were in the tent; near them, so near a man could scarcely walk between, was the boat, containing Meyers and the kayak; but with mischievous intent, the crack run so as to send the boat drifting among the breaking and over-lapping ice. Mr. Meyers could not manage it, of course, under such circumstances, and the kayak was of no use to any but an Esquimo, so he set it afloat, hoping it would drift to the floe-party. Here was a fearful situation! The floe-party, as well as Mr. Meyers, was sure to perish miserably if the boat was not returned. There was only a dim light, and objects at a short distance looked hazy. It was a time for instant and desperate action. Joe and Hans took their paddles and ice-spears and started for the boat, jumping from one piece of floating, slippery ice to another. They were watched in breathless suspense until they *seemed*, in the shadowy distance, to have reached the boat, and then all was shut out in the darkness.

The morning came, and the floe party were glad to see that the boat had three men in it. It was a half mile off, and the kayak was as far away in another direction. It was soon clear that the boat could not be brought back without a stronger force. Tyson led the way, and finally all but two of the men made the desperate passage of the floating ice to the imperiled craft. It was with difficulty that, with their combined force, the boat was returned to the floe. The kayak was also recovered.

For a brief time there was quiet all around. The aurora gleamed, and displayed its wonderful beauty of form and motion; while the majestic icebergs, in every varied shape, reflected its sparkling light. The grandeur of sea and sky seemed a mockery to the danger-beset voyagers. The elements might be grand, but they had combined to destroy them, for a new form of peril now appeared. The sea came aboard of their icy craft. They were sitting one evening under their frail tent, the boat near, when a wave swept over their floe, carrying away tent, clothing, provisions—every thing except what was on their persons or in the boat. The women and children had been put on board in fear of such an occurrence, and the men had just time to save themselves by clinging to the gunwale. The boat itself was borne into the middle of the floe. When the wave subsided the boat was dragged back, lest another push by a succeeding one might launch it into the sea from the other side. It was well they did this, for another wave bore it to the opposite edge and partly slipped it into the water. This game of surging the boat from one side to the other of the floe, was kept up from nine o'clock in the evening to seven in the morning. All this time the men were in the water, fighting the desperate battle for its safety, and the preservation of their own lives; the conflict being made more terrible by the fact that every wave bore with it ice-blocks from a foot square to those measuring many yards, having sharp edges and jagged corners, with which it battered their legs until they were black and blue. It was the severest test of their courage and endurance yet experienced. But God was their helper. Not one perished, and when the defeated sea was by his voice commanded to retire, and the day appeared, they were not seriously harmed. But they were cold and wet, without a change of clothes and utterly provisionless.

It is not surprising that after their rough handling on the floe they should seek a larger and safer one. This they did, launching their crowded boat into the turbulent sea, and, working carefully along, succeeded in landing safely on one stronger looking; nothing worse happening than the tumbling overboard of the cook, who was quickly rescued. Here, cold, half-drowned, hungry, and weary to faintness, they tried to dry and warm themselves in the feeble rays of the sun, and wait for their food at the hand of the great Provider in the use of such means as were yet left to them. They had preserved their guns and a small supply of powder and shot. Snow and rain came on, and continued until noon of the next day, April twenty-second. Their hunger was fearful. Mr. Meyers had been slightly frost-bitten when drifting away alone in the boat, his health seemed broken, and he was actually starving.

In the afternoon of this day Joe went as usual with his gun. He had caught nothing on this floe, and now there were no signs of seals, though it was his fourth time out that day. What should they do? God had their relief all arranged. Joe saw what he did not expect to see, and what was seldom seen so far south—a bear! He ran back to the boat, called Hans with his trusty rifle, and the two lay down behind the hummocks. All were ordered to lie down, keep perfectly quiet, and feign themselves seals, the Esquimo helping out the deception by imitating the seal bark. Bruin came on cautiously. He, too, was hungry. What are those black objects, and what is that noise, he seemed to say? They don't look *quite* like seals! The noise is not *just* like the seal cry! But hunger is a weighty reason with men and bears, on the side of what they desire to believe, so the bear came on. When fairly within an easy range both rifles cracked, and he fell dead. The whole party arose with a shout. Polar was dragged to the boat and skinned. His warm blood slaked their raging thirst. His meat, tender and good, satisfied their gnawing hunger. They were saved from a terrible death! Seals were secured soon after, and hope again revived.

It was not long before their ice-craft crumbled away, so they were obliged to repeat the experiment, always full of danger, of launching into the sea and making for a larger and safer one. April twenty-eighth they were beset by a fleet of bergs, which were crashing against each other with a thundering noise, and occasionally turning a threatening look toward the frail craft of our drifters. So angrily at last did one come down upon them that they abandoned their floe and rowed away. Surely there is no peace for them by night or day, on the floe or afloat in their boat. They dare not lie down a moment without keeping one half of their number on the watch. But what is that in the distance? A steamer! A thrill of joy goes through the boat's company. Every possible signal is given, but she does not see them, and another night is spent on the floe. The next morning every eye was straining to see a whaler. Soon one appears. They shout, raise their signals, and fire every gun at once. But she passes out of sight. April thirtieth, as the night was setting in foggy and dark, the shout from the watch of "steamer" brought all to their feet. She was right upon them in the fog before she was seen. Hans was soon alongside of her in his kayak, telling their story as best he could. In a few moments the whaler was alongside of their piece of ice. Captain Tyson removed his old well-worn cap, called upon his men, and three cheers were given, ending with a "tiger" such as the poor fellows had not had a heart to give for many long months. The cheers were returned by a hundred men from the rigging and deck of the vessel. It was the sealer "Tigress," Captain Bartlett, of Conception Bay, Newfoundland. They soon had the planks of a good ship beneath them instead of a treacherous floe; curious but kind friends beset them, instead of threatening bergs; and every comfort succeeded to utter destitution. They had been on the floe six months, and floated more than sixteen hundred miles.

They were speedily conveyed, by the way of Conception Bay and St. Johns, to their own homes, the telegraph having flashed throughout the length and breadth of the land their coming, and the nation rejoiced. But there were tears mingled with the joy, that one, the noble, the true, the Christian commander of the expedition, Charles Francis Hall, lay in his icy grave in the far north.

As speedily as possible the "Tigress" was purchased and fitted out by the United States Government in search of the "Polaris" party. Captain Tyson and Joe were among her men. She reached Life-boat Cove about two months after Captain Buddington and his men had left. They learned that, much to the grief of the natives, the "Polaris" had floated off and sunk. The Buddington party arrived home in the fall, by the way of England.

As we may not meet our Esquimo friends again, with whom we have made so many voyages, the reader will want to know the last news from them. Hans and his family returned to Greenland in the "Tigress." Joe has bought a piece of land and a house near New London, Connecticut, and intends, with his family, to remain there, getting a living by fishing.

Thus ended the last American North Pole Expedition. The last from other Governments have not been more successful. Yet, while we write, England and Austria are reported as getting ready further North Polar expeditions to start in the spring of 1875. It must be allowed that the icy sceptered guardian of the North has made a good fight against the invaders into his dominions. But the nations of the earth are determined to send men to sit on his throne, though they find it a barren and worthless, as well as a cold domain.

THE END.

The Story of a Pocket Bible.
Ten illustrations. 12mo.................... ....$1 25

Historical Souvenirs of Martin Luther.
By Charles W. Hubner. Illustrated. 12mo..... - 00

Words that Shook the World;
Or, Martin Luther his own Biographer. By Charles Adams, D.D. Twenty-two Illustrations. 12mo.. 1 25

Renata of Este.
From the German of Rev. Carl Strack. By Catherine E. Hurst. 16mo................ .... 1 25

Anecdotes of the Wesleys.
By J. B. Wakeley, D.D. 12mo 1 25

Martyrs to the Tract Cause.
A contribution to the History of the Reformation. By J. F. Hurst, D.D. 12mo.................. 75

Palissy, the Huguenot Potter.
By C. L. Brightwell. Illustrated. 16mo......... 1 25

Prince of Pulpit Orators.
A Portraiture of Rev. George Whitefield, M.A. By J. B. Wakeley, D.D. 12mo.................... 1 25

Thomas Chalmers.
A Biographical Study. By James Dodds. 12mo. 1 00

Gustavus Adolphus.
The Hero of the Reformation. From the French of L. Abelous. By Mrs. C. A. Lacroix. Illustrated. 12mo.. 1 00

William the Taciturn.
From the French of L. Abelous. By Professor J. P. Lacroix. Illustrated. 16mo................. 1 25

Life of Oliver Cromwell.
By Charles Adams, D.D. 16mo............. .. 1 25

Lady Huntington Portrayed.
By Rev Z. A. Mudge. 12mo................... 1 25

Curiosities of Animal Life.
Recent Discoveries of the Microscope. 12mo.... 0 75

Glaucia.
A Story of Athens in the First Century. By Emma Leslie. Illustrated. 12mo....................$1 25

Talks with Girls.
By Augusta Larned. 12mo.................... 1 50

Peter, the Apprentice.
An Historical Tale of the Reformation in England. By the author of "Faithful, but not Famous," etc. 16mo. 90

Romance without Fiction.
Or, Sketches from the Portfolio of an Old Missionary. By Rev. Henry Bleby. 12mo.................... 1 75

The Man of One Book;
Or, the Life of the Rev. William Marsh, D.D. By his Daughter. Edited by Daniel Wise. 12mo.......... 1 50

Sunday Afternoons.
A Book for Little People. By E. F. Burr, D.D., author of "Ecce-Celum." 16mo.................... 75

Little Princess,
And other Stories, chiefly about Christmas. By Aunt Hattie. 18mo.................... 65

School-Life of Ben and Bentie.
Illustrated. 18mo.................... 90

Peeps at our Sunday-Schools.
By Rev. Alfred Taylor. 12mo.................... 1 25

Elizabeth Tudor:
The Queen and the Woman. By Virginia F. Townsend. Illustrated. 12mo.................... 1 50

True Stories of the American Fathers.
For the Girls and Boys all over the Land. By Miss Rebecca M'Conkey. Illustrated. 12mo.............. 1 50

Glimpses of our Lake Region in 1863,
And other Papers. By Mrs. H. C. Gardner. 12mo... 1 50

Through the Eye to the Heart;
Or, Eye-Teaching in the Sunday-School. By Rev. W. F. Crafts. 12mo.................... 1 50

Discontent,
And other Stories. By Mrs. H. C. Gardner. 12mo... 1 25

Afternoons with Grandma.

From the French of Madame Carraud. By Mrs. Mary Kinmont. Beautifully Illustrated. Bound in Muslin. 16mo...$1 25

Household Stories.

From the German of Madame Ottilie Wildermuth. By Miss Eleanor Kinmont. With Illustrations. 16mo. Four Volumes. Each.. 1 25

Father's Coming Home.

By the Author of "Weldon Woods." Four Illustrations. 16mo.. 1 00

Agnes Morton's Trial;

Or, the Lost Diamonds. And **The Young Governess.** By Mrs. Emma N. Janvier. 12mo........................ 1 25

My Sister Margaret.

A Temperance Story. By Mrs. C. M. Edwards. Illustrated. 12mo.. 1 25

Lilian.

A Story of the Days of Martyrdom in England Three Hundred Years Ago. Five Illustrations. 16mo...... 90

Ethel Linton;

Or, The Feversham Temper. By E. A. W., Author of "The Home of the Davenports," etc. 12mo.......... 1 25

Simple Stories with Odd Pictures;

Or, Evening Amusements for the Little Ones at Home. With Twenty Illustrations by Paul Konewka. 16mo. 75

Young Life;

Or, The Boys and Girls of Pleasant Valley. By Mrs. Sarah A. Mather, Author of "Itinerant Side," etc. 12mo.. 1 25

Fraulein Mina;

Or, Life in an American German Family. By Miss Mary H. Norris. 12mo.................................. 1 25

Through Trials to Triumph.

A Story of Boy's School-life. By Miss H. A. Putnam. Illustrated. 12mo.. 1 25

www.ingramcontent.com/pod-product-compliance
Lightning Source LLC
LaVergne TN
LVHW020118110826
845151LV00001B/198

* 9 7 8 1 4 2 5 5 4 2 0 1 6 *